What Readers

Women living with deep pain from the past are walking wounded. Walls of defense, fear, loneliness and shame are symptoms. But from the bottom of my heart, I believe there is no wound too deep for God to heal. Tammy's story and life are living proof of God's promises of Isaiah 61, "He gives beauty for ashes." Freedom, joy, peace and new purpose await you as you begin your journey to be healed and set free. I took Healed and Set Free to Australia and New Zealand. We must leave no hostages in the enemy's clutches! JESUS HEALS!

Debbi Bryson, Pastor's Wife
Calvary Fellowship, Vista, CA, CCA Board Member of Pastor's Wives Conferences

We have known Pastor Rick and Tammy Brown for many years, and have had the privilege of working alongside them and watching them minister together as a couple. Tammy exemplifies a woman healed by the grace of God. She extends grace and hope in such a free and inspired manner at all times. Indeed, God doesn't change the past, but He can change the meaning of the past.

With an anointed Bible study like *Healed and Set Free*, those who dive into the Lord's plan for healing can and will be healed. He will use the scars and wounds of our past to create a testimony that will glorify our Him. Through His Word He heals us by digging deep into His truths and our lives. We are thrilled to recommend *Healed and Set Free*, as it will bring anyone into a closer walk with our Savior, Jesus Christ.

Pastor Wayne and Cathy Taylor
Calvary Fellowship, Seattle, CCA Northwest/Alaska Leaders

I highly recommend this inspired book by Tammy Brown! If you know anyone who has been abused sexually, battled anorexia or bulimia, dealing with bitterness, marriage problems or many other issues then Healed and Set Free is a great tool that the Master Potter can use to help set you free! Check it out!

Pam Rozell
Pastor's wife at Potter's Field Ministries, Whitefish, MT, Christian Singer/Songwriter

The Healed and Set Free Bible study by Tammy Brown was given to me many years ago by my pastor's wife. God really used it to transform my life. We have used this study with teenagers and women who have hurting hearts. I always keep some on hand. Thanks for listening to God and allowing yourself to be so vulnerable.

Lisa Merideth
Director of Family Ministry & Women's Ministry, Calvary Chapel Delaware, PA

We are using the Healed and Set Free book overseas in the Philippines where we care for abandoned babies and children, and abused girls/young women. We've used it since about 2003 at Rainbow Village Ministries.

Pastor Trip & Susan Kimball
Directors of Rainbow Village Ministries in the Philippines.

What Readers are Saying

The *Healed and Set Free Bible Study* has been a wonderful blessing for all of us participating. Satan kept whispering lies. He tried to tell me that I couldn't lead other women through this study. I began praying for God's help, and it was wonderful. God is doing a work in my life, as well as in the lives of the ladies in this group study. I am personally able to put pieces of my life back together that have been fragmented. All of God's principles are put together in a way we are all able to apply to our own unique situations. We have grown in love for one another, and can't wait to meet each week to get into *Healed and Set Free*. God is so good and so faithful to move us forward and heal our hearts when they are crippled.

Cheryl, Women's Ministry Leader
Calvary Chapel Minnesota

As I was taking the *Healed and Set Free Bible Study*, I was continually reminded in each chapter that I needed to see what was really going on in my heart and get real with the hurts that still lingered. As I completed the Bible study homework each day, God began to show me that my heart had a junk drawer where I kept all my pain over the years.

Most homes have a junk drawer: a drawer to throw in odds and ends such as screwdrivers, pencils, pens, and all the other items that don't have a home. I didn't realize that I had been keeping a junk drawer in my heart ever since my stepfather sexually abused me at a very young age. Throughout my life, I learned to put broken trusts, painful memories and hurts that still lingered into the junk drawer of my heart.

My heart became filled with unforgiveness, bitterness and wrongs that others had committed against me. After being a Christian for over 20 years, I was now faced with the contents of my heart's junk drawer. I needed to clean out the drawer, and *Healed and Set Free* gave me the tools to do it. I now have a heart that has been healed and set free, and I know how to keep it that way. I lead other women through the *Healed and Set Free Bible Study* to comfort them with God's truth and love.

Debbie, Idaho

I wanted to write to let you know how pleased I am to lead women through the *Healed and Set Free Bible Study*. My husband, Pastor Kurt, and I have looked at many similar studies. This is the best one we've come across for three reasons:

1. Tammy's personal triumph is an incredible story of Christ's transforming power. Because she is willing to share something so personal, others know that she relates to them and their hurts.
2. It's biblical! Modern psychology says that people behave the way they do because of their circumstances. I talk with many women who believe the lie that their past controls them, and that they are doomed to a hopeless future. *Healed and Set Free* gives tremendous hope through Christ, His love and His enduring, eternal Word.
3. *Healed and Set Free* helps a multitude of issues using four powerful tools.

As I read Tammy's story, I wept at God's marvelous healing power. I praise Him for her obedience to produce this material.

Vicki, Pastor's Wife, Ohio

TAMMY BROWN

Healed
AND *set free*

From Past Hurts

God doesn't change the past,
but He can change the meaning of the past

Healed and Set Free is a ministry of Watersprings Church of Idaho Falls, Idaho.

Watersprings Church is one of thousands of Calvary Chapel churches which are international, non-denominational fellowships of believers in Jesus Christ. Our mission is to reach, disciple and equip people to know Jesus Christ and to make Him known through successive generations.

Healed and Set Free is a Bible study written to help people with painful hurts that still linger, by teaching biblical truths they can apply to their lives so Jesus Christ can set them free.

© Copyright 2012, © Copyright 2000, © Copyright 1998 by Tammy Brown.

All rights reserved. No part of this Bible study may be reproduced in any form without written permission from the author.

All scripture quotations, unless otherwise indicated, are taken from the New King James Version, © Copyright 1982 by Thomas Nelson, Inc. Used by permission. All rights reserved.

Brown, Tammy
Healed and Set Free: A Bible Study by Tammy Brown

Cover title: *Healed and Set Free*

Published by: Seek First Publications
ISBN-10: 1545536155
ISBN-13: 9781545536155

Editor-in-Chief: Ashley Brown
Editing: Christa Landon, Rhondalyn Moran, Shelley Spady, Proofreading Team
Design: Christa Landon, Shelley Spady, Ashley Brown
Cover Design: Christa Landon, Alicia Hoskins, Ashley Brown, Jessica Sprague
Printed in the United States of America

To Order:

THE *HEALED AND SET FREE* BIBLE STUDY
(Leader's Guide is at the back of the *Healed and Set Free* **Bible Study**)

visit us online at www.hsfministries.org

Contents

How to Use This Study		1
Tools to Become Healed and Set Free
(Repeated At the End of Each Chapter)		5
A Journey Worth Taking by Tammy Brown		6
Chapter 1	Getting Real with God Where I Need Healing	9
Chapter 2	Knowing God's Heart	39
Chapter 3	Letting Go of Anger	75
Chapter 4	Forgiving the Unacceptable	103
Chapter 5	Conquering Depression	139
Chapter 6	Body Image	169
Chapter 7	Remembering to Forget	203
Chapter 8	Two Become One: God's Design for Marriage	231
Chapter 9	Healed and Set Free	269
Q & A on Everlasting Life and How to Pray		300
Definitions		301
Scripture References		302
Leader's Guide		311
For Leaders, From Leaders		321
Acknowledgments		340
Q & A with Tammy		341
About the Author		343

Dedication

I dedicate this book to the only one who heals and sets our souls, hearts and lives free: my Lord and Savior, Jesus Christ. The truth found within these pages are simply the application of His timeless wisdom and truth.

How to Use This Study

The *Healed and Set Free Bible Study* is user-friendly. It has been designed so that anyone can use it, regardless of their biblical knowledge. Owning a Bible is not mandatory. All Bible verses have either been typed directly into each section, or in the scripture reference section at the back of the book, making it easy to follow. So whether you are a Bible scholar or have never opened a Bible before, you can complete this study and receive a fresh beginning: through God's Word.

Individual Study

1. Begin each day with prayer. Ask God to help you understand the passage and apply it to your life. Prayer is simply having a conversation with God - listening and talking to Him. Believers can pray freely from the heart, spontaneously, and in their own words. Go to page 300 if you would like to learn more about prayer.

2. Develop daily quiet times with the Lord. Use this time to do your study without distraction. Read and reread the passage(s). Remember, you must know what the passage says before you can understand what it means and how it applies to you. Once you have read the passage, take a moment to think about how it may apply to your life.

3. This study includes daily questions with space provided for your answers. It may be a good idea to keep a notebook on hand in case you run out of room. Keeping track of your thoughts, insights and prayers (asked or answered) is not only a great opportunity for healing, but provides an opportunity to track your progress, and see how God is working in your life.

4. Daily questions are an important part of this study, and completing each question is vital to your healing process. Remember, the more you give to something, the more you will benefit from it.

Suggestions for Group Study

1. Groups meet once a week, with members having answered the chapter questions prior to coming to the study.

2. Come to each week's study prepared. Careful preparation will greatly enrich your time in group discussion.

3. Group leaders are not there to lecture, but to encourage group members to keep focused on the study: specifically, to focus on how God is working in each individual's life, and what they have learned from each passage. Group leaders will encourage discussion from all who are ready to share. Think and pray about your answers and insights before sharing with your group.

4. This study is meant to encourage you to feel comfortable sharing your "true self," your hurts, sins and fears with God. You will never be forced to share with your group, although when you do, your whole group will benefit.

5. Try to stay focused on the passages being studied during meetings. This will allow everyone the best opportunity to get the most out of each question. Base your answers on the verses or reflections being discussed.

6. Try to be sensitive to other members in the group. Listen attentively when others speak, and encourage them when you can.

7. Be careful not to dominate the discussion. It's important for you to participate, but also allow others to have equal time.

8. As you begin this study of God's Word, you will be given many opportunities to see His healing power in your life, as well as in the lives of others.

9. Remember to encourage and comfort one another; cry and rejoice together in this journey to becoming healed and set free.

Your devotional time is not a gift you give to God, it is a gift God gives to you.

Group Accountability to Confidants

(Read with your group and sign)

Agape Love:

The commitment that I make to each individual in our group will be in the spirit of God's love that says, "Nothing you say or do will make me stop loving you."

"...If we love one another, God abides in us, and His love has been perfected in us" (1 John 4:12).

"But above all these things put on love, which is the bond of perfection. And let the peace of God rule in your hearts, to which also you were called in one body; and be thankful" (Colossians 3:14-15).

Prayer:

I will pray for each member of our group consistently.

"Likewise the Spirit also helps in our weaknesses. For we do not know what we should pray for as we ought, but the Spirit Himself makes intercession for us with groanings which cannot be uttered" (Romans 8:26).

Confidentiality:

I will make the commitment to not share anything outside our group that has been shared inside the group, including the names of group members, not even with my spouse or best friend.

"A talebearer reveals secrets, but he who is of a faithful spirit conceals a matter. Where there is no counsel, the people fall; but in the multitude of counselors there is safety" (Proverbs 11:13-14).

Openness:

I understand that I can't know those in my group, and they can't know me, unless we tell each other who we are. I will make the commitment to tell my group who I am, my strengths and my weaknesses.

"Confess your trespasses to one another, and pray for one another, that you may be healed. The effective, fervent prayer of a righteous man avails much" (James 5:16).

Sensitivity:

I will ask God to make me sensitive to the needs of each person in our group. I will make the commitment to consciously listen to each person every time they speak, whether in words, actions or attitudes.

"Let nothing be done through selfish ambition or conceit, but in lowliness of mind let each esteem others better than himself. Let each of you look out not only for his own interests, but also for the interests of others" (Philippians 2:3-4).

Honesty:

I understand that speaking the truth in love is both positive and constructive for spiritual growth. I will allow God to use me in our group's growth process by telling my group when I agree and when I disagree.

"That we should no longer be children... but, speaking the truth in love, may grow up in all things into Him who is the head—Christ— from whom the whole body, joined and knit together by what every joint supplies, according to the effective working by which every part does its share, causes growth of the body for the edifying of itself in love (Ephesians 4:14, 15-16).

Accountability:

It's my conviction that God has placed me in our group for the purpose of building up the body of Christ. From time to time, it will be necessary for me to seek the mind of the Lord through the counsel and advice of those in our group. I will accept responsibility for applying their counsel and advice in my life, and report to them as to what I have done with their collective wisdom.

"Where there is no counsel, the people fall; but in the multitude of counselors there is safety" (Proverbs 11:14).

Signature and Date: _____

Before We Begin

Thinking about the past will never change the past, but you can change your future and be SET FREE from past hurts that linger in your heart.

(Circle your answers)

- Do you have a true desire to get real with God?

    Yes or No

- Have you decided that you can't continue living the way you've been living?

    Yes or No

- Are you ready to have hope win out over despair?

    Yes or No

- Have you lost perspective in relationships, or with your children or marriage?

    Yes or No

- Are you ready to spend time each day in this Bible study?

    Yes or No

Tools to Become Healed and Set Free

To equip yourself in God's truth, look over the tools and verses that will be introduced in the coming weeks. Thinking about the past won't change it, but you can change your future by being set free from your past.

TOOL #1 - SEE: (Covered in chapters 1 and 2) I must SEE the truth about what is in my heart so I am not defiled.

Definition: To defile means to make filthy or dirty; to pollute.

Bible Verse: "Looking carefully lest anyone fall short of the grace of God; lest any root of bitterness springing up cause trouble, and by this many become defiled" (Hebrews 12:15).

TOOL #2 - GIVE: (Covered in chapter 3) I must GIVE my sin to God through repentance, knowing that Christ is waiting to take it. I must be sorry enough to change, and choose to go God's way over my own.

Definition: To repent means to feel such sorrow for sin or fault as to be disposed to change one's life for the better; be penitent.

Bible Verse: "For godly sorrow produces repentance leading to salvation, not to be regretted; but the sorrow of the world produces death" (2 Corinthians 7:10).

TOOL #3 - FORGIVE: (Covered in chapter 4, tools 1-3 reviewed in chapters 5 & 6) I must FORGIVE as I am forgiven by Christ: Forgiving those who hurt, bruised, wronged, rejected, betrayed or harmed me, whether unintentionally or deliberately. I must ask God to forgive me for holding on to unforgiveness and know that He will.

Definition: To forgive means to stop feeling angry or resentful toward someone for an offense, flaw or mistake.

Bible Verse: "...Bearing with one another, and forgiving one another, if anyone has a complaint against another; even as Christ forgave you, so you also must do" (Colossians 3:13).

TOOL #4 - FORGET: (Covered in chapter 7, tools 1-4 reviewed in chapters 8 & 9) I must FORGET by no longer dwelling on the hurt or the painful reminders, such as: phrases, smells, places, songs and comments. Instead, I am putting my mind on the higher calling that Christ has for me.

Definition: To forget means to choose not to remember or notice, "forgive and forget".

Bible Verse: "Brethren, I do not count myself to have apprehended; but one thing I do, forgetting those things which are behind and reaching forward to those things which are ahead" (Philippians 3:13).

Be Healed and Set Free: (Covered in chapter 9) Christ will heal me from my past, showing me the truth, so I can become a cleansed vessel, healed and set free.

Definition: To set free means to make free; set at liberty; release from bondage, imprisonment, or restraint.

Definition: To heal means to make whole and healthy; to cure; to remedy or repair.

Bible Verse: "And you shall know the truth, and the truth shall make you free" (John 8:32).

A Journey Worth Taking

God loves you. He is with you on the good days, the bad days, the boring days, the unexpected days, whether they bring true joy and laughter, or pain and sorrow.

As we take this journey together, we will learn to recognize His voice in our story. We will see His hand in our lives and His loving arms there to embrace us, taking all our hurts, disappointments and pain.

I am reminded of Corrie Ten Boom, a victim of Nazi Germany who survived imprisonment in a concentration camp. She was able to hear God's voice in the midst of complete despair: "There is no pit so deep that God's love is not deeper still. God will give us the love to be able to forgive our enemies."[1]

Through her words, Corrie teaches us that God is always there, and no situation is too dark for His light to shine. God has used Corrie's story to help thousands of people around the world see His miraculous power, and to show how He uses everything in our lives for His purpose. Every experience God gives us, every person He puts in our lives, is part of His perfect preparation for our future.

He is ready to be the hero of our story, as we allow Him to change our hearts day by day. He is patient, and only wants the best for us. "For I know the thoughts that I think toward you, says the Lord, thoughts of peace and not of evil, to give you a future and a hope" (Jeremiah 29:11).

He loves us deeply and forever. So yes, even on the bad days when life is hard, frustrating and emotionally draining, God is there, waiting for us to look up and ask for help. He is ready to set us free from our pain, and to take the journey with us.

"I can do all things through Christ who strengthens me" (Philippians 4:13).

HEALING... it's what God does.
Invigorating others about His healing power in our lives... it's what He longs for us to do.

Healed and Set Free,
Tammy

Chapter 1

Getting Real With God Where I Need Healing

This Week's Focus

This week we will be learning Tool #1. We will be inviting God into our lives to shed light on things of which we have been previously unaware. He will help us to **SEE** the true condition of our hearts, which is the first step towards becoming healed and set free.

Tool #1 - SEE: I must SEE the truth about what is in my heart, so I am not defiled.

Definition: To defile means to make filthy or dirty; to pollute.

Bible Verse: "Looking carefully lest anyone fall short of the grace of God; lest any root of bitterness springing up cause trouble, and by this many become defiled" (Hebrews 12:15).

Week 1: Day 1

Prayer: Bow your heart before the Lord in prayer prior to completing today's Bible study and ask Him to guide you as you begin the *Healed and Set Free* journey.

I love my girlfriends. I love experiencing life with friends who "get me." I love having conversations over long walks. Friends are like pearls strung together with light-hearted laughter, loads of love, gifts of time, deep revelations and a great deal of grace.

Though sharing beautiful life moments is always a highlight, some of the most powerful blessings of friendship for me have been found in the trenches and in the broken places. Those are the places where our fears and problems need the understanding heart of a loyal friend. Those are the times when we rise up to encourage one another, speak hope to a sister who is hurting, offer prayer for troubles or extend challenges to believe and trust in God's promises.

Healed and Set Free was originally written in 1998 for two friends who opened up to me about deep hurts they had been carrying since childhood. Courageously, one of the ladies shared that her three brothers had sexually abused her during her childhood. At the age of twelve, fear gripped her at the possibility of an incestuous pregnancy. The other friend had been battling with the pain and devastation of anorexia. As we prayed and cried together, my heart broke for them. I could relate to their pain. I wanted to share the comfort and healing God had given me through my secret, painful past.

God Never Wastes a Hurt

I was a young pastor's wife in the '90s. Being fairly new to life in the ministry, I was utterly mystified to discover a handful of women I served with were gossiping about me. They were doing everything they could to cause dissension in the church. It was one of the most difficult times I had faced in ministry up to that point.

Few things sow division more quickly than gossip. It damages relationships, divides teams, and destroys unity. In short, nothing good comes from gossip. The Bible cautions us that "a perverse person stirs up conflict, and a gossip separates close friends" (Proverbs 16:28). Yet many people are so filled with a love of gossip that they begin to see it as normal and natural. Gossip is a very dangerous tool of the devil, and we should be aware of the gossiper and not be greedy to hear the gossip. It's a cycle that needs to be broken. Words hold the power of life or death—both for those who speak them and those who receive them (Proverbs 18:21). Cut the gossip out of your workplace, church, house, and watch them come alive with unity and peace.

Looking back, I realize I didn't handle the gossip situation in my life properly. I started to disengage from ministry and grow an unforgiving heart. The wound was lodged in my soul, and Satan was trying to take me out of the ministry. But God never wastes a hurt, and it backfired on the enemy: My life changed for the better when I let Jesus heal the hurts and help me forgive the offense. Then I pressed in to Jesus, and weeks later God guided me into a new ministry as He moved on my heart to develop Healed and Set Free for two hurting women in our church. He was helping me look upward to Him and outward toward others. You see, sometimes in the midst of brokenness and darkness God uses us in a more purposeful way. God is not only working to heal us, but to heal others through us. God is raising up an army of once-wounded Healed and Set Free warriors to take a message to women and men of all ages: Jesus heals!

Have you been wounded by someone in the faith? While the pain can seem unbearable, it is not unconquerable. You can be healed and set free from such a wound. Jesus stated, "You have heard that it was said, 'Love your neighbor and hate your enemy. But I say to you, love your enemies, bless those who curse you, do good to those who hate you, and pray for those who spitefully use you and persecute you" (Matthew 5:43-44). That's far-reaching wisdom for our souls: If you really absorbed the meaning of Christ's words, when everything inside you wants to get even with the person who hurt you or spoke badly of you, choose to react with love, goodness and prayer. Handle criticism and bitterness with godly wisdom and skill. God never wastes a hurt, as we are reminded in Romans 8:28, "We know that all things work together for good to those who love God, to those who are called according to His purpose."

Wherever today finds you, look around for someone in need, someone who needs a touch of compassion, someone who needs to know that Jesus died on the cross for them. If we can't prevent pain, we can at least lighten the load with compassion and God's love. Pastor Alan Redpath has been known to say, "You can never lighten the load unless you have first felt the pressure in your own soul." Are you willing to let God use you?

Getting Started

My question for you today is this: Can you let go of the battle? Do you want to become all that God created you to be? Do you want to love fearlessly? Are you ready to allow God into the secret places of your heart to set you free? "And you shall know the truth, and the truth shall make you free" (John 8:32).

There are times when it's appropriate to get angry. However, God's word says, "Do not let the sun go down on your wrath" (Ephesians 4:26). Staying angry, holding grudges and drinking the poison of unforgiveness is a life of bondage! Life is too short not to be healed of our past hurts and set free to live the abundant life. The four powerful tools and nine chapters in *Healed and Set Free* can point you to the only one who can change everything.

In this study, you will be introduced to four tools to help overcome difficulties such as:

- Betrayal
- Guilt
- Divorce
- Sexual abuse
- Inability to love
- Abortion
- Rejection
- Rape
- Verbal abuse
- Depression
- Adultery
- Shame
- Physical abuse
- Cruel words
- Abandonment
- Bitterness
- Church conflict
- Anger
- Bullying
- Addiction
- Incest

God will be faithful to do His part, but we have to do our part as well. The four biblical tools to freedom can only set you free when you apply them. "He heals the brokenhearted and binds up their wounds" (Psalm 147:3).

Once this study was composed, I had a burning question for my two hurting friends. Before the three of us began the *Healed and Set Free* Bible study, I asked if they would be comfortable if we announced the study at church to reach more hurting women. They didn't even hesitate to say, "Yes! Please invite anyone who is hurting."

The Lord filled my living room with hurting women. The Holy Spirit opened eyes and changed hearts. You will find many of their beautiful stories woven throughout *Healed and Set Free*. To read my friend's story, one of the two whom *Healed and Set Free* was originally written for, turn to page 194 and look for "A Brand New Woman."

Healer of the Broken

"He heals the brokenhearted and binds up their wounds" (Psalm 147:3).

Calvary Chapel Magazine Reprint of Tammy's Story:

First as a child, then as a new Christian, and later as a pastor's wife, a young woman tried to forget the pain too deep for words... until she turned it over to God.

Tammy Brown sobbed uncontrollably at the kitchen table as her husband Rick wrapped his arms around her. This was the first time that she had unlocked 20 years' worth of memories from her secret past.

"Every night for years I would watch passing car lights creep past my window. I would lie there and wonder if my uncle was coming to get me, or even kill me," Tammy said. "I lay in bed at the age of seven, scared to fall asleep, and planned over and over how I would tell my mom about my secret. But my planning was always stopped by the haunting words of my uncle: 'I'll kill your parents if you ever tell. If they find out what a dirty little girl you are they'll be so ashamed of you.' I was silenced by shame and fear. Each time my uncle would come near me I would run as fast as I could from him thinking, 'Get away from me!'

"From that moment, I tried to FORGET those unspeakable memories. First as a child, then as a new Christian, and later as a pastor's wife, I tried to forget the pain, but the memories kept me angry and bitter. As I recalled the repeated sexual abuse by my uncle and his sons, and later being date-raped as a teenager, I was kept prisoner to my past. I was good at keeping the memories a secret."

But abuses and secrets left deposits on her heart which were not easily removed. Tammy's future husband, Rick, led her to Christ during her senior year of high school. She hoped that becoming a Christian, and later being involved in her husband's ministry, would take away her crippling insecurities, bitterness, and shame. It didn't work.

"I would sing songs about how God heals, but they were empty words because I'd never experienced it," she said. Tammy is thankful that those ugly deposits are gone after God tenderly led her on a journey of healing and forgiveness. Tammy described herself as "a self destructive woman going nowhere in life."

Frustration led her to God's Word, which showed that before she could FORGET the abuse and FORGIVE her abusers, she first had to SEE the condition of her embittered heart so she wouldn't remain defiled (Hebrews 12:15). However, Tammy warned, "Simply reading God's Word is not enough—you have to purposely obey, then you experience true healing." She admitted, "There were times I didn't want to obey. I wrestled, wept, and questioned, 'How could the sin of hatred be equal to the sin of abuse in God's eyes?' I thought I was justified. Surely God hated [my abusers] too."

When she realized her bitterness, she wondered, "Now what am I supposed to do?" The answer was to GIVE it to Christ in repentance. She had to be deeply sorrowful about her bitter response, enough to change her thinking (2 Corinthians 7:10).

"It's completely opposite of how we think humanly," she noted. "Repentance cleans out the sin in our hearts." Tammy was quick to add that taking this step did not justify the abuse or betrayal. We live in a fallen world where sin abounds and hurts from others can affect our lives. Satan continually tries to get us to hate, not FORGIVE. But God's Word helps us grow and move away from the destruction Satan desires to do.

Forgiveness was finally possible, but she needed the Lord to show her how. Again the Word showed her that when we pray, we must FORGIVE others (Mark 11:25). By choosing forgiveness, we are choosing God's way and showing that we trust Him. Forgiveness releases you from the past and opens the door for His healing and restoration.

The final step to healing was to FORGET, now possible by her repentance and forgiveness. In Philippians 3:13, Paul tells us to fully "FORGET those things that are behind and put our minds on the higher calling of Jesus." We live in a world where hurt is part of life. We can become bitter and offended in a split second even by other Christians," Tammy said. "I'm so thankful those things in the past don't define us. It's not what happens to you that matters most, it's what happens in you."

"It's an amazing opportunity when unfair things happen in our lives," Tammy added "because the Lord can be glorified. He is a good God who wants to heal the world, and He is the only true Healer."

Growing Strong in the Broken Places
He never wastes a hurt. Perhaps you need a word of encouragement today. Perhaps you know a friend who needs this word. The best thing we can do for our friends is to love them and point them to Jesus. There is a common phrase, "Growing strong in the broken places." The idea behind these words is that where a bone is broken and heals, it becomes the strongest part of the bone.

> It's not what happens *to* you that matters most,
> it's what happens *in* you.

Tools to Become Healed and Set Free

There are four tools that will help you become set free. Each tool will be defined when the time comes. It is crucial to memorize these powerful tools and review them regularly in order to apply them to your daily life.

#1 - SEE: I must SEE the truth about what is in my heart so I am not defiled.

#2 - GIVE: I must GIVE my sin to God through repentance, knowing that Christ is waiting to take it. I must be sorry enough to change, and choose to go God's way over my own.

#3 - FORGIVE: I must FORGIVE as I am forgiven by Christ: Forgiving those who hurt, bruised, wronged, rejected, betrayed or harmed me, whether unintentionally or deliberately. I must ask God to forgive me for holding on to unforgiveness and know that He will.

#4 - FORGET: I must FORGET by no longer dwelling on the hurt or the painful reminders such as: phrases, smells, places, songs and comments. Instead, I am putting my mind on the higher calling that Christ has for me.

Be Healed and Set Free: Christ will heal me from my past, showing me the truth, so I can become a cleansed vessel, healed and set free.

This Week's Focus

Prayer: Ask God to help you be willing to SEE what's in your heart.

By Memory: My challenge to you is to be able to recite this week's tool and Bible verse without looking. I know that by hiding these words of wisdom in your heart you are providing yourself with tools to truly be healed and set free. May we rise up to be women of the Word.

Tool #1 - SEE: I must SEE the truth about what is in my heart, so I am not defiled.

Definition: To defile means to make filthy or dirty; to pollute.

Bible Verse: "Looking carefully lest anyone fall short of the grace of God; lest any root of bitterness springing up cause trouble, and by this many become defiled" (Hebrews 12:15).

"And you shall know the truth, and the truth shall make you free" (John 8:32).

Week 1: Day 2

Prayer: Bow your heart before Christ in prayer prior to answering these questions. Ask Jesus to help you SEE the wounds that need to be healed.

Which tool comes first: SEE or FORGET?

Does it surprise you that the first tool is "SEE", not "FORGET"? Many times we want to jump ahead to FORGET because the hurt is so painful that we want to push it away, acting as if nothing has happened. It doesn't work that way. Those lingering pains have a way of negatively impacting our lives and the lives of those around us. In order to be healed and set free from our past, we must first be able to clearly SEE the condition of our hearts towards those who have wronged us along the way or personal regrets so that we can bring all of it to God, our ultimate Healer.

Satan Wants to Keep Us in Shackles

The opposite of God's compassion and healing is Satan's lies and destruction. Some of us have been shackled down with burdens of guilt, shame, bitterness, fear and discouragement since childhood. We are tired of trying to stand, let alone walk under a heavy load. You need to know that hurt doesn't go away by itself. God is right there ready to heal your broken places. If we put on a smile and pretend nothing bothers us, we are lying to God and to ourselves. This allows Satan to keep us in shackles to those lingering hurts. We must SEE what is affecting us today from our past so we can be set free. Examine your heart, examine your way of thinking and compare it to God's way of thinking.

The Ways Satan Steals, Kills and Destroys

Satan works through hurt, shame, guilt and fear to destroy our lives. Christ has come to offer us new life free from the weight and torment of hidden pain. Pray for God to show you the hurts in your life that need to be healed. Invite Him into the deep places of your heart where you hide your pain. That is when true healing can begin!

Forgetting Wasn't Enough

"The Thief does not come except to steal, and to kill and to destroy" (John 10:10). After becoming a Christian, I didn't understand why my heartache and trouble wouldn't vanish. I loved Christ with all of my heart, so why were the painful thoughts still in my mind? Why was the hatred still in my heart? Why couldn't I forget? I soon learned that just forgetting my past wasn't enough. I needed God to help me SEE that my heart and mind were grieved by the resentment and hatred I was harboring towards those who had violated and wronged me.

Sin is sin. I had to see that even though the crime committed against me was sin, living with anger and bitterness toward any person would never help me move past the pain and receive God's restoration.

> "Your word I have hidden in my heart,
> that I might not sin against You"
> (Psalm 119:11).

Ways Satan Tried to Steal, Kill and Destroy My Life - A Note from Tammy

- My innocence was *stolen* as a child through sexual abuse.
- My dreams of being a virgin bride were *killed* as a teenager through date rape.
- My spirit was *destroyed* by shame, resentment, unforgiveness and revenge as I suffered in silence for over 20 years.

1. Write down the ways Satan is trying to steal, kill and destroy your life.

    - What has been stolen?

    _____
    _____

    - What has been killed?

    _____
    _____

    - What has been destroyed?

    _____
    _____

Tool #1 - SEE what is left over in your heart from the hurt or regret. Hebrews 12:15 says, "Looking carefully lest anyone fall short of the grace of God; lest any root of bitterness springing up cause trouble, and by this many become defiled."

2. Write down the definition of "defile" from page 301.

    _____
    _____
    _____

Maybe someone has wronged or hurt you. You are not to seek revenge because bitterness and hatred will do more harm to you than the person you are directing it towards. It will defile you and eat you up inside. It will destroy your life. It will hinder your time in prayer with God. It will hinder your worship.

3. Is God allowing you to SEE that your heart is defiled from past hurts or shame? Write down your thoughts.

    _____
    _____
    _____

4. What changes are you willing to trust God to make in your life?

    _____
    _____
    _____

Stories of Real People and a Real Savior

Freedom in Christ
Sherry, Minnesota

"Bearing with one another, and forgiving one another, if anyone has a complaint against another, even as Christ forgave you, so you also must do" (Colossians 3:13).

My childhood was one of great fear. I grew up with an alcoholic father who frequently had bouts of drinking followed by fits of rage. I learned at an early age to run and hide in the safest place I could find in our home, but the truth is, there really was no place to escape. Even though my mother tried to hold the home together, I withdrew more and more. In the midst of my father's alcoholic rage, he would often say very abusive and demeaning things to me and my siblings. It caused me to live in fear, with a deep sense of rejection, mistrust and hopelessness, even into my adult years. How I longed to be loved by my father.

When I was a young girl, my uncle came to our home and shared the love of Jesus with me. He gave me a small white Bible, and prayed with me. I cried out to Jesus. I remember having a sense of joy, but the excitement would dissipate in time. There would be no one to teach or mentor me for many years. I know now, looking back, that God loved that broken little girl in the alcoholic home.

As a hurting young woman I looked for any circumstance that would help me escape my volatile home life. A man came into my life and offered me what looked like love and safety. I moved in with him and we eventually married. Soon I realized that he had the same stronghold of alcoholism in his life. To my horror, the nightmare went on and my life became one of day-to-day survival.

When I held our first baby in my arms, I desperately needed some reassurance and hope, knowing I was now responsible for this little life. I began to think about that little white Bible and the things my uncle shared with me those many years ago. I decided to go to church and learn more about Jesus. I was excited about learning God's Word for the first time, and yet terrified of anyone finding out what my home life was like. I continued my pattern of hiding even in the midst of believers.

Then God did something beautiful in my life. I heard there was a Bible study called "Healed and Set Free" being offered in our church, and that there was one opening left. The Lord moved upon my heart and I was able to set my fear aside and sign up. It was a decision that would change my life forever. This beautiful study took me back to God's Word, and for the first time I really understood what Jesus did for me at the cross. I realized that the sin of not forgiving my dad broke God's heart just as much as my dad's sin. I began to see my dad now through the eyes of Christ—with love and forgiveness. I could pray for my dad now that I felt the love of Christ for him. I would visit with him without the bitterness or fear in my heart. Then a miracle happened. My dad chose to stop drinking after he became seriously ill. He began to seek the Lord and read the Bible. I would visit with him and he would talk to me about the Lord and ask me questions. Then one incredible day, my dad asked me to forgive him for all the wrong he had done to me. I was able to look at him with all sincerity and tell him that I had already forgiven him. It was a beautiful moment for both of us, and the thought of it still brings me to tears to this day. My dad would pass away not long after this miracle. Because the Lord showed me the way of freedom and forgiveness, I was able to have those final days of relationship with my dad. I will be forever grateful.

The Lord continued to show me the way of forgiveness. My husband continued to drink, and that bondage finally destroyed our home. After our last separation, my husband filed for divorce and our 25 year marriage ended. It was devastating, but I was prepared as God had shown me the way of freedom. I know now that forgiveness is the greatest form of love.

I try to always look at the blessings in my life. I have beautiful grown children and precious grandchildren which I praise God for. My heart is to be a witness of God's love to them and to see them follow hard after Jesus. My "Healed and Set Free" Bible study leader would also become a most treasured friend. We went on to serve together in ministry and have witnessed many women enter into freedom in Christ. I have so much to be thankful for. Above all I praise God for showing me the way to forgiveness and freedom.

The Bible: Your User's Guide for Life

I recently read a wonderful Bible study from Harvest Ministries called "Start! to Follow."[1] It defined perfectly what makes the Bible worth reading:

> Like any good instruction manual, the Bible tells us how things fit together and what we need to keep our spiritual life in good working condition. God knows we need help, so He has given us the Bible—complete with operating instructions, real-life illustrations and warning labels. Everything we need to know in order to live and grow can be found in this God-inspired book.
>
> The Bible never stops speaking to us. It cuts across the surface, penetrating to the heart of the matter. It has been said that the heart of the matter is the matter of the heart. God's Word reveals all that's in our hearts, good or bad. The Bibles gives us insight into our own lives—what is broken, what needs to change and what must absolutely go. Only God's Word can pierce through sin's barrier and answer the need of every human heart.
>
> Some people have the idea that the Bible is an outdated book filled with moral fables and endless lists of "do's" and "do not's." They don't believe the Bible is relevant for today. As you begin to study the Bible for yourself, you will discover the great value, benefit and promises given to you, as a child of God, in the pages of this living book.

> "Let us search out and examine our ways, and turn back to the Lord; let us lift our hearts and hands to God in heaven"
> (Lamentations 3:40-41).

Week 1: Day 3

Prayer: Bow your heart before the Lord prior to completing today's Bible study. God, give me a heart to SEE the truth about what has made me sad, disappointed, angry and a prisoner to my past. "The spirit of a man will sustain him in sickness, but who can bear a broken spirit?" (Proverbs 18:14).

God Heals the Brokenhearted

"He heals the brokenhearted and binds up their wounds" (Psalm 147:3).

1. "To heal" means to mend, to get better, to put right, to restore, cure, cause to heal or be healed. Are you ready to open up all of your heart to the only One who can heal it? Yes or no?

    What area of your life do you need to work on the most?

    _____

    _____

    What concerns or fears keep you from opening your heart to God?

    _____

    _____

2. Let's take a look at Hebrews 12:12-13: "Therefore strengthen the hands which hang down, and the feeble knees, and make straight paths for your feet, so that what is lame may not be dislocated, but rather be healed."

    Write down the definition of "lame" from page 301.

    _____

    _____

3. Write down the ways that lingering, unacceptable hurts cause your heart and mind to be lame.

    _____

    _____

    _____

    _____

> Don't waste the pain, use it to drive you deeper into God.

Preparing for Heaven

John 3:16 says, "For God so loved the world that He gave His only begotten Son, that whoever believes in Him should not perish, but have everlasting life."

If you are anything like me, you sometimes have difficulty believing you are who God says you are. The more we learn about Jesus and His thoughts toward us, the more we realize we have a heavenly Father who loves us, wants to have a relationship with us, and thinks of us as His treasure, despite our shortcomings.

Jesus said, "If anyone loves Me, he will keep My Word; and My Father will love him, and We will come to him and make our home with him" (John 14:32). That is an amazing statement. God the Father and God the Son are saying they want to make their home with you and me.

Do you have a desire to go to heaven and have a relationship with God? If you are ready to receive Christ as your Savior, pray the life-changing prayer below.

Dear Lord Jesus,
I know I am a sinner and need Your forgiveness. I want to turn from my sins. I believe You died for my sins, and I invite You to come into my heart and life. I want to trust You and follow You as my Lord and Savior.
In Jesus' name, amen.

Welcome to God's Family

"For I know the thoughts that I think toward you, says the Lord, thoughts of peace and not of evil, to give you a future and a hope" (Jeremiah 29:11).

Questions and answers about everlasting life are available on page 300.

Don't start your day with the broken pieces of yesterday.
Every day is a fresh start.
Each day is a new beginning.
Every morning we wake up is the first day of our
NEW LIFE.

- Unknown

Why Does Love Cover All Sins?

In the devotional "Sweeping Statement,"[2] The Active Word explains why we need God's unfailing love, and why we can be forgiven in Him. Taking their cue from Proverbs 10:12, "Love covers all sins," they write:

> Earth can be a very difficult place. It's filled with sinners. And where there are sinners, there's sin, corruption, injustice, backstabbing, stealing, infidelity, abuse, torture, genocide, and the list goes on and on.
>
> But as powerful as sin is, there is something more powerful: love. Proverbs 10:12 unmistakably and unapologetically says, "Love covers all sins." In other words, there's no sin under the sun that can't be overcome and eventually forgiven through the power of love. In most of us, there's an instinctive, "Yeah, but…" that wells up in response to such a sweeping statement. "Yeah, but you don't know what someone once did to me. Yeah, but I've been wounded more deeply than you can ever imagine. Yeah, but the things I've been through are so horrible, so heinous, they can't possibly be covered by love."
>
> My point isn't to minimize anything that may have happened to you. However, we minimize love's power when we presume there's any sin or combination of sins greater than love. And while *our* love is often unable or unwilling to forgive sin, Romans 5:5 says God's love is different. It is poured out on our lives by His Spirit, and it's more than able to cover over anything that happens here on earth.
>
> Yes, God's love covers all sins. If we ask for it, experience it and extend it, we're able to fully enter into what Proverbs 10:12 is telling us: We don't have to be bound or held captive by the sins that have been committed against us. The "Yeah, but…" disappears and is overcome by something infinitely greater.

What a powerful meditation on the power of God's love. Indeed, as the Active Word team alluded to, Romans 5:5 says, "Now hope does not disappoint, because the love of God has been poured out in our hearts by the Holy Spirit who was given to us." Thank God for a hope that does not disappoint!

Stories of Real People and a Real Savior

A Life-Changing Accident

Brenda, Idaho

As I was going through *Healed and Set Free,* and was ministered to by close friends who love God, I was able to see that I needed to grieve through some things that happened in my past. If I had not been encouraged to be honest with myself and admit I was angry and sad about a semi-truck crashing into us and taking away my life as I knew it, I would have never been able to forgive the driver. But God is gracious and merciful. He has walked with me through every step of the healing process. He has also helped me to accept that some things are changed forever, but it is not the end of the world. I can minister to others who will suffer similar things.

Personal Questions

The questions in this section are geared towards people who have had painful experiences. In reading through these questions, be aware of any emotional or physical responses you have and record them. Answering these questions honestly will put you in touch with areas of your life that have been affected by your past issues like sexual abuse, rape, premarital pregnancy, abortion, divorce, rejection, betrayal or abuse.

Be Honest with Yourself

4. Which of the following statements describe what is in your heart, mind and life from hurts that linger? Circle those that apply and ask God to help you be honest with yourself.

    - I am angry; I hate them for hurting me.
    - It was wrong.
    - I am justified to hold hatred in my heart because of what they did to me.
    - I am overwhelmed with emotion thinking about what happened to me.
    - I am tired of the emotions consuming my life.
    - I feel numb when I think about what happened to me.
    - I need God to lead me to His truth and purify my heart.

5. Which of the following words describe how past hurts have manifested themselves in your life? Circle those that apply and ask God to help you see what could be defiling your heart.

    - Fear
    - Hurt
    - Negative thoughts
    - Defensiveness
    - Need to control
    - Resentment
    - Doubt
    - Pride
    - Anxiety
    - Insecurity
    - Bitterness
    - Desire to get even
    - Guilt
    - Self-pity
    - Feeling dirty

6. Are you struggling to turn off the negative feelings connected to your past, telling yourself to forget them or trying to sweep them under the rug?

7. Do you react physically by tightening your stomach muscles, clenching your jaw, or holding your breath when molestation, rape, abortion, divorce or the name of the one who hurt you is mentioned? If so, what happens?

8. Are you affected by physical reminders such as: smells, phrases, places, songs, etc.? (Recognize it as an attempt by Satan to make you a prisoner of your past).

9. Do you feel uncomfortable trusting others? If so, why?

10. Are you resentful and unforgiving toward anyone for his or her involvement in your painful memories? This may include parents or stepparents, children or stepchildren, past romantic interests, spouses or ex-spouses, brothers, sisters, extended family members, friends or ex-friends, bosses or co-workers. Ask God to help you examine your heart. "Let us search out and examine our ways, and turn back to the Lord; let us lift our hearts and hands to God in heaven" (Lamentations 3:40-41).

Write down your thoughts.

The Quilt

One of the greatest gifts we can give ourselves on our journey is to realize that it is our choice in how we allow the past to affect us. In her powerful piece, *The Quilt*,[3] my dear friend Shelley Spady expresses so beautifully how even the most painful past can turn into something beautiful with God's healing.

> Words like pain, heartache, suffering, disappointment and sorrow are not often connected with the thought of life's greatest moments. Yet we must understand that these emotions are part of the thread that makes up the fabric of our lives. Enduring life's twists and turns allows these threads to knit together to form the quilt that is our story.
>
> As time goes on, we can look back and see the patterns, the color and the beauty that a lifetime of experience brings—knowing with all certainty that the absence of just one thread would render the quilt incomplete. This is what makes our quilt unique and creates the picture of our life's journey.
>
> Wrap yourself in your quilt today and enjoy each moment. Both joys and sorrows can be beautiful if we have the right perspective.

Week 1: Day 4

Prayer: Bow your heart before the Lord prior to completing today's Bible study. Christ Jesus, help me SEE what wounds need to be healed. "He heals the brokenhearted and binds up their wounds" (Psalm 147:3).

Stories of Real People and a Real Savior

Letting Go of Shame and Guilt

Cheryl, Idaho

As a victim of child abuse, I carried a heavy burden around - if my own parents didn't love me or want me, then who would? I felt like beaten, damaged, used goods. I carried these feelings into my marriage and it affected my relationship with my husband and children. I was a high-maintenance wife and mother with uncontrolled anger, which burned out everyone around me! During this study I got on my knees, and for the first time in my life I begged the Lord to help me see what was in my heart and heal it so I could live the rest of my life in peace rather than torment. A mind-transforming miracle happened to me during this precious Bible study. I learned that Jesus Christ loves me and always has! For once in my life I looked beyond my self-absorbed world of fear and bitterness and gave those feelings of inadequacy to Christ. I learned that I didn't have to live as a victim of a horrible crime forever, but with Christ's love and God's truth, I could now live as an enlightened survivor, truly healed and set free.

By God's truth, my whole mindset has changed. I could never go back to that life again! It's as if the dark cloud that hung over my entire life has been completely evaporated by the power of God's light. I have learned how to forgive. To all those beautiful sisters of mine who have suffered the loss of innocence, I want to say to you, "Do not fear letting go of your shame, guilt or anger. Fear is of the enemy! Christ died for all sins including yours and He is waiting for you to come to Him. He is pure love. Wouldn't you love to walk in His pure love?"

Living for Today

Sindy, Idaho

The Healed and Set Free Bible Study gave me a new beginning to live for today and look forward to the future. It taught me what true forgiveness is and how to become free from my past. Jesus mended my broken heart, a heart I thought was shattered and would never be healed. He set me free from my past hurts. The Lord also showed me why I would lash out in anger toward others - I was so weak and brokenhearted that my thinking and judgment were impaired. I didn't realize how it affected others and that I was hurting them. I didn't know I was sinning. Thank You, Lord, for Your forgiveness, which is total, complete and absolute. "He has sent Me to heal the brokenhearted, to proclaim liberty to the captives" (Luke 4:18). "Therefore, If the Son makes you free, you shall be free indeed" (John 8:36). You can't change the past, but you can make a better tomorrow by living for today!

Hurt doesn't go away by itself. If you are denying the hurt, it will find ways to express itself, forming roots of bitterness that can injure you and others in your life. You can try to bury your heartache by putting on a smile, but your heart will still be filled with fear, shame, guilt, unforgiveness, self-centered desires, jealousy, and uncontrolled anger. It's time to get real with God about what is in your heart.

Emotional scars can affect other areas of your life, too. Your marriage, your children, your friendships, and your school or job performance all will suffer. Those scars can manifest in your life in ways such as drug and alcohol abuse, deep depression, suicidal tendencies, eating disorders, outbursts of anger, or rebellion.

1. Are your emotions out of control, specifically anger or sorrow? If so, explain.

   _____

   _____

2. Do you avoid friendships for fear of getting hurt?

   _____

   _____

3. Are memories of past sexual acts committed against you or by you causing difficulty with intimacy in your marriage? If so, what happened?

   _____

   _____

   _____

   _____

4. Do you find sexual intimacy a burden to you in your marriage? Yes or no?

5. Have you used illegal or prescription drugs or alcohol? Yes or no?

6. Have you had suicidal thoughts? If so, have you told anyone? How have you coped with these thoughts?

   _____

   _____

7. Have you experienced any flashbacks related to the memories of your past? If so, what?

   _____

   _____

   _____

   _____

8. Are you grieving the loss of something in your life? For example, a spouse, a child, your virginity, a trust, a position, or anything else.

9. When talking about your hurt, are you overcome with shame, sorrow, anger, or guilt?

10. Are you compelled to conceal your pain and suffering from certain people in your life or are you compelled to tell many people about your experience?

11. If you have children, do you smother them with your love and overprotect them or are you unable to show affection and bond with them?

12. Do you see repeating patterns such as outbursts of anger or depression in your behavior? Explain.

13. Do you struggle with overeating, starving yourself, or making yourself vomit?

14. Do you look at your life in terms of "before and after" the painful memories?

15. Did the painful event(s) bring you closer to God or turn you away from Him? Explain.

   _____

   _____

16. "Looking carefully lest anyone fall short of the grace of God; lest any root of bitterness springing up cause trouble, and by this many become defiled" (Hebrews 12:15). Bitterness is a root! I find it gripping that bitterness is described as a root. Roots grow underground. They are there, you just can't see them. The root of bitterness begins to grow very quietly. By the time it sprouts up, a lot has already taken place "underground" to destroy your heart. Let's face it. It can feel really good to stay mad at someone! It can also feel really good to plan out in your mind what you would do to this person if you had the chance. I know this all too well! We must SEE the root of bitterness in our own heart. This is absolutely critical so that God can set us free.

    - How do you know you may have a root of bitterness?
    - Do you find yourself trying to turn others against someone you dislike?
    - Are you continually thinking destructive thoughts about someone?
    - Do you feel sick to your stomach when you see a person you don't like?

    Determine to deal with this stuff NOW and don't put it off. Don't let your heart be bitter against anyone. Ask God to show you how to SEE the bitter root you may be holding onto. No one ever gets to the end of their life and thinks, "I wish I stayed bitter longer." Pain and tragedy can bring out the worst in humanity, but it can also bring out the best if we let God heal and set us free.

17. Read Luke 18:9-14: "Also He spoke this parable to some who trusted in themselves that they were righteous, and despised others: 'Two men went up to the temple to pray, one a Pharisee and the other a tax collector. The Pharisee stood and prayed thus with himself, "God, I thank You that I am not like other men—extortioners, unjust, adulterers, or even as this tax collector. I fast twice a week; I give tithes of all that I possess." And the tax collector, standing afar off, would not so much as raise his eyes to heaven, but beat his breast, saying, "God, be merciful to me a sinner!" I tell you, this man went down to his house justified rather than the other; for everyone who exalts himself will be humbled, and he who humbles himself will be exalted.'"

    Do you see yourself as the Pharisee or tax collector in the story? Explain why.

    If so, why do you need God's mercy?

This Week's Tool and Memory Verse

Tool #1 - SEE: I must _____ the truth about what is in my _____, so I am not defiled. To _____ means to make filthy or dirty; to _____.

"Looking carefully lest anyone fall short of the grace of God;
lest any root of bitterness springing up cause trouble,
and by this many become defiled" (Hebrews 12:15).

Week 1: Day 5

Prayer: Bow your heart before the Lord prior to completing today's Bible study. Christ Jesus, help me SEE what wounds need to be healed. Help me to forgive others as You have forgiven me.

After finishing yesterday's questions, you may be aware of other areas in your life that have been affected by unresolved hurts. Use the space provided on this page to write down what continues to flood your mind about the hurts that still linger. Don't stop the tears or the pain as this is part of the process God uses to reveal your heart. It is how you get real with Him. It is what will help you to SEE the depths of your pain. Allow God into the secret rooms of your heart. He is not looking for a performance, just the truth. God is serious about His love for you. Let's be people who are serious about being honest with Him because He cares for us and wants to completely heal our deepest wounds.

Open Your Heart and Let the Healer In

1. Write down what continues to flood your mind about your lingering hurts.

The Power of Forgiveness

A Reflection from Pastor Rick Brown,[4]
Tammy's husband

There is one of Rick's messages that, to this day, makes me realize how crucial forgiveness is. Focusing our attention on Matthew 18:21-35 (on page 302), he says:

One of the things you are going to experience when you fall in love with Jesus is being overwhelmed by His forgiveness for you. You'll be blown away that God can forgive you for everything: for your past—no matter how rotten you were, your present—no matter what you're struggling with, and your future—His forgiveness even awaits the things yet to come. Past, present and future—the cleansing blood of Jesus is there to change and transform our hearts.

So when we discover and embrace Jesus' forgiveness in our lives, it follows with good logic that we shouldn't be mere recipients of His forgiveness. We shouldn't just be a dead-end of grace, but grace should also flow through us to others. We not only become a forgiven people, but we should become a forgiving people.

Yet for some, there's a disconnection between what God has done for them and what they should extend to others. And this is where a question arises in the Apostle Peter's mind. You see, earlier in the text, Jesus was talking about offenses. He'd been talking about when people sin against you, and how you work through that conflict resolution. That's what prompted Peter to ask this question.

It says in Matthew 18:21, "Then Peter came to Him and said, 'Lord, how often shall my brother sin against me and I forgive him? Up to seven times?'" Again, Jesus had just been talking about reconciliation: You confront somebody, they say they're sorry, you say you're sorry, and you reconcile. Peter then says, "How many times should I go through the process of forgiveness with a brother or sister? Seven times?"

Realize, Peter has grown up listening to the rabbis, who believed three times was the maximum number of times you need to forgive someone, or that if you tried to work through a conflict three times, then you didn't have to forgive any more. Perhaps that's where the original "three strikes and you're out" came from.

So Peter thinks he's onto some really incredible spiritual truth. Can you imagine his thought process? Now he's been hanging out with Jesus, who seems a lot more gracious, merciful, loving and forgiving than all the rabbis he had grown up around. He guesses that perhaps Jesus is a little more than twice as forgiving as the rabbis, so he suggests forgiving others up to seven times.

Peter probably thinks that's as generous as a person needs to be with forgiveness. So he says, "Lord, how many times should I forgive my brother? Seven times?" I think at that moment he is sitting there waiting for the praise, "Oh Peter! Unbelievable! How magnanimous of you! How generous! I didn't realize what was going on in your spirit, Peter, you're really coming along well. Atta boy!"

But Jesus blows his mind. He says, "I do not say to you up to seven times, but up to seventy times seven" (v.22). Peter gets his rudimentary Galilean calculator out: seventy x seven = 490 times?! Now he is in shock. He thought he was being generous—the rabbis said three, he thought seven, but Jesus said *seven times seventy?!*

That had to take the breath right out of Peter's lungs! And yet, is Jesus saying, "Well, Peter, it's seventy times seven, so get your notebook out and start recording and keeping track of people"? Was Jesus trying to teach His disciples to become good counters, good record-keepers? Not at all!

Yet some people think that's what relationships are about. They become counters. They get a notebook (although they might not need a notebook, because they have a mind like a steel trap) and start keeping a record of wrongs. How are we going to get through life if Jesus is teaching us that He doesn't want us to keep score?

Before you came to Christ, maybe you felt like I did. I grew up without Jesus in my life. Because of the difficulty of life, I was quite jaded and hard-hearted from an early age. Three strikes from the rabbis was way too generous for me. If you hurt me once, unless you were in my family, you were done. Then I got saved, and all of the sudden I'm basking in God's forgiveness. I realized He wanted forgiveness to flow through me to others. In life, there will be a lot of conflict but through the grace of God we can be changed.

When Tammy was young, she used to go over to her cousins' house a lot. Her parents thought they were taking her to the safest place possible, because it was her aunt and uncle's daycare. Tammy was in first or second grade at the time. But what her parents didn't know was that when they dropped Tammy off, her uncle was molesting her and the other children in the daycare. They kept dropping off their precious little girl at a pervert's house.

Tammy was so traumatized by this perverted uncle that in second grade she totally shut down. She couldn't learn because of what was going on in her life. Her teacher called her parents for a parent-teacher conference and said, "I'm sad to inform you that your daughter is retarded." It wasn't that she was retarded, but that she was so traumatized by what her uncle was doing to her.

Tammy was 19 years old when we got engaged. She had never shared her entire story with anyone until she told me. And at that point we realized the daycare was still there, and this uncle was still doing these things. He was a predator and his wife had a daycare where he could molest all these little kids. I was incensed and enraged over the issue. I wanted to kill the guy!

It was before the TV series "Cold Case," so I couldn't learn how to do it and not get caught. I'm good with a rifle at long range, I thought about that. I thought about poison, but I'm not really a good chemist. While I was thinking about how I could kill this guy, Tammy's mom went one step further: She drove to his house with her husband's police revolver. She thought about it, but at the last minute went home.

Meanwhile, we discovered that not only had this guy molested Tammy and all the kids in the daycare, but all Tammy's cousins as well. So we found one cousin that was within the statute of limitations, and we pressed charges. We thought it would be great; he would be arrested and off the streets so the kids would be safe.

But you see, he had children of his own that he had been molesting all those years. The day he was arrested, Tammy's cousin Nicki, a popular, cute, 16-year-old whose father had been molesting her all her life, went home and hung herself on her closet door. Nicki's funeral was the same week her dad was arrested.

His son Steve killed himself several years later because of the perversion his father had tortured him with all those years. His other son Tim, was in a mental institution for years and in 2013 he ended his life by jumping off a bridge. His other daughter is a meth addict.

When we chose to take this crime to the law to get this predator off the streets, it destroyed our family. It absolutely obliterated the family because of what he did. He went to prison for 15 years in the Idaho State Penitentiary. On the day of his sentencing, the judge sentenced him for 30 years, then realized he could only give him 15, and said, "Well, I want to give you 30." I was filled with such hatred toward this guy for what he had done to Tammy. I've never wanted to murder anyone in my life, but I wanted to kill him.

You know what changed my life? When Tammy and I started praying. Tammy, having learned in His Word that the Lord wanted her to forgive, said, "Father I forgive Tom, and I pray for his salvation. I pray that you would save his soul in prison, that he might go to Heaven and not go to Hell."

I wanted him to go to Hell. I wanted him to have the hottest spot. I wanted him to be the Walmart greeter in Hell: "Hi, you're in Hell—I'm Tom." But when Tammy made the choice, the decision of the will, to forgive him, I thought, "Who am I to harbor any unforgiveness?" I realized I needed to pray, "Lord, please forgive me, I need to forgive him. I need to let it go because it's eating me alive." And when forgiveness flowed through us, we were no longer in bondage.

Now, this guy had never asked for forgiveness. He didn't want forgiveness. Just because Tammy and I forgave him, doesn't mean what he did was okay. When his parole hearing came up 10 years into his sentence, our forgiveness didn't stop us from testifying against him to protect other children. We realized he is a predator and if given the chance, he would not only molest children, but he'd probably kill them this time like he had threatened before. This guy is that wicked.

There are going to be people throughout your entire life whom you need to forgive. I want you to know that on a regular basis I have somebody in this category that I am praying for as I go through struggles in my life. That's just the way it is. That's real life. With Christ's help, and the forgiveness He has given to us, we are able to extend forgiveness to others.

Jesus has come that you might have forgiveness, but once you taste and see that the Lord is good and experience His forgiveness, you are now able to extend forgiveness. Watch your blood pressure drop, watch your appetite come back, and your sleep be sweet again.

"Bearing with one another, and forgiving one another, if anyone has a complaint against another; even as Christ forgave you, so you also must do" (Colossians 3:13).

There is a choice in pain, an opportunity in every trial. Pain makes us focus either inward or outward. It makes us either martyrs or merciful. The choice is ours.

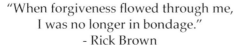

"When forgiveness flowed through me,
I was no longer in bondage."
- Rick Brown

Chapter Review

1. Read the commentary below.

How to Be a Slave

Start by hating someone

The moment you start hating someone, you become their slave

They control your thoughts and invade your dreams

They absorb your creativity, determine your appetite and affect your digestion

They rob you of your peace of mind and take away the pleasure of your work

You can't get away from the person you hate

They are with you when you are awake and when you sleep

They influence the tone of your voice when you speak to your wife, children or boss

They require that you take medicine for your indigestion and headaches

They steal time and energy

Your hatred will keep you from forgiving

Your unforgiveness will make you a slave

2. Do you want to be a slave and continue to hate, or do you want to forgive and be set free?

This Week's Focus

Prayer: Ask God to help you SEE what's in your heart.

By Memory: My challenge to you is to fill out this week's tool definition and Bible verse without looking. I know that by hiding these words of wisdom in your heart you are providing yourself with the truth to truly be healed and set free. May we rise up to be women of the Word.

Tool #1 - SEE: I must SEE the _____ about what is in my _____, so I am not _____.

Definition: To defile means to make filthy or dirty; to pollute.

Bible Verse: "Looking carefully lest anyone fall short of the _____ of God; lest any root of _____ springing up cause trouble, and by this many become _____" (Hebrews 12:15).

Stories of Real People and a Real Savior

From a 22 Year-Old Rape Survivor
By Kay, Pennsylvania

When I left my parents' house in Pennsylvania that afternoon, danger was the furthest thought from my mind. A few girls on my basketball team invited me to a small party, and I was determined to go. After all, fitting in with the upperclassmen was important to me. I had been to parent-supervised parties back home, but they were tame compared to the scene I witnessed shortly after arriving. I was abandoned almost as soon as I stepped through the door. There were countless people pouring into the house, loud music booming. At this point, I think even the hostess of the party was beginning to feel a tinge of anxiety. My confidence over being invited to such an event quickly evaporated as I watched reckless behavior evolve.

I honestly considered heading back home, but feeling pressured to fit in, I shrugged it off and stayed. I mingled, trying to find familiar faces. I finally did, and was thankful to discover I wasn't the only person abstaining from alcohol and other deviant behavior. Crammed into a corner and feeling suffocated from all the people around me, I began to feel thirsty. I made my way to the kitchen and asked the hostess where I could find something non-alcoholic to drink. She guided me to the refrigerator and told me to help myself. I found a Gatorade and quickly chugged the entire bottle in a matter of seconds. Having quenched my thirst, I re-entered the living room to find friends. But soon I began to feel strange, almost nauseated and sick feeling. My palms started to sweat; I could feel my heartbeat quickening. Thinking I was going to become sick, I asked where I could lie down for just a moment until the nausea faded. I was directed to a bedroom upstairs where I was told I wouldn't be bothered. My concept of time ends here.

Have you ever felt so tired you can't keep your eyes open to save your life? Your whole body seems to be "gone"? Dizziness, overwhelming fatigue, blackouts, moments of lucidity followed by blank spots, feeling as if in a dream, not hearing sounds-only voices with an echo as if they are far away, memory lapses, inability to cry out or even talk, paralysis of your entire body, difficulty breathing... Realizing what is happening to you, and not being able to do anything to make it stop; feeling the clothes being stripped from your body, and not having the physical strength to fight back; feeling your body being violated, fearing you are dying, that this person on top of you is going to kill you; feeling a force of intense pain, trying to stay awake to yell for help, trying to say stop, to muster a NO, trying to survive... I experienced all this, then proceeded to fall into a deep sleep.

When I finally woke up I felt foggy, scared, like I was experiencing the worst hangover ever. I had fallen victim to a drug that left me completely helpless. After the effects wore off, I was in a state of complete shock. I knew what had happened to me... I could feel the pain; honestly, I could hardly walk. Nevertheless, I walked right out of that house without saying a word to anyone, got in my car, and drove two hours back to my parents' house. I got home, jumped in the shower, and went straight to bed without saying a thing. I looked at the bruising between my legs, the bleeding. I cried myself to sleep that night and woke up Christmas Eve morning to find that my whole body was sore. I felt like I had been hit by a bus, literally. I did everything I could to make sure nobody knew the pain I was feeling. I was embarrassed, ashamed, scared, I felt dirty, I didn't want to get in trouble for going to a party. So I remained silent. I remained silent for a long time. But the silence was killing me.

I began making life-destroying decisions. I distanced myself from good friends and family. I wanted nothing to do with God, nothing to do with the only people who would love me no matter what. I began having inappropriate relationships with other females. I was drawn to the nurturing, the attention, feeling loved. I craved love and attention, yet I refused the love of my family, my church, my friends, and most importantly, God. For about three years I lived a life of debauchery. I found myself sitting in bars having drink after drink, trying so hard to fill this horrible emptiness I was feeling. I was at a very low point, I had even considered ending my life just to shut off the constant emotional and mental torment I was in. I had opened my life up to darkness, and darkness happily reigned in my soul.

My parents tried everything they could. They loved me unconditionally and prayed without ceasing that the Lord would take hold of my life. I had begun seeing a therapist, but it became a waste of time and money because I wasn't willing to be truthful or open to change. Out of pure desperation, my dad ordered Healed and Set Free in an attempt to reach me. I loved to read, and I knew they were just grasping at straws. I agreed to give it a try. I would have fleeting intentions of wanting to get my life back. I would read, but my heart was so hard nothing was truly penetrating. I decided to leave my parents' house, to walk out of their lives for good so I could continue living the dark life I had become so accustomed to. I was a prodigal, and had left my parents no choice but to give my life over to the Father; it was out of their hands.

After three years of living a chaotic, out-of-control life, not speaking with my family for months, God graciously and miraculously put His people into my life. I had reached a breaking point, stripped of everything, and God in His perfect timing set everything in place so I couldn't deny His loving presence. I cried out to Him, I couldn't take this burden I had been carrying anymore. I needed His love, His grace and His comfort. But most of all, I needed His forgiveness; I needed repentance. I remember calling my mother; I was afraid to talk to her after literally putting my family through hell, but to my surprise I was greeted with kindness and love. I cried, and it was at that point that I made the commitment to give my life back to Christ, to restore the years I had lost to sin and silence.

I was making all the right moves, yet I still had a lot of work to do. I knew it was imperative that I see my therapist again. I was ready to get my life back, the life Christ had for me. I had a lot of skeletons in my closet to reveal-to bring every secret, every hurt, every shame into the light. I began to unravel the tangled mess I had allowed to reside within me.

Healed and Set Free became a crucial tool in my healing process. Reading it this time was different: Every page, every word began to penetrate my heart. The clear gospel message of the book began to illuminate all the disgrace I had felt and its effects. By reading [the study] I learned that God is strong even when I am weak, and He is close to the brokenhearted. There is such powerful, clear hope there. I felt God using Healed and Set Free to give me grace from Jesus that ran deeper than the wounds I had experienced. Reading this book was a huge tool that God used to change my life. That sounds cliche, but it is so true. Healed and Set Free is dripping with divine knowledge; it is overwhelmingly full of the evidence of God's grace, promises of restoration and the healing power of the Holy Spirit. Here are just a few of the many truths I took from Healed and Set Free:

God cares about what you went through. His own Son, although He didn't experience violence in a sexual form, was a victim of violent assault. No matter how awful your attack, no matter how long and slow your recovery, God is your Redeemer. He is able to redeem terrible wrongs and make them right. Psalm 147:3 tells us, "He heals the brokenhearted and binds up their wounds."

Face your reactions to what happened. You must be willing to let God enter into your reactions—to feel what you feel. A violation makes you feel violated. When something overpowers you, you feel weak and overwhelmed. You need to be able to enter into your grief, hurt, confusion, fear and anger. Tell God all about your anguish as the psalmist does: "My heart is in anguish within me" (Psalm 55:4).

Don't try to face what happened and deal with your reactions by yourself. Invite Jesus into your struggle. Take hold of His promise of good: "When you pass through the waters, I will be with you; and through the rivers, they shall not overwhelm you; when you walk through fire you shall not be burned, and the flame shall not consume you" (Isaiah 43:2). You are walking in deep waters; God will walk with you. You are walking through fire; God will not let the flames consume you. Turn to Him every day, take His promises to heart each day. Every time you remember, every time you struggle, every time you feel your heart breaking under the weight of what happened to you, ask Him to help you. Say His promises out loud. Speak them back to the One who is your hope. Having faith in Jesus is not something you do just once. He's the person toward whom you reach, toward whom you cry, toward whom you bring your pain, confusion, anger, and fear. He is the direction in which you face. He's the direction in which you live. He can bear the weight of your trouble and heartache. He also suffered at the hands of evil people. He knows what a broken heart feels like.

Another crucial step in your healing is forgiveness. What happened to you was a great evil, so forgiveness won't come easily or in a moment. It will be a journey of many small steps. True forgiveness for a true evil is only possible because of God's forgiveness of you. Paul explains it like this, "Be kind to one another, tenderhearted, forgiving one another, just as God, in Christ, has forgiven you" (Ephesians 4:32).

I am a huge advocate for Healed and Set Free and its ministry, and I will be forever blessed by it. As I celebrate year one of being healed and set free, I have committed my life to being a nameless servant of Christ. Praise be to Him.
December 23, 2008

Tools to Become Healed and Set Free

To equip yourself in God's truth, look over the tools and verses that will be introduced in the coming weeks. Thinking about the past won't change it, but you can change your future by being set free from your past.

TOOL #1 - SEE: I must SEE the truth about what is in my heart so I am not defiled.

> **Definition**: To defile means to make filthy or dirty; to pollute.
>
> **Bible Verse**: "Looking carefully lest anyone fall short of the grace of God; lest any root of bitterness springing up cause trouble, and by this many become defiled" (Hebrews 12:15).

TOOL #2 - GIVE: I must GIVE my sin to God through repentance, knowing that Christ is waiting to take it. I must be sorry enough to change, and choose to go God's way over my own.

> **Definition**: To repent means to feel such sorrow for sin or fault as to be disposed to change one's life for the better; be penitent.
>
> **Bible Verse**: "For godly sorrow produces repentance leading to salvation, not to be regretted; but the sorrow of the world produces death" (2 Corinthians 7:10).

TOOL #3 - FORGIVE: I must FORGIVE as I am forgiven by Christ: Forgiving those who hurt, bruised, wronged, rejected, betrayed or harmed me, whether unintentionally or deliberately. I must ask God to forgive me for holding on to unforgiveness and know that He will.

> **Definition**: To forgive means to stop feeling angry or resentful toward someone for an offense, flaw or mistake.
>
> **Bible Verse**: "...Bearing with one another, and forgiving one another, if anyone has a complaint against another; even as Christ forgave you, so you also must do" (Colossians 3:13).

TOOL #4 - FORGET: I must FORGET by no longer dwelling on the hurt or the painful reminders such as: phrases, smells, places, songs and comments. Instead, I am putting my mind on the higher calling that Christ has for me.

> **Definition**: To forget means to choose not to remember or notice, "forgive and forget".
>
> **Bible Verse**: "Brethren, I do not count myself to have apprehended; but one thing I do, forgetting those things which are behind and reaching forward to those things which are ahead" (Philippians 3:13).

Be Healed and Set Free: Christ will heal me from my past, showing me the truth, so I can become a cleansed vessel, healed and set free.

> **Definition**: To set free means to make free; set at liberty; release from bondage, imprisonment, or restraint.
>
> **Definition**: To heal means to make whole and healthy; to cure; to remedy or repair.
>
> **Bible Verse**: "And you shall know the truth, and the truth shall make you free" (John 8:32).

Knowing God's Heart

This week we will be growing in our understanding of Tool #1 and how to apply it to our lives. Inviting God into our lives and **SEE**ing the truth within our hearts is the first step towards becoming Healed and Set Free.

Tool #1 - SEE: I must SEE the truth about what is in my heart so I am not defiled.

Definition: To defile means to make filthy or dirty; to pollute.

Bible Verse: "Looking carefully lest anyone fall short of the grace of God; lest any root of bitterness springing up cause trouble, and by this many become defiled" (Hebrews 12:15).

Prayer: Ask God to help you SEE what's in your heart. Continue to ask God to fill you with the knowledge of His will through all the wisdom and understanding that the Spirit gives.

Week 2: Day 1

Prayer: Bow your heart before the Lord in prayer prior to completing today's study. Ask Him to draw near to you.

When everything is lost—loved ones, possessions, jobs—many people feel hopeless. I want you to know that God has a cure for every kind of trouble we face, because God gives us a hope unlike any in the entire world. So let me ask you a question: Do you have a problem? Well, God has the cure"says Greg Laurie.[1] God does have the cure. I'm encouraged by Psalm 147:3; it says that Jesus "heals the brokenhearted and binds up their wounds."

Long ago, before antibiotics and modern medicine, wounds were dealt with very differently. Instead of just putting a couple stitches in a wound or applying a Band-Aid, special care had to be taken to ensure that a possibly life-threatening infection didn't set in. If an infection did set in, a caregiver would often have to reopen the wound in order to get the infection out.

The same could be said of our own wounds. Sometimes we have to reopen the deep, dark wounds of our hearts again to deal with the "infection" that has set in. These wounds may not be visible from the outside, but their effect is the same: they hurt us and keep us from being well.

Our memory verse this week is Hebrews 12:15: "Looking carefully lest anyone fall short of the grace of God; lest any root of bitterness springing up cause trouble, and by this many become defiled."

The first step to becoming set free is to SEE our wounds. This process will take courage and may hurt a little, but the promise of being set free will be worth it all.

> "Looking carefully lest anyone fall short of the grace of God;
> lest any root of bitterness springing up cause trouble,
> and by this many become defiled"
> (Hebrews 12:15).

Tools to Become Healed and Set Free

This week we will be growing in our understanding of **Tool #1 - SEE** and learning how to apply it to our lives.

These four tools will help you become set free. Each tool will be defined when the time comes. It is crucial to memorize these powerful tools and review them regularly in order to apply them to your daily life.

#1 - SEE: I must SEE the truth about what is in my heart so I am not defiled.

#2 - GIVE: I must GIVE my sin to God through repentance, knowing that Christ is waiting to take it. I must be sorry enough to change, and choose to go God's way over my own.

#3 - FORGIVE: I must FORGIVE as I am forgiven by Christ: Forgiving those who hurt, bruised, wronged, rejected, betrayed or harmed me, whether unintentionally or deliberately. I must ask God to forgive me for holding on to unforgiveness and know that He will.

#4 - FORGET: I must FORGET by no longer dwelling on the hurt or the painful reminders such as: phrases, smells, places, songs and comments. Instead, I am putting my mind on the higher calling that Christ has for me.

Be Healed and Set Free: Christ will heal me from my past, showing me the truth, so I can become a cleansed vessel, healed and set free.

This Week's Focus

Prayer: Ask God to help you SEE what's in your heart. Continue to ask God to fill you with the knowledge of His will through all the wisdom and understanding that the Spirit gives.

By Memory: My challenge to you is to be able to recite this week's tool and Bible verse without looking. I know that by hiding these words of wisdom in your heart you are providing yourself with tools to truly be healed and set free. May we rise up to be women of the Word.

Tool #1 - SEE: I must SEE the truth about what is in my heart so I am not defiled.

Definition: To defile means to make filthy or dirty; to pollute.

Bible Verse: "Looking carefully lest anyone fall short of the grace of God; lest any root of bitterness springing up cause trouble, and by this many become defiled" (Hebrews 12:15).

"And you shall know the truth, and the truth shall make you free" (John 8:32).

God's Heart to Counsel

God invites us to draw close to Him. Knowing God's heart encourages us to be like Him, to bring our needs to Him, to love and trust Him, and to respond to Him in joyful obedience. We must lay our will down and apply the truth of His Word to our lives, one day at a time, choice by choice. We trust that He is all-knowing, the Provider, Counselor, Healer and the Prince of Peace.

But how do we draw near to God's heart? How can we put ourselves in a position to allow God to heal and set us free?

Developing a Habit of Drawing Near to God

The answer is to develop a habit of drawing near to God by devoting ourselves daily to reading His Word and to prayer. This is called our devotional time. It is through daily time with God and reading His Word that we gain the spiritual nutrients we need to grow in our faith and understanding of Him. But, as Elizabeth George remarks in *A Woman After God's Own Heart*,[2] it's too easy to let life get ahead of our time with the Lord:

> I know firsthand how hard it is to develop the habit of drawing near to God, how easy it is to skip and miss. For some reason, I tend to think I'll spend time with God later, or I'll just miss this one day, then catch up with God tomorrow! I've learned, however, that my good intentions don't go very far. It's easy for me to start the day planning to have my devotional time... After I've done a few things around the house, made some phone calls, tidied up the kitchen, started the dishwasher, made the bed, picked up those clothes on the floor, and—oh, I almost forgot—wiped off the bathroom counter. Suddenly I'm off and running. Somehow I never get the time for the most important relationship in my life—my relationship with God! That's why I have to be firm with myself and aim for scheduled time with God, whether I feel like it or not.

A dear friend of mine has her devotional time every morning after dropping the kids off at school. Some mothers have their time while their children are asleep. I set aside time at 7:00 a.m. every morning for my devotions and Bible study. Remember, the only wrong time for being alone with God is no time! So pick a time that matches your schedule and go for it!

1. Read Deuteronomy 7:6-8: "For you are a holy people to the LORD your God; the LORD your God has chosen you to be a people for Himself, a special treasure above all the peoples on the face of the earth. The LORD did not set His love on you nor choose you because you were more in number than any other people, for you were the least of all peoples, but because [He] loves you..."

    Who chose you? Do you believe God loves you?

    _____

2. Why are you a special treasure to Him?

    _____

    _____

3. Do you trust God with your hurts, struggles and disappointments: yes or no?

4. Read Psalm 1:1-2: "Blessed is the man who walks not in the counsel of the ungodly, nor stands in the path of sinners, nor sits in the seat of the scornful; but his delight is in the law of the Lord, and in His law he meditates day and night."

   Are you to seek ungodly counsel from those who don't follow God's counsel? Why or why not?

5. Does ungodly counsel set you free? Yes or no?

6. Read Psalm 1:6: "For the LORD knows the way of the righteous, but the way of the ungodly shall perish."

   What happens when you follow ungodly ways of counsel?

7. When or where are you most often prompted to make a choice between dwelling in God's counsel or lingering in the ungodly counsel of a friend, spouse or your own thinking?

8. Read Proverbs 1:5: "A wise man will hear and increase learning, and a man of understanding will attain wise counsel."

   Where is wise counsel found?

9. What happens when you apply God's wisdom to your life?

10. In John 5:6 Jesus asks, "Do you want to be made well?" Before you move on in this journey, you need to know the answer to the question Jesus has asked you. Search your heart—don't look to your dad or mom, stepfather or stepmother, boyfriend, or the heart of the person who hurt you. You must take a stand in your own heart to be made well from the hurts that still linger. This is critical! Do you desire to be healed and set free? If so, how great is your desire? Be specific.

Stories of Real People and a Real Savior

The Lord Rescued Me From Myself

Renee, Idaho

Watching the Lord heal and comfort my mother's heart made me wonder if He could do the same for me.

I had just rededicated my life to Christ. However, I still hung on to what I felt were justified pain and anger. I was hurting so bad because my heart had been misled by so many guys so many times. I lived in fear of getting close to anyone because getting close meant getting hurt and getting walked on.

I was sick of hurting and not trusting anyone. I wanted to be free from my past but I didn't know how to get there. So I signed up for *Healed and Set Free*. I thought just signing up and going to the study would be enough to heal my heart. It wasn't! I needed to actively choose to apply the tools and the Word to my own life.

When I realized I couldn't do it on my own, I let Jesus heal me and I applied the things I learned in the study. I became totally aware of God's awesome power, and being healed was an amazing experience. The Lord rescued me from myself. He was preparing my heart to love again. I was amazed.

He is continually working in my life. Being healed doesn't mean that I'll never be hurt or fall down again, but it does cause me to see how much I truly needed the Savior to save me from falling.

This Week's Tool and Memory Verse

Tool #1 - SEE: I must _____ the truth about what is in my _____, so I am not defiled. To _____ means to make filthy or dirty; to _____.

"Looking carefully lest anyone fall short of the grace of God;
lest any root of bitterness springing up cause trouble,
and by this many become defiled" (Hebrews 12:15).

Week 2: Day 2

Prayer: Bow your heart before the Lord in prayer before completing today's study. Ask God to prepare and soften your heart to listen to His still, small voice.

God's Heart to Heal

In Mark 2:17 Jesus says, "Those who are well have no need of a physician, but those who are sick. I did not come to call the righteous, but sinners, to repentance." In Greg Laurie's devotional "Our Great Physician,"[3] he explains how the Lord ministers to us in ways specific to our needs:

> Every person Jesus had conversations or contact with was in a different situation, and He dealt with each one differently, because He recognized that every man, woman and child is different: Though they have many of the same problems and the same basic needs, He recognized there were unique things about them that needed ministry. In His encounters with people, Jesus was like a physician.
>
> He basically said, "I didn't come to bring the righteous to repentance, I came to bring sinners, because those who are whole do not need a physician."
>
> Jesus is the Great Physician. He came to heal the brokenhearted, to preach deliverance to the captives, give sight to the blind and freedom to the oppressed. He is going to find your area of need, whatever it may be, and He is going to minister to you as an individual.

Jesus captures it perfectly in John 3:16: "For God so loved the world that He gave His only begotten Son, that whoever believes in Him should not perish but have everlasting life." Again, as Greg Laurie aptly describes in "You are Loved by God:"[4]

> Although God loves us as we are, He doesn't want to leave us this way. He wants us to turn from our sin, and believe in and follow Him. When we do, we become His adopted child. He refers to us "in the Beloved" (Ephesians 1:6), meaning we are in a special relationship with Him because of Jesus' death for each of us, and our acceptance of Him as Savior and Lord.
>
> God loves you more than you realize: When Jesus was baptized by John, God said, "This is my beloved Son, in whom I am well pleased" (Mark 3:17). Jesus said, "The glory which You gave Me I have given them, that they may be one just as We are one: I in them, and You in Me; that they may be made perfect in one, and that the world may know that You have sent Me, and have loved them as You have loved Me" (John 17:22-23). It's hard to believe God loves us that much. The truth about the Christian—the one who is in Christ and adopted into God's family, made accepted in the Beloved—is that God the Father loves him as He loves His own Son.
>
> Let that sink in: That's an amazing thought, don't you think? So be blessed today, you who have trusted in Christ. Know that you are His dear beloved children.

1. Read Psalm 107:19-20: "Then they cried out to the Lord in their trouble, and He saved them out of their distresses. He sent His word and healed them, and delivered them from their destructions."

   In the space below, name the hurts that cause trouble and distress in your mind and heart. Write down your thoughts.

   _____
   _____
   _____
   _____
   _____
   _____
   _____

2. Do you believe that God can be your personal Healer with the issues that trouble your heart?

   _____
   _____

3. Do you desire to see the truth about what is in your heart?

   _____
   _____

4. Write down what God has already revealed to you.

   _____
   _____
   _____
   _____
   _____
   _____
   _____
   _____

> I'm thankful I'm going on this journey,
> even though it will be one of the most
> difficult journeys I'll ever make.

5. Read James 5:13,15-16: "Is anyone among you suffering? Let him pray... And the prayer of faith will save the sick, and the Lord will raise him up. And if he has committed sins, he will be forgiven. Confess your trespasses to one another, and pray for one another, that you may be healed. The effective, fervent prayer of a righteous man avails much."

   After meditating on James, what do you need to do to be obedient to God in your healing? Write down that which applies to you:

   _____
   _____
   _____
   _____

6. In the midst of the heartache, you must apply the message of James 5 to your healing. Christ must be the center of every conversation concerning your hurt in order to heal. The memories, heartache, anger and resentment may be deep inside your heart, and once you begin to talk about it you may be overwhelmed by grief. But once it is out, it feels good. Pray for God's help to heal from the past. Pray to find one close, godly, Christian friend who is a good listener to pray with you. Name this person:

   _____

7. Read Isaiah 53:4-5: "Surely He has borne our griefs and carried our sorrows; yet we esteemed Him stricken, smitten by God, and afflicted. But He was wounded for our transgressions, He was bruised for our iniquities; the chastisement for our peace was upon Him, and by His stripes we are healed."

   All the unacceptable, gross sin that's happened in your life has been laid on Christ Jesus. Write down what is flooding your heart toward Him after seeing what He went through in order for you to receive healing for your soul.

   _____
   _____
   _____
   _____
   _____
   _____

> "Your truths are simple, sweet Jesus, and may we all understand that Satan doesn't want us to see just how easy it is to be free."
> -T.J., Idaho

8. Read 1 John 2:1: "My little children, these things I write to you, so that you may not sin. And if anyone sins, we have an Advocate with the Father, Jesus Christ the righteous." Who is your Advocate when you sin?

_____

_____

9. Read Matthew 9:9-13 on page 302, and write the definition of "righteousness" from page 301. Based on this scripture and definition, why do you think Jesus said He didn't come into this world for the righteous?

_____

_____

_____

_____

_____

10. In Matthew 9:12, it reads: "He said to them, 'Those who are well have no need of a physician, but those who are sick.'" The Great Physician is waiting to touch your heart. Write down the areas of your life that need Christ Jesus.

_____

_____

_____

_____

_____

_____

_____

_____

11. Take an inventory of your heart. What do you see still lingering (circle):

- Resentment
- Self-absorption
- Hatred
- Pride
- Unforgiveness
- Guilt
- Personal failures
- Out-of-control anger
- Shame
- Fear
- Holding grudges
- Jealousy

It's not easy to admit or even to see the inventory of our hearts, but it is so necessary that we examine our hearts every day, to keep us from being defiled by sin. Write down your thoughts.

_____

_____

_____

_____

Stories of Real People and a Real Savior

From Tears of Sorrow to Tears of Freedom

T.J., Idaho

Dear Lord,

As Your hand guides me, may I share the truth of Your love, mercies and joy with anyone who is seeking to be healed by Your mighty power.

There were dark corners of my life where words were not allowed: deep hurts, incest and betrayal. At first, they were just dirty memories of the sins that were put on me, never to be spoken of again. But from those sins and memories, which I call the trunk, a tree grew. Just a few branches at first, but then through the years, an enormous sinful tree made of sexual immorality, abortion, theft, lying, manipulation, judging, condemnation, pride, self-absorption, self-pity and deep roots of bitterness.

Sweet Jesus, knowing all, You never left me behind. You drew me in like a fish on a line. You put a hunger in my heart that nothing would satisfy but You, and bit by bit, I started to know Your truths, and I cried many tears of sorrow.

At the time, I thought the tears were those of self-pity, but now, as I'm growing in knowledge, I realize they were tears to set me free (2 Corinthians 7:10).

You, Lord, showed me that I was lacking something vital. I know now why I am here—to further Your kingdom. I know why I suffer—to draw near to You—although I sometimes still ask the question, "Why do bad things happen?" You always answer, and I know You are love and that You created us to love us. Finally, I understand Your love for me. Thank You, Lord.

As I started to see what was hiding in my tree of sin, You revealed the deep hurts that were there. You helped me to forgive the weaknesses of others, because that is Your desire. You also helped me to see the real agony and pain of my memories—which I had used to rationalize my own sin—that needed to be forgiven.

Oh Lord, I can SEE, looking closely. I can GIVE, knowing You are waiting to take it. I can FORGIVE, as I am forgiven for Your "mercies' sake" (Psalm 6:4). I can FORGET, until You, Lord, want to use my memories for Your glory.

My tree is no longer dead, dark and broken, but has buds of love, forgiveness and mercy sprouting up all around it.

Your truths are simple, sweet Jesus, and may we all understand that Satan doesn't want us to see just how easy it is to be free.

I found this list from *God Is in the Small Stuff*[5] to be so simple and powerful. God really is part of our "everyday life." Read and meditate on the following items:

- Whenever you feel insignificant, remember how important you are to God.

- We love God because we know who He is. God loves us despite who we are.

- Be teachable every day when it comes to love.

- Love yourself as the unique individual that God created you to be—nothing more, nothing less.

- Unconditional love comes only from our Heavenly Father.

- God does not help us because we deserve it, He helps us because He loves us.

- Find your self-worth in God's love for you, not in your accomplishments.

- The love of God has no limits.

- The reason we can love God is because He loved us first.

- His unconditional love for us should motivate us to love others unconditionally.

- Never confuse love with lust.

- Love isn't an option; we are commanded by God to love others.

- Loving God is the greatest thing we can do.

> With Christ's help and the forgiveness He has given us, we are able to extend forgiveness to others.

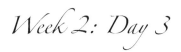

Week 2: Day 3

Prayer: Bow your heart before the Lord in prayer prior to completing today's study. Ask Him to reveal what areas in your heart need to be examined.

God's Heart to "SEE"

"And there is no creature hidden from His sight, but all things are naked and open to the eyes of Him to whom we must give account" (Hebrews 4:13).

1. Read Psalm 10:14,17: "But You have seen, for You observe trouble and grief, to repay it by Your hand. The helpless commits himself to You; You are the helper of the fatherless. Lord, You have heard the desire of the humble; You will prepare their heart; You will cause Your ear to hear."

   What do the Psalms reveal about what God sees and hears? What are the ways that He responds to what He sees and hears?

2. Why is it so important to humble yourself before God according to the scripture above?

3. What thoughts are constantly bombarding you? Are they thoughts about betrayal, sexual abuse, rape, guilt, shame, abortion, an eating disorder, premarital pregnancy, past failures or painful memories? You need to examine your heart and get real with God. Pray for God to show you the reason for your heartache, then write it down.

4. Do you desire to do evil to another person? Explain below, being totally honest so you can see what God already sees in your heart.

Tammy's Reflections

Trapped in a Horrifying Nightmare

I was raped a very long time ago, but in some ways it still seems like yesterday. Maybe you are a victim too. If so, I don't presume to know how you feel. Every attack is different. But my heart breaks for you, and I understand the devastation that rape, or any attack, can bring.

One thing I want you to know is that many times, as when I was raped, I was also controlled and manipulated. This can be very confusing. Please understand, some people are very skilled at manipulation, and we can become prey in that sense as well. When someone says, "I was raped," those words only state a small fraction of the damage done to them as rape victims. Even if you were raped long ago, I know the suffering can last for years. I hope my story brings you some comfort and healing.

At 15 I Was Raped

When I was 15 years old, I had hopes and dreams of one day marrying as a virgin bride. The groom would be a wonderful, handsome man who I would love and cherish for the rest of my life. My future was exciting. I felt wonder and anticipation when I thought about the special man who would come into my life. Then one night, this dream came to a crashing halt when, on a casual date with a friend from school, I was raped.

The rape caused deep-seated anger, resentment and rebellion in my heart. This "friend" threatened to tell everyone we had slept together, which would have destroyed my reputation. I was confused, angry and filled with hatred. My life fell into a downward spiral of depression.

He knew I didn't want a reputation of being someone who slept around, so he used my fear to trap me into a relationship with him. The nightmare continued day after day as he physically abused me and threatened me with what he would do if I ever left. He played mind games and continued to force himself on me sexually. I was going through the first rape experience over and over again. I couldn't believe he had bullied his way into my life and was controlling me with fear. I hated him! He talked about marriage and having kids together. The thought of marrying and spending the rest of my life with this guy, whom I despised, overwhelmed me. I vowed I would never marry him, and for the first and only time in my life, I contemplated killing myself.

Trapped in silence for an entire year, I lost 20 pounds. I was depressed and stressed from my horrifying nightmare. I didn't tell anyone what I was going through—not even my best friend. Why didn't I break the silence? Maybe I was ashamed. Maybe I was trying to bury my sick, shameful past of being sexually abused by my uncle as a child. Whatever the reason, I remained silent, trying to live a halfway normal life, all the while feeling worthless.

Then, through a number of difficult circumstances, this sick relationship ended as quickly as it started. My best friend saw the bruises on my arms and asked what had happened. I finally told her how I was being shoved around and controlled.

She told some of our friends, including Rick Brown, who wasn't even a Christian yet. One thing led to another, and Rick ended up beating him to a pulp. Right then and there, the nightmare ended. I was released from my silent prison and the control this guy had over my life. He never messed with me again. He probably thought he'd better keep his mouth shut or Rick would be looking for him.

Although the nightmare was finally over, the painful, abusive relationship continued to have its effect on me for years. The terror had ended physically, but emotionally it haunted my every moment. My only solace was to numb the pain. I began to party hard and became rebellious toward my parents. I was angry and critical, not trusting anyone. I kept the pain of the rape locked up tight. I didn't tell anyone until after I married my high school sweetheart, Rick Brown. Only then did I finally break the silence and tell him about my hidden past.

"Justified" Wrongs

I felt entitled to hate the guy who had controlled my life, raped and abused me. I was overwhelmed with resentment and bitterness toward him. I was unforgiving, unmerciful and desired to do evil. I felt driven to get even. I kept a long list of the wrongs he had done to me. I was consumed with hatred and allowed my sin to become a part of my everyday life in the name of "justice."

In my heart the list of wrongs he had done continued to grow longer and longer. He became a close friend of my parents. They had no idea what he had done to me, because the only other person who knew was my husband. So now this guy was invited to family gatherings and celebrations. He would show up at my parents' home and give them pictures of his family, which they would display. Each time I went to my parents' house I was slapped in the face by a picture given to my parents by my abuser. My hatred and bitterness were growing, and my loving parents, with no knowledge of the hatred I held in my heart toward this guy, would even talk about getting our kids together to play. I would smile to hide my true heart, but in my mind I would think, "Over my dead body!"

As my mind and spirit were overcome with hatred, I was being robbed of my joy. It wasn't pleasing to the Lord and I knew I had to stop thinking about the abuse and stop holding a grudge.

Then One Day

Then one day, in the silence of my mind and heart, I got real with God and myself: No more putting on a fake smile and acting like everything was normal, because it wasn't. I began to meditate on two important scriptures: Romans 1:21-22 and Hebrews 12:15.

> "...Although they knew God, they did not glorify Him as God, nor were thankful, but became futile in their thoughts, and their foolish hearts were darkened. Professing to be wise, they became fools" (Romans 1:21-22).

I learned that one of the most important steps I had to take was to look into my own heart and be willing to see what was in it. I saw sins stemming from roots of bitterness, unforgiveness and futile thoughts of getting even. As a result, I was blocking God out of my life in the very moments I needed Him most! I was a Christian woman, a pastor's wife and a child of God, but I was full of hatred that was destroying me.

> "...Looking carefully lest anyone fall short of the grace of God; lest any root of bitterness springing up cause trouble, and by this many become defiled" (Hebrews 12:15).

Like the book of Romans describes, my heart had been darkened. God shined His spotlight on my self-centered heart and I saw that it was foolish. I had never realized how my bitterness, hatred and unforgiveness prevented God's love from coming in.

Totally broken, I repented and gave it all to God. I asked for forgiveness and in His mercy and grace, He forgave me. After that, forgiveness flooded my heart for the man who raped me. Where I was once blind in my sin, now I could SEE.

He Is Faithful to Forgive

5. As Jesus hung on the cross He said, "Father, forgive them, for they do not know what they do" (Luke 23:34). Are you dealing with your painful experiences in the wrong way through grudge holding, resentment, bitterness, judgement, hatred, jealousy? Confess now and ask for God's forgiveness. What does God promise to do? "If we confess our sin, He is faithful and just to forgive us our sins and to cleanse us from all unrighteousness" (1 John 1:9). This scripture is the Christian bar of soap. Write down your thoughts.

_____

_____

_____

If you deny your hurt, it will find ways to express itself, forming roots of bitterness that injure you and others. Get real with God about what's in your heart. You can try to bury your heartache by putting on a smile, but you will still be filled with fear, shame, guilt, unforgiveness, self-centered desires, jealousy and anger.

Emotional scars can affect other areas of your life too: your marriage, your children, your friendships, and your school or job performance. You may have turned to harmful behaviors like illegal or prescription drugs or alcohol abuse. Maybe it's caused deep depression, suicidal tendencies, eating disorders, outbursts of anger or rebellion. Stop and think about how the effects of deep hurt and the unacceptable actions of others have manifested in your life. I understand. I, like you, didn't want it to affect me or manifest itself in destructive behavior, but it did! I just had to stop long enough to be honest with myself about how it was destroying me.

It was hard to look at who I was becoming and realize how my wounded heart was hurting others around me. I wanted to live the rest of my life understanding and applying forgiveness so I could be set free from bitterness and hatred. Forgiven people should be forgiving people. I wanted to celebrate the life God had given me. I wanted to love and care about people without fear of being hurt.

So please, if your hurt is making you miserable, take the first steps to be set free from the pain. Allow God to bring healing and freedom to your heart through forgiveness. I learned that one of the most important steps I could take was to look at my heart and see what was in it. I saw sins stemming from roots of bitterness, unforgiveness and futile thoughts of revenge. As a result, I was blocking God out in the very moments I needed Him most!

Thankful

"Finally, brethren, whatever things are true, whatever things are noble, whatever things are just, whatever things are pure, whatever things are lovely, whatever things are of good report, if there is any virtue and if there is anything praiseworthy—meditate on these things" (Philippians 4:8).

It is never right to rape someone, but God helped me to see there were things to be thankful for, even in my year of terror brought about by the date rape. I wrote out a list of ten things He showed me. I encourage you to do the same. It will help to change your perspective and begin the process of becoming free from this hurtful experience.

1. I am thankful the abuse stopped.

2. I am thankful I didn't get pregnant.

3. I am thankful I didn't get a disease.

4. I am thankful I wasn't trapped into getting married.

5. I am thankful the silence was broken.

6. I am thankful God gave me the strength to tell my husband the painful truth.

7. I am thankful Christ gave me spiritual eyes to SEE the truth about the sin of unforgiveness.

8. I am thankful I learned to forgive, and press toward the higher calling in Christ.

9. I am thankful I can comfort others with the comfort I received through the healing power of Christ.

10. I am thankful that through Christ and by His stripes (the punishment He received) I have been healed and set free. The old is gone, and the new has come.

> "Although they knew God, they did not glorify Him as God, nor were thankful, but became futile in their thoughts, and their foolish hearts were darkened. Professing to be wise, they became fools"
> (Romans 1:21-22).

6. Write down a list of things you are thankful for today.

1. _____
_____

2. _____
_____

3. _____
_____

4. _____
_____

5. _____
_____

6. _____
_____

7. _____
_____

8. _____
_____

9. _____
_____

10. _____
_____

This Week's Tool and Memory Verse

Tool #1 - SEE: I must _____ the truth about what is in my _____, so I am not defiled. To _____ means to make filthy or dirty; to _____.

"Looking carefully lest anyone fall short of the grace of God; lest any root of bitterness springing up cause trouble, and by this many become defiled" (Hebrews 12:15).

Week 2: Day 4

Prayer: Bow your heart before the Lord in prayer prior to completing today's study. Ask God to help you know Him better.

Today, we will look at some of God's characteristics and what it's like to know Him as the Almighty God. He will encourage you to trust Him with the pain and sorrow you've experienced.

The Ultimate Priority

So often, we seem to think what's important in our lives is filling our time with people. But in *A Woman After God's Own Heart*,[6] Elizabeth George explains how God needs to be our number one priority.

> If God is going to be first in our hearts and the 'Ultimate Priority' of our lives, we must develop a root system anchored deep in Him. Just like a plant with its roots hidden underground, you and I—out of public view and alone with God—are to draw from Him all that we need to live the abundant life He has promised His children.

> [But] we are always with people: people at work, people on campus, people in the dorms, people from Bible studies, people in discipleship or fellowship groups. But the truth is, 'the greater the proportion of your day spent hidden in quiet, in reflection, in prayer, in study, in preparation, the greater will be the effectiveness, the impact, the power, of the part of your life that shows.' You cannot be with people all the time and have a ministry. The impact of your ministry to people will be in direct proportion to the time you spend away from people and with God.

God is Never Changing

1. Read Malachi 3:6 and Hebrews 13:8:

    - "For I am the LORD, I do not change; therefore you are not consumed, O sons of Jacob" (Malachi 3:6).

    - "Jesus Christ is the same yesterday, today, and forever" (Hebrews 13:8).

    Does God ever change according to Malachi and Hebrews? Yes or no?

2. Fill in the following blanks with the characteristics of God that never change. Scriptures found on page 302 and 303.

    "The _____ of God never changes" (Numbers 23:19).

    "His _____ never fails" (Lamentations 3:22-23).

    "His _____ never fails" (Psalm 18:50).

    "The _____ of God never changes" (2 Peter 3:9).

    Which of God's characteristics do you find comforting?

God is All-Powerful

3. Read Jeremiah 32:17: "...Behold, You have made the heavens and the earth by Your great power and outstretched arm. There is nothing too hard for You."

   Describe God's power according to Jeremiah 32:17.

   _____
   _____
   _____

4. Read Psalm 77:13-15: "Your way, O God, is in the sanctuary; Who is so great a God as our God? You are the God who does wonders; You have declared Your strength among the peoples. You have with Your arm redeemed Your people, the sons of Jacob and Joseph."

   What are some ways God displays His power?

   _____
   _____
   _____

5. Read Acts 1:8: "But you shall receive power when the Holy Spirit has come upon you; and you shall be witnesses to Me in Jerusalem, and in all Judea and Samaria, and to the end of the earth."

   How do you have access to the power of God?

   _____
   _____

6. What is one way God intends for you to use His power?

   _____
   _____

7. Are you a witness to those around you at home, work or school? Yes or no?

God is All-Knowing

8. Read John 3:19-20: "And this is the condemnation, that the light has come into the world, and men loved darkness rather than light, because their deeds were evil. For everyone practicing evil hates the light and does not come to the light, lest his deeds should be exposed."

   Does God know everything? How do you practice evil in your heart concerning your past?

   _____
   _____
   _____

9. Read Psalm 44:20-21 and 1 Corinthians 4:5:
    - "If we had forgotten the name of our God, or stretched out our hands to a foreign god, would not God search this out? For He knows the secrets of the heart" (Psalm 44:20-21).
    - "Therefore judge nothing before the time, until the Lord comes, who will both bring to light the hidden things of darkness and reveal the counsels of the hearts. Then each one's praise will come from God" (1 Corinthians 4:5).

    Which areas of your life does God know about?

    _____
    _____

10. Read Hebrews 4:13 and Daniel 2:22:
    - "And there is no creature hidden from His sight, but all things are naked and open to the eyes of Him to whom we must give account" (Hebrews 4:13).
    - "He reveals deep and secret things; He knows what is in the darkness, and light dwells with Him" (Daniel 2:22).

    What areas of your life do you think are hidden from God? Pray and ask God to help you see the secrets that are in your heart and write them down.

    _____
    _____
    _____

11. Read 1 Chronicles 28:9: "As for you, my son Solomon, know the God of your father, and serve Him with a loyal heart and with a willing mind; for the LORD searches all hearts and understands all the intent of the thoughts. If you seek Him, He will be found by you; but if you forsake Him, He will cast you off forever."

    God knows everything. What is one way you can respond to this truth?

    _____
    _____

12. According to 1 Chronicles 28:9, who are we to serve with a loyal heart and a willing mind? Who searches our heart and understands all the intents of our thoughts?

    _____
    _____

13. What can you see more clearly about your own heart?

    _____
    _____
    _____

God is Able to Protect

14. Circle the words that imply that David felt God's protection from the following Bible verses.

    - "I will love You, O LORD, my strength. The LORD is my rock and my fortress and my deliverer; my God, my strength, in whom I will trust; my shield and the horn of my salvation, my stronghold. I will call upon the LORD, who is worthy to be praised; so shall I be saved from my enemies" (Psalm 18:1-3).

    - "He sent from above, He took me; He drew me out of many waters. He delivered me from my strong enemy, from those who hated me, for they were too strong for me. They confronted me in the day of my calamity, but the LORD was my support. He also brought me out into a broad place; He delivered me because He delighted in me" (Psalm 18:16-19).

15. Read the following scriptures:

    - "You are my hiding place; You shall preserve me from trouble; You shall surround me with songs of deliverance" (Psalm 32:7).

    - "I sought the LORD, and He heard me, and delivered me from all my fears" (Psalm 34:4).

    - "But the Lord is faithful, who will establish you and guard you from the evil one" (2 Thessalonians 3:3).

    What does God promise to protect you from if you seek Him?

    _____
    _____
    _____

16. How does God protect you?

    _____
    _____
    _____

17. Read John 10:27: "My sheep hear My voice, and I know them, and they follow Me."

    What does God ask of you in order for Him to protect you?

    _____
    _____

> What do you need today? Courage, healing or comfort?
> Is it love, contentment or peace? Look to God. He will
> supply. Quiet your mind now. Talk to God about those
> things your heart is wrestling with.

Hope for Those Facing Crisis

"Crisis. It hits hard. It hits fast. It takes no prisoners," writes Greg Laurie. Indeed, for many of us, it's as if pain has knocked at our front door, moved in without our permission and refuses to leave. As Greg continues, "Sometimes a crisis is so epic that you eventually look back on it as a dividing point in your life."[7] You wouldn't wish this on your worst enemy, but it's your reality. Here are a few things to keep in mind about crisis and adversity from Greg Laurie's "Preaching Through Pain."[8]

Practical Principles

1. Adversity levels us, keeps us humble. Prosperity has a tendency to make people proud and self-sufficient. It's easy to get caught up in success and think we're pretty good. But when trials come, we are brought to our knees and reminded that we are weak and need God. It's often through pain that we draw nearer to God, and then He strengthens us to face those challenges. As the psalmist said, "Before I was afflicted I went astray, but now I keep your word" (Psalm 119:67).

2. Adversity teaches us eternal lessons we might not otherwise learn. It'd be wonderful if everything we needed to know about God was learned through "mountaintop" experiences. But some lessons can only be learned in the valley, in the midst of a trial. Those lessons can be passed on to others in the same position, or they can help you be an example to unbelieving friends or family.

3. We gain a new compassion for those in pain. Face it, the world is full of pain. When we are able to empathize with those who are suffering, it creates a relational bridge. Paul writes that God comforts us in our pain so we can comfort others in the same way (2 Corinthians 1:3-4).

Relevant Reminders

Isn't it true that when crises hit, we are often blindsided? But remember:

- Storms will come into our lives no matter what. Don't spend time thinking, "Why is this happening to me?" Instead, focus your attention on, "What am I supposed to do now that a crisis has hit?"

- We tend to want a cause and effect for everything, but that can be dangerous, because some things are never going to make sense. Sometimes bad things just happen without explanation and we must trust that God is sovereign.

- The big picture is all about God's glory, not our personal happiness.

Applicable Actions

When you are in the middle of life's storms, cry out to God and trust in Him. Remember, He is in the miracle business. Recognize that through your hardships He can accomplish great things. One day we will get to the other side; not just the other side of our problems. I'm talking about Heaven, if you are a follower of Christ.

Stories of Real People and a Real Savior

Set Free from the Garbage In My Heart

A Mom, Minnesota

My biggest struggle as a mom has been guilt and fear. Since I have gone through *Healed and Set Free*, God freed me from so much garbage. I told my daughter recently, "Honey, I am just figuring out this parenting thing. Could you stay a couple more years and see me do it right?"

We had a great laugh out of it all, but it is so true. I never knew I feared so many things for my children and fear is sin. I had never really entrusted my children to the Lord's hands until I was set free. I was always afraid they would turn out like other family members, that they wouldn't serve the Lord, that I would be embarrassed or be an awful parent.

Now, on a daily basis, I take those thoughts captive and realize there is NO perfect parent. God has a wonderful way and we must entrust our lives to Him, then take our leadership roles as parents seriously. I have never seen a pastor lead his flock in strength when he had fear in his heart. I now know that the same principle applies to leadership in the home. There is no perfect parent—only a perfect God.

A Real Friend

Praise Report from a Women's Retreat

God will never stop loving me. He is a real friend! A friend who can love you in spite of who you are. A friend who can comfort you wherever you are. A friend who can speak to you in honesty, but then encourage you to move to the next step. God has shown me, by what He has done in my life and the lives of so many people I know, that I can really trust Him. Again and again in the face of pain, doubt and despair, my God has proven Himself trustworthy.

God is using *Healed and Set Free* to heal lives, marriages, friendships and families. Women who have no hope are now seeing that God has given them freedom through His Word to walk in victory.

Loving God is the greatest thing we can do!

Week 2: Day 5

Prayer: Bow your heart before the Lord in prayer prior to completing today's study. Ask Him to help you love Him with all your heart.

God's Unfailing Love for You

It is so important to your healing to know and believe that God loves you. If you don't learn to love and to be loved as He intended, you have truly wasted your life. When you serve and obey the Lord's will, you will be set free. "He who does not love does not know God, for God is love" (1 John 4:8).

"Love suffers long and is kind; love does not envy; love does not parade itself, is not puffed up; does not behave rudely, does not seek its own, is not provoked, thinks no evil; does not rejoice in iniquity, but rejoices in the truth; bears all things, believes all things, hopes all things, endures all things. Love never fails. But whether there are prophecies, they will fail; whether there are tongues, they will cease; whether there is knowledge, it will vanish away" (1 Corinthians 13:4-8).

1. Read 1 John 4:18-19: "There is no fear in love; but perfect love casts out fear, because fear involves torment. But he who fears has not been made perfect in love. We love Him because He first loved us."

   Fill in the blanks from 1 John 4:18-19.

   "There is no _____ in love; but perfect love casts out _____, because _____ involves torment. But he who _____ has not been made perfect in _____. We _____ Him because He first _____ us."

2. Read 1 John 4:7: "Beloved, let us love one another, for love is of God; and everyone who loves is born of God and knows God. He who does not love does not know God, for God is love. In this the love of God was manifested toward us, that God has sent His only begotten Son into the world, that we might live through Him."

   In a few sentences, describe God's love for you.

   _____
   _____
   _____
   _____
   _____
   _____
   _____
   _____

Realize God Loves You

For a better understanding of how much God loves you, read 1 John 4:10: "In this is love, not that we loved God, but that He loved us and sent His Son to be the propitiation for our sins." His love for us is overwhelming. I love this piece from *God Is in the Small Stuff*,[10] as it explains God's heart for us:

> Love is a powerful emotion, perhaps the strongest of human emotions. People will go to great lengths to express love, and they will do almost anything to get love. So if love is in such demand, why does it seem in such short supply?
>
> The problem with human love is that it's usually self-centered. Much of the so-called love we feel could be summarized by the phrase: "What's in it for me?" We may think we love someone, but in reality we may simply love what he or she does for us.
>
> In *The Four Loves*, C. S. Lewis identified four different kinds of love, all but one of which are basically self-centered. First, there's affection, which is the kind of love we can have for something other than people, such as a dog or a home or a car. Then there's friendship, a valuable love that is the basis of most human relationships. There's erotic love, which is the beautiful love shared between a husband and wife. All three of these are wonderful and necessary loves, but each of them depends on the object of our affection for complete fulfillment.
>
> The only love that is completely other-centered is called *agape* love. This is love of the highest order. It's what Lewis called, "Divine Gift-love." When we love with *agape* love, we desire the best for the people we love. We are even able to love those who are unlovable.
>
> We are capable of *agape* love only to the extent that we give our lives over to God and allow Him to work in us. But even before that can happen, we must realize that God loves us, and that He can only love us with this kind of love. God's love is never self-centered, and God's love is always sacrificial. While we were enemies of God, He loved us. When we ran from God, He loved us. He loved us so much that He sacrificed the Son He loved most, so that we could experience eternal life.
>
> Love is the essence of God. Love is what motivates Him to do what He does for us—down to the last detail—even when we don't love Him in return. Knowing that should give tremendous meaning to our lives.

> "An infinite God can give all of Himself to each of His children. He does not distribute Himself that each may have a part, but to each one He gives all of Himself as full as if there were no others."
> - A.W. Tozer

God's Promise to Never Leave You

3. Read Hebrews 13:5: "Let your conduct be without covetousness; be content with such things as you have. For He Himself has said, 'I will never leave you nor forsake you.'"

   What does Hebrews 13:5 say about God being there for you?

   _____
   _____
   _____

4. Read John 14:16-18: "And I will pray the Father, and He will give you another Helper, that He may abide with you forever—the Spirit of truth, whom the world cannot receive, because it neither sees Him nor knows Him; but you know Him, for He dwells with you and will be in you. I will not leave you orphans; I will come to you."

   What promises does God give to you during the times you feel alone, rejected and abandoned?

   _____
   _____
   _____

5. Read Deuteronomy 31:6: "Be strong and of good courage, do not fear nor be afraid of them; for the Lord your God, He is the One who goes with you. He will not leave you nor forsake you."

   Name something you can do when you think God isn't there for you.

   _____
   _____
   _____

The Father

God wants to be your Father. Does that idea comfort you, or does the word "father" bring feelings of hurt and bitterness? Accepting God Almighty as your heavenly Father may be difficult, especially if you have broken relationships with authority figures here on earth, or if your parents weren't there for you for various reasons, such as divorce, death or addiction. You may have a hard time believing there is a heavenly Father who cares for you and who is always there.

God's promise is to care for His children, and He keeps His promises! He promises to be a Father to all of us and He never changes His mind. He longs for you to come to Him with your needs. He wants to meet your need for love and acceptance.

6. Read the following scriptures:

    - "For unto us a Child is born, unto us a Son is given; and the government will be upon His shoulder. And His name will be called Wonderful, Counselor, Mighty God, Everlasting Father, Prince of Peace" (Isaiah 9:6).

    - "Therefore, do not be like them. For your Father knows the things you have need of before you ask Him. In this manner, therefore, pray: Our Father in heaven, Hallowed be Your name" (Matthew 6:8-9).

    How do these verses describe God?

7. Read Psalm 68:5: "A father of the fatherless, a defender of widows, is God in His holy habitation."

    To whom will God be a Father?

8. Read 1 John 2:23: "Whoever denies the Son does not have the Father either; he who acknowledges the Son has the Father also."

    In what ways could you deny the Son in your life?

9. Read Galatians 3:26: "For you are all sons of God through faith in Christ Jesus."

    Have you by faith received Christ into your heart? If so, when?

10. Have you told others about Christ? If so, give an example.

11. Read John 1:12: "But as many as received Him, to them He gave the right to become children of God, to those who believe in His name..."

    Who can be called children of God?

12. Read Romans 8:12-16: "Therefore, brethren, we are debtors—not to the flesh, to live according to the flesh. For if you live according to the flesh you will die; but if by the Spirit you put to death the deeds of the body, you will live. For as many as are led by the Spirit of God, these are sons of God. For you did not receive the spirit of bondage again to fear, but you received the Spirit of adoption by whom we cry out, 'Abba, Father.' The Spirit Himself bears witness with our spirit that we are children of God."

    How are you able to call Him "Father"?

13. Read Galatians 5:19-21: "Now the works of the flesh are evident, which are: adultery, fornication, uncleanness, lewdness, idolatry, sorcery, hatred, contentions, jealousies, outbursts of wrath, selfish ambitions, dissensions, heresies, envy, murders, drunkenness, revelries, and the like; of which I tell you beforehand, just as I also told you in time past, that those who practice such things will not inherit the kingdom of God."

    What is the flesh? Write down each "work of the flesh" from Galatians above and ask yourself if the flesh is at work in your life.

14. "For godly sorrow produces repentance leading to salvation, not to be regretted; but the sorrow of the world produces death" (2 Corinthians 7:10).

    Give the sinful burden of the works of the flesh to the Lord in repentance. We must be sorry enough to change and choose to go God's way over our own. Do you desire to walk in the flesh, or to apply 2 Corinthians 7:10 to your daily life and actions?

15. Galatians 5:22-23 says, "But the fruit of the Spirit is love, joy, peace, longsuffering, kindness, goodness, faithfulness, gentleness, self-control. Against such there is no law."

    What is the fruit of the Spirit? Write down each fruit of the Spirit from above and ask yourself if the fruit of the Spirit is at work in your life.

16. In what practical ways will you apply the fruit of the Spirit to your life?

The Father's Discipline

God is like a parent to you. Consequently, He disciplines you. But His discipline is wiser than your parents' discipline.

17. Write down the definition of "discipline" from page 301.

    _____

    _____

18. Read Hebrews 12:5-11 on page 303.

    Describe the difference between the way God disciplines us and the way our earthly parents disciplined us.

    _____

    _____

19. Read Hebrews 12:6: "For whom the Lord loves He chastens, and scourges every son whom He receives."

    Whom does God discipline?

    _____

20. Write down the definitions of "sin" and "iniquity" from page 301.

    _____

    _____

    _____

    _____

21. In order to SEE what is really in your heart, ask God to expose the root cause of your sinful thoughts and actions. Read Hebrews 12:15, Proverbs 27:5-6 and Romans 2:5-11:

    - "...Looking carefully lest anyone fall short of the grace of God; lest any root of bitterness springing up cause trouble, and by this many become defiled" (Hebrews 12:15).

    - "Open rebuke is better than love carefully concealed. Faithful are the wounds of a friend, but the kisses of an enemy are deceitful" (Proverbs 27:5-6).

    - "But in accordance with your hardness and your impenitent heart you are treasuring up for yourself wrath in the day of wrath and revelation of the righteous judgment of God, who will render to each one according to his deeds: eternal life to those who by patient continuance in doing good seek for glory, honor, and immortality; but to those who are self-seeking and do not obey the truth, but obey unrighteousness; indignation and wrath, tribulation and anguish, on every soul of man who does evil, of the Jew first and also of the Greek; but glory, honor, and peace to everyone who works what is good, to the Jew first and also to the Greek. For there is no partiality with God" (Romans 2:5-11).

If anger, unforgiveness, bitterness, hardheartedness or disobedience takes over your heart and you choose not to deal with it, your heart will grow cold. When that happens, God's love cannot flow through you, and you will become a phony Christian. Genuine love demands toughness in moments of crisis.

What happens to the chains on your heart if you reject God's truth about SEEING and examining your heart?

22. Is there partiality with God if you are a stay-at-home mom, business woman or a pastor's wife, according to Romans 2:5-11 above?

23. Read 1 John 1:9: "If we confess our sins, He is faithful and just to forgive us our sins and to cleanse us from all unrighteousness."

    Brokenness before Christ drives us to confession. What then does God do for us?

24. Fill in the blanks: "If we confess our sins, He is _____ and _____ to forgive us our _____ and to cleanse us from all unrighteousness" (1 John 1:9).

25. What first step must you take to begin healing in your heart? Circle the one that applies to you.

    - Live in bitterness and unforgiveness, reliving what others have done to me, or beating myself up over my own failures.
    - Embrace God's healing truth from His Word to **SEE, GIVE, FORGIVE, FORGET** and **BE SET FREE**.

26. Read Psalm 119:101-104: "I have restrained my feet from every evil way, that I may keep Your word. I have not departed from Your judgments, for You Yourself have taught me. How sweet are Your words to my taste, sweeter than honey to my mouth! Through Your precepts I get understanding; therefore I hate every false way."

    What should we restrain our feet from according to this scripture?

27. God is serious about you. Let's be people who are serious about God. Read 1 John 1:6-7: "If we say that we have fellowship with Him, and walk in darkness, we lie, and do not practice the truth. But if we walk in the light, as He is in the light, we have fellowship with one another, and the blood of Jesus Christ, His Son, cleanses us from all sin."

    What does getting serious about God mean to you?

    _____
    _____
    _____

28. I must SEE what is really in my heart, asking God to expose the root cause of my sin, so I am not defiled and I don't defile others.

    - "Looking carefully lest anyone fall short of the grace of God; lest any root of bitterness springing up cause trouble, and by this many become defiled" (Hebrews 12:15).

    - "I sought the LORD, and He heard me, and delivered me from all my fears" (Psalm 34:4).

    Which of the following tend to control the way you react? Circle those that apply and write down your thoughts.

    - Negative thoughts
    - Comparing to others
    - A need to control
    - Insecurity
    - Defensiveness
    - Pride
    - Guilt
    - Hurt
    - Anger
    - Grudge holding
    - Lack of trust
    - Self-pity

    _____
    _____
    _____
    _____
    _____
    _____
    _____
    _____
    _____
    _____

Chapter Review

While you review this chapter on knowing God's heart, reflect on the truths you have learned.

1. What have you learned about God's heart toward you?

2. What encouraged you?

3. What challenged you?

This Week's Tool and Memory Verse

Tool #1 - SEE: I must _____ the truth about what is in my _____, so I am not defiled. To _____ means to make filthy or dirty; to _____.

"Looking carefully lest anyone fall short of the grace of God; lest any root of bitterness springing up cause trouble, and by this many become defiled" (Hebrews 12:15).

Stories of Real People and a Real Savior

Learning How to Forgive People in My Past
By a Woman in the United States

Before I became a Christian, I had some Christian friends, but I thought, "They have to be faking it!" I thought their happiness had to be a cover up; their joy had to be phony! But I thought that because I had been faking it most of my adult life; I was the phony. I had a great job, a husband and family, a nice home… At work, I was a fun, flirty girl. With friends, I was the life of the party. With family, I was the wise older sister, always ready with advice. The outside package seemed fine, but inside I was hurting. My thoughts were dark; I had so many painful memories of sexual abuse, loneliness, depression, bad choices, bitterness, resentment… I had feelings of disgust and hatred for people in my past and for myself. There was a battle going on in my heart, and not a word ever surfaced about my inner struggles.

Right after we found out we were having our first baby, I laid in bed all day through the summer, with the shades down and the TV blaring. I could only muster enough strength to go to work for those few hours in the morning. I'd go home exhausted from trying to seem happy, trying to feel happy, trying to be normal. I wasn't engaged in my life at all. I tried to will myself to come out from under the dark cloud that seemed to hang over me. My family bore the brunt of my frustrations: The only emotion that made sense to me was anger. I was quick to anger and slow to show mercy. I expected my husband to understand. I can't count the number of times I thought, "No one understands! No one helps me around here. My husband doesn't get it! My kids are like leeches that suck the energy right out of me. I never get time to myself…" I played little games to get what I wanted; I'd have an angry look and barely speak to my husband, trying to get him to see that I "needed help around here!" I got annoyed with my kids constantly. I blamed them for the anger that raged inside me. I told my friends about my woes at home, spouting off about how unfairly I was treated and complaining about my kids. Inside, there was a constant fountain of anger. I knew it was wrong, but I didn't know how to change it. I hated what I had become, and I didn't know how to dig myself out of it.

Even though I had been raised in church, I had never studied the Bible. But those Christian friends God had placed in my life were making me curious. I surprised myself by signing up for a Bible study—the first substantial Bible study I'd ever taken—called Healed and Set Free. I was scared to admit just how badly I needed it. From the time I signed up until the study began, everything was coming to the surface. I remember asking the leader of our study, "When will I be healed and set free?" I laugh about that now, but it was an honest question from a desperate woman waiting for something to save her. And guess what? HE did; He saved me. I told Jesus, "Here's the worst stuff that happened to me: It's bad, it's sick, it's wrong. Here is the worst stuff that I did to others; this stuff is bad too, sick and wrong. See what You can do with it, because I've got no ideas left. I quit!" Well, it turns out that the freedom is real. The joy is real. The love is real. I saw the truth of Jesus for the first time, and I ran to Him. He gently and lovingly helped me see what was in my heart. He took all that pain, anger, sorrow, disgust, hatred, and threw it into the deepest part of the sea. He forgave me, and I forgave everyone in my life because He taught me how. All those years I had been searching for the one trick to take away the pain, but absolutely nothing worked until I gave it to HIM. It's good to remember what God has done. He's still working on me, and I still use the steps from Healed and Set Free. But God is ALWAYS faithful. God is ALWAYS trustworthy. He never changes His ways. He is the same saving God that opened my eyes when I took Healed and Set Free for the first time.

Tools to Become Healed and Set Free

To equip yourself in God's truth, look over the tools and verses that will be introduced in the coming weeks. Thinking about the past won't change it, but you can change your future by being set free from your past.

TOOL #1 - SEE: I must SEE the truth about what is in my heart so I am not defiled.

> **Definition**: To defile means to make filthy or dirty; to pollute.
>
> **Bible Verse**: "Looking carefully lest anyone fall short of the grace of God; lest any root of bitterness springing up cause trouble, and by this many become defiled" (Hebrews 12:15).

TOOL #2 - GIVE: I must GIVE my sin to God through repentance, knowing that Christ is waiting to take it. I must be sorry enough to change, and choose to go God's way over my own.

> **Definition**: To repent means to feel such sorrow for sin or fault as to be disposed to change one's life for the better; be penitent.
>
> **Bible Verse**: "For godly sorrow produces repentance leading to salvation, not to be regretted; but the sorrow of the world produces death" (2 Corinthians 7:10).

TOOL #3 - FORGIVE: I must FORGIVE as I am forgiven by Christ: Forgiving those who hurt, bruised, wronged, rejected, betrayed or harmed me, whether unintentionally or deliberately. I must ask God to forgive me for holding on to unforgiveness and know that He will.

> **Definition**: To forgive means to stop feeling angry or resentful toward someone for an offense, flaw or mistake.
>
> **Bible Verse**: "...Bearing with one another, and forgiving one another, if anyone has a complaint against another; even as Christ forgave you, so you also must do" (Colossians 3:13).

TOOL #4 - FORGET: I must FORGET by no longer dwelling on the hurt or the painful reminders, such as: phrases, smells, places, songs and comments. Instead, I am putting my mind on the higher calling that Christ has for me.

> **Definition**: To forget means to choose not to remember or notice, "forgive and forget".
>
> **Bible Verse**: "Brethren, I do not count myself to have apprehended; but one thing I do, forgetting those things which are behind and reaching forward to those things which are ahead" (Philippians 3:13).

Be Healed and Set Free: Christ will heal me from my past, showing me the truth, so I can become a cleansed vessel, healed and set free.

> **Definition**: To set free means to make free; set at liberty; release from bondage, imprisonment, or restraint.
>
> **Definition**: To heal means to make whole and healthy; to cure; to remedy or repair.
>
> **Bible Verse**: "And you shall know the truth, and the truth shall make you free" (John 8:32).

Letting Go of Anger

This week we will be learning **Tool #2 - GIVE** which shows us how to give our faults and failures to God so He can show us a new way to walk.

Tool #2 - GIVE: I must GIVE my sin to God through repentance, knowing that Christ is waiting to take it. I must be sorry enough to change, and choose to go God's way over my own.

Definition: To repent means to feel such sorrow for sin or fault as to be disposed to change one's life for the better; be penitent.

Bible Verse: "For godly sorrow produces repentance leading to salvation, not to be regretted; but the sorrow of the world produces death" (2 Corinthians 7:10).

Prayer: Ask God to help you SEE what's in your heart and GIVE Him the strongholds that our thinking and pride can cause. "If we confess our sins, He is faithful and just to forgive us our sins, and to cleanse us from all unrighteousness" (1 John 1:9).

Week 3: Day 1

Prayer: Bow your heart before the Lord in prayer prior to completing today's Bible study. Ask God to help give you understanding about the truth of anger.

Anger: a strong feeling of annoyance or hostility. It often begins as something small: a ticking clock in the room. An annoyance. An aggravation. Nothing huge, just a small frustration. Your hair stylist is twenty minutes behind schedule, disrupting your carefully planned day. The cashier at the supermarket is slow, the line is long and you're in a hurry. Your dinner guests will arrive in five minutes, and dinner is burned. The ticking clock—*tick tock, tick tock, tick tock*.

Keep stacking up these frustrations and annoyances, however, and before long you've got a trash can full of hostility, bitterness and anger. You become a ticking bomb, with uncontrolled rage that's ready to explode at any minute. Anger is powerful. It can lead us into so many other destructive behaviors. Being angry isn't just bad for your heart, it's bad for your health: it can make you physically sick, or shorten your life.

Anger doesn't go away on its own. If left alone, it will find ways to express itself, hurting those who get in the way, or burrowing into your heart in roots of bitterness. You might be angry with someone who made a mistake. Maybe you're angry with yourself, someone you trusted, maybe even God.

This week we will learn how to express our anger with self-control, and without lashing out and hurting those around us. Through God's Word, we will learn how our anger can turn into bitterness, crippling us and keeping us in bondage to what is really behind the anger: our past and present hurts.

Tammy's Reflections

Boiling Pot

I hated those who hurt me so much! I prayed God would send them to Hell to burn! The bitterness affected all areas of my life; I became a pot of boiling water—those around me never knew when a splash of "hot water" would spill out and burn them. Bitterness, rage, hatred, resentment, defensiveness and insecurities filled my heart. I was tired of being filled with malice and sin.

I knew it was time to face the pain of my unforgiving heart. It was taking over my life, and I could no longer accept the way I was living. I was ready to get real with Jesus and ask for help. I needed to become broken before Him, and I needed to trust Him with my hurts. I wanted a new beginning.

It was then that Jesus started moving me on a journey toward healing. I'm so thankful I went on that journey, even though it was one of the most difficult journeys I've ever made.

Tools to Become Healed and Set Free

In this chapter, we will continue to use **Tool #1 - SEE**, as we learn **Tool #2 - GIVE**.

These tools will help you to become set free. Each tool is defined as the time comes. It is crucial to memorize these powerful tools and review them regularly in order to apply them to your daily life.

#1 - SEE: I must SEE the truth about what is in my heart so I am not defiled.

#2 - GIVE: I must GIVE my sin to God through repentance, knowing that Christ is waiting to take it. I must be sorry enough to change, and choose to go God's way over my own.

#3 - FORGIVE: I must FORGIVE as I am forgiven by Christ: Forgiving those who hurt, bruised, wronged, rejected, betrayed or harmed me, whether unintentionally or deliberately. I must ask God to forgive me for holding on to unforgiveness and know that He will.

#4 - FORGET: I must FORGET by no longer dwelling on the hurt or the painful reminders such as: phrases, smells, places, songs and comments. Instead, I am putting my mind on the higher calling that Christ has for me.

Be Healed and Set Free: Christ will heal me from my past, showing me the truth, so I can become a cleansed vessel, healed and set free.

This Week's Focus

Prayer: Ask God to help you SEE what's in your heart and GIVE Him the strongholds that our thinking and pride can cause. "If we confess our sins, He is faithful and just to forgive us our sins, and to cleanse us from all unrighteousness" (1 John 1:9).

By Memory: My challenge to you is to be able to recite the tool, definition and Bible verse from this chapter without looking. I know that by hiding these words of wisdom in your heart you are providing yourself with tools to truly be healed and set free. May we rise up to be women of the Word.

Tool #2 - GIVE: I must GIVE my sin to God through repentance, knowing that Christ is waiting to take it. I must be sorry enough to change, and choose to go God's way over my own.

Definition: To repent means to feel such sorrow for sin or fault as to be disposed to change one's life for the better; be penitent.

Bible Verse: "For godly sorrow produces repentance leading to salvation, not to be regretted; but the sorrow of the world produces death" (2 Corinthians 7:10).

"And you shall know the truth, and the truth shall make you free" (John 8:32).

God is Slow to Anger

1. Read Psalm 78:38: "But He, being full of compassion, forgave their iniquity, and did not destroy them. Yes, many a time He turned His anger away, and did not stir up all His wrath."

    Why are you grateful for God's compassion towards you?

2. Read Isaiah 48:9: "For My name's sake I will defer My anger, and for My praise I will restrain it from you, so that I do not cut you off."

    Why is God slow to anger?

3. Read 1 Kings 11:9-10: "So the Lord became angry with Solomon, because his heart had turned from the Lord God of Israel, who had appeared to him twice, and had commanded him concerning this thing, that he should not go after other gods; but he did not keep what the Lord had commanded."

    Why was God angry with Solomon?

4. How can you tell when you have turned from the Lord?

5. You may have allowed other gods into your life as a source of comfort. Little gods such as: self-absorption, gossip, being critical of others, wanting to be better than others, spiritual pride, compulsive overeating, compulsive spending, abusing drugs, alcohol or other things. What false gods do you see that may have crept into your life?

    - Do you: criticize or encourage?

    - Do you: use people or develop people by strengthening and helping them grow in their walk with the Lord?

    - Can you forgive or do you have ill feelings toward those who injure you?

6. Are you willing to give up false gods? Explain how to do this in God's will.

Stories of Real People and a Real Savior

Grace and Redemption after Adultery

Vicki, Idaho

Our second child, a beautiful boy, was born when I was 29—about 28 years ago. I had been a Christian for four years. David Judah was born deaf.

I was scared: "How do I raise a deaf child?" I was angry: "Why me, Lord, when I have been trying to follow You?" I was confused: "Why would a good God who loves me allow my child to be deaf?" I was disappointed: "Why is my husband not responding to David's deafness the way I think he should?"

Because I was a Christian, I knew these feelings were wrong, so I began to stuff them down. I pretended I was okay. I didn't know how to apply God's Word to my personal life. It seemed to me there were no other Christians with my bad attitude and feelings. I didn't see my negative, judgmental and unforgiving thoughts as sin. I felt like this "Jesus/Christian thing" did not work or make me happy. I chose my own way of dealing with my hurts and disappointment—adultery. I thought another man would make me happy. I was WRONG.

My life began a downward, self-absorbed cycle. I was tearing down my house with my own hands. I was trying to ease my pain, but instead my pain became much worse. I fought with my kids and husband. I didn't provide meals or a welcoming environment in our home. "Me, me, me," consumed my thoughts. I was so tormented that I couldn't sleep at night, and I finally ended up in a mental hospital. It was there that I finally turned back to the Lord.

At that time, I wasn't familiar with the *Healed and Set Free* tools: SEE, GIVE, FORGIVE, FORGET and BE SET FREE. But looking back, God showed me the same basic principles before I was even in the study. He led me to: 1) Recognize and acknowledge my negative thoughts. I had to get alone with God to vent and cry, telling Him everything. 2) Confess and repent all my sinful thoughts, actions and emotions. In that process, the Lord gave me the strength to unconditionally forgive—myself and others. 3) I gave it all over to God, surrendering my will and asking Him to help me see and obey His will. And, 4) I needed to read God's Word daily to renew my mind with the truth.

I felt that Jesus was asking me to confess my sin of adultery to my husband and ask him for forgiveness. It was so hard to trust Jesus and tell my husband. I thought he would divorce me and take our two children. He had every right; I knew the Bible said divorce was okay if adultery was involved. I was depressed, lost and I really felt like I was crazy. But I knew trusting Jesus had to be better than how I felt at the time, so I finally surrendered to His will. The day I told the truth to my husband, he took me home from the mental hospital and we began a new life together.

Jesus has restored my sanity, my marriage and my relationship with my children. He has truly made something beautiful out of my life. When I first completed the *Healed and Set Free Bible Study*, I knew God was giving me confirmation that I needed to be honest with Him every day and apply His Word to my life. So every day for the past 17 years, I have tried to SEE, GIVE, FORGIVE, FORGET and BE SET FREE.

I try to tell Jesus daily about all my feelings and ask Him to make me obedient to Him. I never, ever, ever want to lean on my own understanding again. Jesus has given me peace, a good marriage and a purpose for living. The Bible says God shows no partiality. What Jesus has done for me, He will do for you. As I facilitate *Healed and Set Free* studies, I see many women begin to live victorious lives. Just as Hebrews 9:14 says, "How much more shall the blood of Christ, who through the eternal Spirit offered Himself without spot to God, cleanse your conscience from dead works to serve the living God?"

Stories of Real People and a Real Savior

Taking It Out on My Husband

Pam, Idaho

I was molested in the third grade, and because of this sin against me, I responded in my teenage years by being sexually active. I was trying to fill the void in my heart, but ended up getting pregnant. I had an abortion, piling sin on top of sin. I didn't realize these sins affected every area of my life, including my relationship with God, and later my relationship with my husband. I felt dirty, like I had a smelly stain covering my whole life.

God knew that I couldn't go on like that, so He led me to this Bible study—even though I thought I didn't need it. He opened my eyes and revealed things to me I never realized I was doing. I was taking out all the pain from the abortion and molestation on my husband for twenty years. Every time I looked at him, it reminded me of my past hurts.

Through this study, I am free. That is the word that keeps coming to my mind: "free!" By being obedient to God, being in the Word and studying this workbook, God has set me free. Follow these steps and you can be healed, too!

Jesus' Anger

"Jesus had the same emotions we do," writes Linda Cochrane. "He wept, was angry when He saw things that were wrong in the world, and used His anger to see justice done. We must follow His example when expressing our own anger."[1]

7. Read Hebrews 4:14-15: "Seeing then that we have a great High Priest who has passed through the heavens, Jesus the Son of God, let us hold fast our confession. For we do not have a High Priest who cannot sympathize with our weaknesses, but was in all points tempted as we are, yet without sin."

    Did Jesus ever sin when He was angry?

    _____

8. What should we hate or be angry at: the sin or the sinner?

    _____
    _____
    _____

9. Is there anything about your painful memories that you are still angry about? Describe what still lingers.

Do Unto Others

Our natural tendency as humans is to respond to others in the same fashion they treat us: If someone is nice to us, we are nice. If someone is friendly, we are friendly. If someone is hateful, we hate in return. But does getting back at others make things better? Do you feel good after a verbal fight? Satan would like us to believe that the answer is yes, but that is a lie. Let's look at some powerful scriptures to find out how we should treat others in response to how they treat us:

> "But I say to you who hear: 'Love your enemies, do good to those who hate you'" (Luke 6:27).

> "But I say to you, love your enemies, bless those who curse you, do good to those who hate you and pray for those who spitefully use you and persecute you" (Matthew 5:44).

After reading these verses, our actions don't seem right or fair: From our perspective, if someone hurts us, we want to get angry or get even. But Jesus wants us to have the power to overcome evil with love, and to have the joy and freedom that this love brings. We can learn to follow Jesus by looking at His act of love on the cross. His suffering was so great that He cried out in agony; yet when He looked at the angry mob, He didn't hate them. Instead, He loved and forgave them, and prayed for God to forgive them. "Father, forgive them, for they do not know what they do" (Luke 23:34). His enemies hated Him, but Jesus forgave them. This is Jesus' example of love: overcoming hatred and forgiving.

10. How did Jesus respond to those who hated Him, beat Him, verbally abused Him, physically abused Him, and, yes, even sexually abused Him as they removed his clothes and hung Him naked on the cross for everyone to see? How are you affected by His example?

11. Give practical ways that Christ wants your attitude toward those who hurt you to reflect Matthew 5:44.

Week 3: Day 2

Prayer: Bow your heart before the Lord in prayer prior to completing today's Bible study. Ask God to help you SEE what is in your heart that may still be making you angry.

Pulling Out the Bitter Roots

When we forgive others, it is often only from our mouths, not from our hearts. The problem with this approach is that it only cuts off "the top of the plant," so to speak, leaving the deep roots of bitterness, hatred and unforgiveness untouched. To be free from this stronghold, we need to aggressively pull out the plant from its roots. Only then will we know the true meaning of forgiving the unacceptable, not just with our mouths, but with our hearts. How do we do this? When we humble ourselves before Christ in brokenness and repentance, we can replace the bitter root with God's good seed, and become truly set free to live the abundant Christian life.

1. Write down the definition of "bitterness" from the definitions on page 301.

   _____

   _____

2. What is in your heart that may still be making you angry about your hurt?

   _____

   _____

   _____

3. Read Psalm 34:18-19: "The Lord is near to those who have a broken heart, And saves such as have a contrite spirit. Many are the afflictions of the righteous, But the Lord delivers him out of them all."

   Define the following three words from the definitions on page 301.

   - Contrite: _____

   - Remorseless: _____

   - Relent: _____

4. What is the condition of your heart today? (Contrite, remorseless or relenting?)

   _____

   _____

5. What do you want to be delivered or set free from? Explain.

_____

_____

_____

_____

Resentment

Doug Easterday writes, "Resentment begins with the prefix 're.' Re-sent. So resentment is something that happens to me when I say, 'Well, if you're going to do that to me, I'll send it right back!' It's an exchange. 'They never call me, so I won't call them!' This stalemate is resentment." When someone's mere presence makes your blood boil, that's resentment. When you hear someone's name and your mood instantly changes, that's resentment. These little "checks" are evidence that something is wrong in your spirit, "an indication of something in your past that's not resolved. The Lord may be trying to show you that you haven't forgiven."[2]

6. Take a moment to search your heart for times resentment has surfaced in your life and write them down.

_____

_____

_____

_____

Tammy's Reflections

Over the Edge

We are so programmed to bury our true feelings that we never really let go of them. We bury them deeper and deeper, never realizing that these hurts will eventually begin to creep into our actions: We are sent "over the edge" with no control of our emotions, lashing out at those who love us most.

That's exactly what happened to me. Rather than being the loving wife I wanted to be, I would lose control and go "over the edge" by picking a fight with my husband. I felt exactly how Romans 7:15 describes, "For what I am doing, I do not understand. For what I will to do, that I do not practice; but what I hate, that I do."

The bitter memories of being molested and raped continued to creep into my mind, and were choking the peace from my life. I would become depressed, or get mad at the world (my world consisting of my loving husband and two sweet kids). I just couldn't seem to control how I reacted. The buried feelings were always right there, ready to explode. I needed to learn to get a grip on my emotions, and I wondered if I could ever change.

Sometimes I yelled in anger, and my family would look at me with fear-filled eyes. I was completely blind. I would think to myself, "What's wrong with them?" I never thought for a moment that *I* might actually be the problem.

Anger, frustration and hurt consumed me. I didn't know it at the time, but my anger was simply a deep root of bitterness from my past. My life was filled with silent secrets. I thought to myself, "I'm okay with my past," meanwhile mulling over old hurts in my mind. I was afraid to open my heart to anyone, so I continued to send myself into a tailspin of bad moods, a critical spirit and a bad attitude, especially toward my husband and kids.

My raging emotions were caused by wounds I wasn't willing to see. I needed to see what was in my heart, then I could begin to deal with the anger.

Looking back, it was a wonder that my husband, Rick, would even come home at night. I was living Proverbs 14:1: "The wise woman builds her house, but the foolish pulls it down with her hands." Foolishly, I was destroying my home.

It Was Time

I was finally willing to get real with God and truly SEE what was in my sinful heart. God's grace and forgiveness flooded into my life, changing my heart toward those who had hurt me. He showed me I was hanging on to the hurts and wrongs others had committed against me; I had become infected with the deadly poison of bitterness. It felt like a huge weight had been lifted from my shoulders when I finally got rid of the bitterness and chose to be healed and set free.

Forgiving those who molested and raped me didn't make those crimes any less wrong, but forgiving them allowed me to have what I needed—a right relationship with Jesus. I traded my hurt for wholeness in Him.

7. Read Psalm 34:18-19: "The Lord is near to those who have a broken heart, and saves such as have a contrite spirit. Many are the afflictions of the righteous, but the Lord delivers him out of them all."

    Are you ready to see what is in your heart? Are you ready to see how your pain is affecting others around you? List three areas of your life that need improvement:

    1. _____

    2. _____

    3. _____

A World Gone Wrong

There is no escape from pain and heartache in the world we live in. But there's also a way to have peace and joy. As I reflect on Verdell Davis' words in *Let Me Grieve But Not Forever*,[3] I am reminded of how much we need God's help to open our hearts and forgive:

> We live in a world gone wrong, one that was created perfect but now suffers the ravages of sin: death, violated relationships, children born with disabilities and deformities, disease, man's inhumanity to man, moral failures, tragedies of major proportions, chaos...

It is one thing to shake our heads at the mess the world is in; it is quite another to confront the reality of sin in our own lives... When we stand in the middle of a lifestorm, it seems as if the storm has become our way of life. We cannot see a way out. We feel defeated and broken. Will that brokenness produce a cynicism that keeps us in the mire of 'if only' thinking forever? Or will we yield up that brokenness to the resources of One who calms the winds and the waves, heals the brokenhearted, and forgives the most grievous of sins?

8. Will your brokenness produce a destructive, angry person or will you yield to Jesus, who heals and forgives the most grievous of sins? Write down your thoughts regarding the person who sinned against you.

_____

_____

_____

_____

An Anchor in the Storm

As Shelley Spady shares in "An Anchor in the Storm,"[4] we have many reasons to be thankful that God is in control of each storm we face. She writes:

> Sometimes life is like a storm. The raging sea wages war on our vessel. The rain cascades from the dark clouds above, which oppress us with brutal force. The furious wind tries to tatter and tear our sails. It is dark and dim and feels as if the sun will never shine again. But there is hope. A firm and immovable force that cannot be shaken. A rock upon which we stand. An anchor in the storm.

> God's Word says:[5] "In this world you will have trouble" (John 16:33), but "do not let your hearts be troubled and do not be afraid" (John 14:27), "For our light and momentary troubles are achieving for us an eternal glory that far outweighs them all" (2 Corinthians 4:17). "...In the day of trouble he will keep me safe in his dwelling; he will hide me in the shelter of his tabernacle and set me high upon a rock" (Psalm 27:5). "God is our refuge and strength, an ever-present help in times of trouble" (Psalm 46:1, GW). "He makes me lie down in green pastures, he leads me beside quiet waters, He restores my soul" (Psalm 23:2-3). "A righteous man may have many troubles, but the Lord delivers him from them all" (Psalm 34:19). "Is any one of you in trouble? He should pray" (James 5:13).

> So when the storms come, dance in the rain. When the thunder roars, lift up your voice and shout with praise. When the wind tries to blow you away, take flight in the unexpected beauty and wisdom that trials can bring. For this storm will surely pass. There will be sunshine again. There will be a new day. Our Heavenly Father is always there to guide you, to lift you up and to be an anchor in the storm. "Shout for joy, O heavens; rejoice, O earth; burst into song, O mountains! For the Lord comforts His people and will have compassion on his afflicted ones" (Isaiah 49:13).

Week 3: Day 3

Prayer: Bow your heart before the Lord in prayer prior to completing today's Bible study. Ask Him for the strength to be honest about how you express your anger.

Changing Behavior

The effects of my past hurts and "over-the-edge" emotions were a part of my life for such a long time that I continued the pattern of overreacting even after realizing that it was wrong. I didn't know any other way to react when I was stressed or disappointed, so I would just blow up. I was a Christian woman who knew God had spoken specifically to women about pulling their houses down with their hands or mouth (Proverbs 14:1), but I did it anyway! I knew it was sinful for me to act this way, and I was afraid my kids would grow up seeing me as a hypocrite. I realized I must live out my faith, and the best way to achieve that was to have a strong daily walk with God.

That's when I cried out to God to help me put an end to my destructive behavior. I couldn't continue to tell others, "Do as I say, but not as I do," so I started praying daily for self-control. That's when real change began in my life. I confessed it as a sin each time I lost control, and asked God to cut the destruction out of my life. Purging my life of this sin began when I faced my sin regularly in prayer. Do you see the progression? Sin led to confession, which led to change and purification. As 1 John 3:3 says, "...Everyone who has this hope in Him purifies himself, just as He is pure."

Tools for Change

"For godly sorrow produces repentance leading to salvation, not to be regretted; but the sorrow of the world produces death" (2 Corinthians 7:10).

SEE: Why am I letting myself get so upset? Either I'm not trusting God or I am holding a grudge toward another person.

GIVE: I have to give my struggle of uncontrolled anger to God in prayer daily.

FORGIVE: Every time I lose control, I must apologize to God, and then to my husband, my kids or whomever my anger affects. I will begin to have control over my actions and destructive emotions. I know I have to practice self-control, one day at a time.

BE SET FREE: I'll still have stress, disappointments and failure, but now I can choose to act or react in a godly way, and ask for forgiveness when I get it wrong.

Be angry with the sin, but forgive the sinner.

1. Examine your heart to SEE if you are imposing your pain on those who love you most. Write down your thoughts.

2. Take a moment to GIVE your destructive behavior to God. Take responsibility for your actions, ask the Lord to forgive you and know that He will. Write down your thoughts about your destructive behavior.

Our Parents' Example

Anger is an emotion. As children, we watched and imitated the way our parents expressed their anger. We can't blame our parents for the way we express our anger, but it may help us to understand how our behavior has been learned. Answer these questions to discover what you may have learned from your parents.

3. In what ways did your father or stepfather express his anger?

4. In what ways did your mother or stepmother express her anger?

5. What was it like to be around each of your parents when they were angry?

6. How do you express your own anger?

7. Which of your parents are you most like when you express your anger? Why?

> "The north wind brings forth rain,
> and a backbiting tongue an angry countenance"
> (Proverbs 25:23).

8. Ask those who live with you or know you best what it is like for others to be around you when you express your anger. What are their responses?

_____
_____
_____

9. In what ways would you like to express your anger differently?

_____
_____
_____

God's Example

10. God gives us guidelines to follow in expressing anger. Look up these Proverbs on page 303 and match the Proverb with the correlating scripture reference.

    1. Proverbs 15:1

    2. Proverbs 16:32

    3. Proverbs 29:11

    4. Proverbs 29:22

    A. "A fool vents all his feelings, but a wise man holds them back."

    B. "An angry man stirs up strife, and a furious man abounds in transgression."

    C. "A soft answer turns away wrath, but a harsh word stirs up anger."

    D. "He who is slow to anger is better than the mighty, and he who rules his spirit than he who takes a city."

11. How can you apply Proverbs to express your anger more appropriately?

_____
_____

This Week's Tool and Memory Verse

Tool #2 - GIVE: I must GIVE my sin to God through repentance, knowing that Christ is waiting to take it. I must be sorry enough to change, and choose to go God's way over my own.

"For godly sorrow produces repentance leading to salvation, not to be regretted; but the sorrow of the world produces death"
(2 Corinthians 7:10).

Week 3: Day 4

Prayer: Bow your heart before the Lord in prayer prior to completing today's Bible study. Ask Him for the strength to be honest about how you express your anger.

Self-Control or Out of Control

You may need to deal with an attitude that, if it were improved and transformed by God, would enhance the atmosphere of your home. This requires both a work of the Lord, and a willingness on your part to do the work to change. Self-control is difficult, but not impossible, as Elizabeth George shares: "For me, gossip was a serious struggle. I knew God spoke specifically to women about not gossiping (1 Timothy 3:11 and Titus 2:3), but I did it anyway. Convicted of my disobedience and aware that my gossip didn't please God, I tried some practical remedies like taping little notes on the telephone like, 'Is it true, is it kind, is it helpful?' and setting guidelines for my speech. I even prayed each day that I wouldn't gossip, and I still gossiped! Real change began when I started not only to pray about gossip, but to confess it as a sin each time I did it, and ask God to cut gossip out of my life."[6]

"But the fruit of the Spirit is love, joy, peace, longsuffering, kindness, goodness, faithfulness, gentleness, self-control. Against such there is no law. And those who are Christ's have crucified the flesh with its passions and desires. If we live in the Spirit, let us also walk in the Spirit" (Galatians 5:22-25).

1. Write down the nine fruits of the Spirit from Galatians 5:22-25 above.

   1. _____ 4. _____ 7. _____

   2. _____ 5. _____ 8. _____

   3. _____ 6. _____ 9. _____

2. Proverbs emphasizes self-control in expressing anger. What is self-control a result of?

   _____

   _____

3. Read 2 Peter 1:5-8: "But also for this very reason, giving all diligence, add to your faith virtue, to virtue knowledge, to knowledge self-control, to self-control perseverance, to perseverance godliness, to godliness brotherly kindness, and to brotherly kindness love. For if these things are yours and abound, you will be neither barren nor unfruitful in the knowledge of our Lord Jesus Christ."

   What does self-control lead to?

   _____

   _____

4. What are ways you can choose to control what comes out of your mouth when you are angry?

_____

_____

5. Self-control takes effort. Think of a time when you became angry this past week. Did you respond with self-control or were you out of control? If you had used self-control in this situation, what may have happened and what could have been prevented?

_____

_____

6. Read Galatians 5:19-21: "Now the works of the flesh are evident, which are: adultery, fornication, uncleanness, lewdness, idolatry, sorcery, hatred, contentions, jealousies, outbursts of wrath, selfish ambitions, dissensions, heresies, envy, murders, drunkenness, revelries, and the like; of which I tell you beforehand, just as I also told you in time past, that those who practice such things will not inherit the kingdom of God."

Give examples from your own life when the expression of your anger came from your sinful nature.

_____

_____

7. Read 1 John 1:9 and Romans 1:29-32:
   - "If we confess our sins, He is faithful and just to forgive us our sins and to cleanse us from all unrighteousness" (1 John 1:9).
   - "Being filled with all unrighteousness, sexual immorality, wickedness, covetousness, maliciousness; full of envy, murder, strife, deceit, evil-mindedness; they are whisperers, backbiters, haters of God, violent, proud, boasters, inventors of evil things, disobedient to parents, undiscerning, untrustworthy, unloving, unforgiving, unmerciful; who, knowing the righteous judgment of God, that those who practice such things are deserving of death, not only do the same but also approve of those who practice them" (Romans 1:29-32).

Write down each act that could be in your life from Romans 1:29-32 above.

_____

_____

8. What do you need to be healed from?

_____

Tammy's Reflections

Falling Down

When I was a little girl, I loved to go roller-skating with my best friend Karleen. When I first started skating, I would spend most of my time falling down, getting up, falling down, getting up, and falling down again. OUCH! Those falls really hurt! However, each time I went skating, I became a little better. I would keep track of the times I fell down and eventually, with practice, my falls became fewer and fewer. At last, one Saturday, I skated the entire time without falling once. I was very excited to be mastering this new skill, but just a few weeks later I left the skating rink with a broken arm. I had tripped over someone else's skates and down I went. After my arm healed, I was back out there skating. There would be good days when I wouldn't fall at all, and bad days when I would fall often.

I compare my skating days with my Christian walk. The Bible says, "Let him who thinks he stands take heed lest he fall" (1 Corinthians 10:12). The day I gave my life to Christ was the day I started to practice my Christian walk. Most of the early times were spent falling down and getting up, falling down and getting up, and falling down again. With each decision in my life, I was able to choose to follow God's will or my own will. When I gave in to my own negative emotions and wrong thinking, I would fall hard. But praise Jesus! God is a patient teacher, and no matter how many times we fail a test, He always presents us with a new opportunity to take the test again.

God desires for us to learn His ways and then choose to follow them. The more we practice applying His Word, the better prepared we will be when under stress, when hurtful comments come, or when we are in a trial. The more we choose to follow the Spirit and not the flesh, the less we will fall. When we do fall, it is very important not to isolate ourselves; it is easy to get discouraged and believe Satan's lies. During these times, we need other Christian friends to encourage us to turn our eyes back toward Jesus. When we fall, God will use our brokenness to lead us to His righteousness, His will and His plan for us.

God promises to give us the strength when we need to get up again. "I can do all things through Christ who strengthens me" (Philippians 4:13). Just like with skating, the more times we get up and try again, the less we will fall. We'll begin to enjoy standing on our own two feet. The more we get up and try again in our walk with the Lord, the more joy we will have, and the easier it will become to stand for the Lord.

"For we are His workmanship, created in Christ Jesus for good works, which God prepared beforehand that we should walk in them" (Ephesians 2:10).

"Commit your works to the Lord, and your thoughts will be established" (Proverbs 16:3).

The Desire to Get Even

When we get hurt, our first reaction is usually anger. The expression of this anger may be shown by hurting others as they have hurt us. Because we believe that the actions of others are sinful in God's eyes, we feel justified in getting even.

9. Read Proverbs 24:17-18: "Do not rejoice when your enemy falls, and do not let your heart be glad when he stumbles; lest the Lord see it, and it displease Him, and He turn away His wrath from him."

    What does the Bible say about getting even?

    _____

    _____

10. Read Romans 12:19 and 2 Thessalonians 1:6:

    - "Beloved, do not avenge yourselves, but rather give place to wrath; for it is written, 'Vengeance is Mine, I will repay,' says the Lord" (Romans 12:19).
    - "...It is a righteous thing with God to repay with tribulation those who trouble you" (2 Thessalonians 1:6).

    Is there anyone in your life that you would like to see wounded as you have been hurt? If so, how have you responded to this anger?

    _____

    _____

    _____

11. Read Matthew 5:43-46: "You have heard that it was said, 'You shall love your neighbor and hate your enemy.' But I say to you, love your enemies, bless those who curse you, do good to those who hate you, and pray for those who spitefully use you and persecute you, that you may be sons of your Father in heaven; for He makes His sun rise on the evil and on the good, and sends rain on the just and on the unjust. For if you love those who love you, what reward have you? Do not even the tax collectors do the same?"

    What are some ways that God wants you to respond to those who have wronged you?

    _____

    _____

    _____

12. Memorize the three scriptures below. When the desire to get even enters your mind, use these scriptures to remind yourself of God's will for you.

    - "Therefore, if your enemy is hungry, feed him; if he is thirsty, give him a drink; for in so doing you will heap coals of fire on his head. Do not be overcome by evil, but overcome evil with good" (Romans 12:20-21).
    - "And be kind to one another, tenderhearted, forgiving one another, even as God in Christ forgave you" (Ephesians 4:32).

- "Bearing with one another, and forgiving one another, if anyone has a complaint against another; even as Christ forgave you, so you also must do. But above all these things put on love, which is the bond of perfection" (Colossians 3:13-14).

Pray Blessings on Your Enemies

Pray showers of blessings on those who curse you, spitefully use you and persecute you. Pray that God will bless the work of their hands, their family and job. Every time you think of them, don't mull over the pain, pray showers of blessings over them. Apply Matthew 5:43-46 to your prayer life. This scripture is just the opposite of what our flesh wants to do. But when I began doing this with someone who deeply hurt me, my heart was sincerely filled with God's love toward this person. In fact, I wanted to bless them by making them a pumpkin pie for Thanksgiving!

Bitter Roots

Hurtful memories leave many people feeling angry. If your hurtful experience was recent, your anger may be fresh. If your experience was years ago, this anger may have formed roots of bitterness in your life. People often remain angry with those who have betrayed them.

13. Is there anyone in your life with whom you are still angry? Pray and ask the Lord to reveal this truth to you. What issues are still lingering? Write your prayer in the empty space provided. It is important to expose the root cause of your pain.

14. Read Ephesians 4:31: "Let all bitterness, wrath, anger, clamor and evil speaking be put away from you, with all malice."

    - Is there BITTERNESS in your life?
    - Is there ANGER in your life?
    - Is there CLAMOR in your life?
    - Is there EVIL SPEAKING in your life?

15. Read Colossians 3:8: "But now you yourselves are to put off all these: anger, wrath, malice, blasphemy, filthy language out of your mouth."

    What are you to do with your bitterness, clamor, anger or evil speaking?

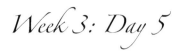

Week 3: Day 5

Prayer: Bow your heart before the Lord in prayer prior to completing today's Bible study. Ask the Holy Spirit to help you SEE what is really in your heart concerning wrong attitudes.

Pain from the Past

Many times when we are filled with anger toward those who have hurt us physically, emotionally or verbally, we end up lashing out at others. It is a painful thing to see how the anger in our hearts can affect all our other relationships. We use that anger on those who live with us, and we strike out at the people who love us most, usually our family members and friends.

1. Is this true in your life? Does pain cause you to lash out at others? Explain.

2. Have you ever been in a situation where people were backbiting you? Or have you been the one who has the backbiting tongue?

3. Pray and confess to the Lord, asking for a new start in this area of your life. Write down your prayer.

4. Read Hebrews 12:15 and 1 John 2:9-11:
   - "Looking carefully lest anyone fall short of the grace of God; lest any root of bitterness springing up cause trouble, and by this many become defiled" (Hebrews 12:15).
   - "He who says he is in the light, and hates his brother, is in darkness until now. He who loves his brother abides in the light, and there is no cause for stumbling in him. But he who hates his brother is in darkness and walks in darkness, and does not know where he is going, because the darkness has blinded his eyes" (1 John 2:9-11).

   What happens if you do not get rid of this anger according to Hebrews 12:15 and 1 John 2:9-11?

5. Has God been speaking to you about any anger or resentment that you have not let go? If so, what do you need to do?

6. Read Ephesians 5:11 and 1 John 1:6-7:
    - "And have no fellowship with the unfruitful works of darkness, but rather expose them" (Ephesians 5:11).
    - "If we say that we have fellowship with Him, and walk in darkness, we lie and do not practice the truth. But if we walk in the light as He is in the light, we have fellowship with one another, and the blood of Jesus Christ His Son cleanses us from all sin" (1 John 1:6-7).

    How do we leave the darkness of anger? Bitterness in your heart cannot be hidden or denied, it must be addressed. God commands you to get rid of it. What areas in your life are hidden in the dark? Bring it out of the darkness and into the light.

7. Quiet your heart and ask God to show you any bitterness from your painful experience. Ask Him to show you any person with whom you may still be angry. In the space below, or on a separate sheet of paper, complete this letter to God, telling Him why you have been angry with this person, and list specific ways in which this person hurt you. What has been in the darkness for so long must be brought into the light.

Dear God,

    I am angry with _____ for hurting me when...

You Can Be Free: A Lifeline of Forgiveness

So often we let our emotions control our lives. Sometimes it feels like we're drowning in them. But I am encouraged by Greg Laurie's words in his devotional "Finding Forgiveness."[7]

> I heard about a man who wasn't a good swimmer, so he went down to a dock and asked a fisherman, "Excuse me, sir, if I were to fall into this water, would I drown?" The fisherman said, "No. Falling into the water doesn't drown anybody. It's staying under the water that drowns them."
>
> You may stumble and fall spiritually, but you don't have to stay under the water. You don't have to stay under the control of sin. You can be free from it, and forgiven of it.
>
> How do you find forgiveness? Remember the words of 1 John 1:9: "If we confess our sin, He is faithful and just to forgive us and cleanse us from all unrighteousness." That is a wonderful promise. What does the word "confess" mean? A more literal rendering would be "agree with God." If you agree with God about your sin, He is faithful and just to forgive you. How does God look at sin? It is abhorrent to Him. It is offensive to Him. Is that how we look at our sin when we confess it?
>
> A lot of people will merely acknowledge their sin, thinking they are confessing it. But confession is seeing sin the way God sees it, and feeling sorry for it—sorry enough to change. The Bible says, "Godly sorrow produces repentance" (2 Corinthians 7:10). So it means that we say, "Lord, I realize what this is. God, I am sorry. Help me." Now we are getting somewhere.
>
> If you will confess your sin, see it as God sees it, be sorry for it and turn from it, then He is faithful and just to forgive you of your sins and to cleanse you from all unrighteousness. Don't stay under that ocean of sin! Grab hold of the lifeline of forgiveness.

Put Off the Old Self

God gives us every opportunity to make the right choices. As Christians we should desire to apply Colossians 3:8 (below), and practice the truth in our Christian walk. When we are obedient in our relationship with Christ, we receive comfort from that obedience. When we go our own way, we're the ones who suffer.

8. Read Colossians 3:8: "But now you yourselves are to put off all these: anger, wrath, malice, blasphemy, filthy language out of your mouth."

    - Have you put off ANGER?

    - Have you put off WRATH?

    - Have you put off MALICE?

    - Have you put off BLASPHEMY?

    - Have you put off FILTHY LANGUAGE?

9. Read Ephesians 4:23-29: "Be renewed in the spirit of your mind, and that you put on the new man which was created according to God, in true righteousness and holiness. Therefore, putting away lying, 'Let each one of you speak truth with his neighbor,' for we are members of one another. 'Be angry, and do not sin': do not let the sun go down on your wrath, nor give place to the devil. Let him who stole steal no longer, but rather let him labor, working with his hands what is good, that he may have something to give him who has need. Let no corrupt word proceed out of your mouth, but what is good for necessary edification, that it may impart grace to the hearers."

    Do you have any ideas of how to practically apply this scripture to your life?

10. Write out the ways that your mind will be renewed if you apply Ephesians 4:23-29 to your relationships, your actions, your hands and your mouth, as you put on the new man.

This Week's Tool and Memory Verse

Tool #2 - GIVE: I must GIVE my sin to God through repentance, knowing that Christ is waiting to take it. I must be sorry enough to change, and choose to go God's way over my own.

"For godly sorrow produces repentance leading to salvation, not to be regretted; but the sorrow of the world produces death"
(2 Corinthians 7:10).

Chapter Review

Finish the following statements.

- God's anger is…

- The thing about my experience that makes me angry is…

- I want to respond to this anger by…

- I will practice self-control when I am angry by…

- For a long time I have had anger toward…

- I desire to know more about forgiving the unacceptable hurts from _____ in the next chapter. (Name the person or people who need to be forgiven.)

The next step is to forgive those who have hurt you. Forgiveness is not easy, especially when the deep hurt has been with you for years. The next chapter will reveal God's plan for learning how to forgive others.

Stories of Real People and a Real Savior

Releasing All the Pain, Anger, Guilt and Shame I'd Kept Inside
By Brooke, Pastor's Wife in Guatemala

At some point in my early childhood, I learned to stuff away the things that brought pain or made me feel ashamed or dirty - like being sexually abused when I was five by my babysitter's son.

My dad was an alcoholic, and much of what I remember from my childhood revolves around him being drunk. I longed for his love and attention, but never received what I was looking for. So I began to search for it in other places in my early teens, looking for a way to ease my pain. Relationships, boyfriends and alcohol became a large part of my life, and by the end of high school, I had developed a double life: being the good girl at school and in front of adults, but the party girl on the weekends.

I had already had several physical relationships with men by the time I started college, and my first semester was one long party: life consisted of parties and guys and fun. I surrounded myself with people who were happy as long as the beer was flowing, who weren't concerned with going deeper than a surface relationship. That was completely fine with me.

I had never truly met Jesus either, although I had believed that I was on good terms with God. I lived life expecting God to come through for me, yet denying Him at every turn, being completely rebellious to what little I did know about His Word and plan for my life.

Not long after starting college, I met my future husband and we began dating. Just after we got engaged, a Christian uncle sat us down after a family member's funeral. He asked what would happen to us if we died the next day, and he shared the gospel with us. You see, we both thought we'd go to heaven since we were 'good people,' but he explained that was not enough. Both my fiance and I met Jesus, and our names were written in the Lamb's Book of Life that day.

We married later that year, and it seemed that life was perfect. We had a nice church home, were very much in love, and now were living life with Jesus. Yet shortly after the births of our first two children, things didn't seem so perfect anymore. Life was hard, money was tight. I thought that with Jesus all the pain and hurt from the past would go away. But it didn't, it was much worse. I had become an angry wife and mother, and it seemed that once again I was living a double life, only this time it was one life at church and around other Christians, and a completely converse life at home. My husband and I fought and seemed to be growing farther and farther apart. I longed for joy and peace in our marriage and home.

After several years of this, the Lord spoke strongly to both my husband and me about our commitment to Him. We both knew we were not fully committed to Him. We served full time on the mission field for five years. I thought all the pain would finally go away once I was a missionary! But it didn't.

Those were lonely, difficult times. Yet the Lord used them to bring me to the point where I was able to release all the pain, anger, hurt, guilt and shame I'd kept inside my whole life. God used the Healed and Set Free Bible Study to truly heal me and set me free! I am a different woman today because of what I learned through this study!

Galatians 5:1 and Philippians 3:13-14 encourage me daily to forget about the past, press on and stand firm in the freedom Christ has given me. I am so thankful for this study and the work of the Lord in my life!

~Sanada y Liberada (healed and freed), Brooke

Tools to Become Healed and Set Free

To equip yourself in God's truth, look over the tools and verses that will be introduced in the coming weeks. Thinking about the past won't change it, but you can change your future by being set free from your past.

TOOL #1 - SEE: I must SEE the truth about what is in my heart so I am not defiled.

> **Definition**: To defile means to make filthy or dirty; to pollute.

> **Bible Verse**: "Looking carefully lest anyone fall short of the grace of God; lest any root of bitterness springing up cause trouble, and by this many become defiled" (Hebrews 12:15).

TOOL #2 - GIVE: I must GIVE my sin to God through repentance, knowing that Christ is waiting to take it. I must be sorry enough to change, and choose to go God's way over my own.

> **Definition**: To repent means to feel such sorrow for sin or fault as to be disposed to change one's life for the better; be penitent.

> **Bible Verse**: "For godly sorrow produces repentance leading to salvation, not to be regretted; but the sorrow of the world produces death" (2 Corinthians 7:10).

TOOL #3 - FORGIVE: I must FORGIVE as I am forgiven by Christ: Forgiving those who hurt, bruised, wronged, rejected, betrayed or harmed me, whether unintentionally or deliberately. I must ask God to forgive me for holding on to unforgiveness and know that He will.

> **Definition**: To forgive means to stop feeling angry or resentful toward someone for an offense, flaw or mistake.

> **Bible Verse**: "...Bearing with one another, and forgiving one another, if anyone has a complaint against another; even as Christ forgave you, so you also must do" (Colossians 3:13).

TOOL #4 - FORGET: I must FORGET by no longer dwelling on the hurt or the painful reminders, such as: phrases, smells, places, songs and comments. Instead, I am putting my mind on the higher calling that Christ has for me.

> **Definition**: To forget means to choose not to remember or notice, "forgive and forget".

> **Bible Verse**: "Brethren, I do not count myself to have apprehended; but one thing I do, forgetting those things which are behind and reaching forward to those things which are ahead" (Philippians 3:13).

Be Healed and Set Free: Christ will heal me from my past, showing me the truth, so I can become a cleansed vessel, healed and set free.

> **Definition**: To set free means to make free; set at liberty; release from bondage, imprisonment, or restraint.

> **Definition**: To heal means to make whole and healthy; to cure; to remedy or repair.

> **Bible Verse**: "And you shall know the truth, and the truth shall make you free" (John 8:32).

Chapter 4

Forgiving the Unacceptable

This Week's Focus

This week we will discover **Tool #3 - FORGIVE** which demonstrates the purpose and importance of receiving God's forgiveness and forgiving others as we ourselves have been forgiven by Christ.

Tool #3 - FORGIVE: I must forgive as I am forgiven by Christ. Forgiving those who hurt, bruised, wronged, rejected, betrayed or harmed me, whether unintentionally or deliberately. I must ask God to forgive me for holding on to unforgiveness and know that He will.

Definition: To forgive means to stop feeling angry or resentful toward (someone) for an offense, flaw or mistake.

Bible Verse: "Bearing with one another, and forgiving one another, if anyone has a complaint against another; even as Christ forgave you, so you also must do" (Colossians 3: 13).

Prayer: Ask God to help you SEE what's in your heart and GIVE Him the strongholds that our thinking and pride can cause.

Week 4: Day 1

Prayer: Bow your heart before the Lord in prayer prior to completing today's Bible study. Ask Him to help you see and understand the truth about forgiveness.

It's been said that harboring unforgiveness makes us a slave. But do you truly believe that? Meditate on how choosing not to forgive can enslave you as you read this reflection from James Blanchard Cisneros' *You Have Chosen to Remember*:[1]

> You can choose not to forgive your brother. But what good has this kind of behavior brought to your life? You might be trying to consciously or unconsciously punish that person by not forgiving him or her. But who are you really punishing? Who carries that judgment with him wherever he goes? My friend, you might not consciously recognize that you are carrying this judgment, but it does simmer below the surface, coloring everything and everyone with whom you interact.
>
> Little by little, these judgments add up and weigh you down. You may be quick to anger, feel tired or stressed, and not understand why. Comments to friends or family may become nasty, and your patience may fade. All this is due to your attempt to punish that person by not forgiving him. My friend, again I ask you, who are you really punishing? Do you realize what anger can do to you?

Day by Day

Getting real with God is the first step when facing the deep, dark hurts that have chipped away at your heart. Whether it has been one year or 50, God's love is bigger than our hurts and fears. He is waiting for you to let go of it all and trust Him so you can receive restoration, freedom and peace.

On a day-by-day basis, let's continue to go over the four steps that will keep our hearts free! They are: SEE, GIVE, FORGIVE and FORGET. Thinking about the past will never change the past, but you can change the future and be set free from your past. As you deal with your past and present hurts, you can either embrace the truth and let go of the burdens you carry, or carry your burdens and reject the truth and freedom that it brings. The choice is yours.

> "I choose gentleness... Nothing is won by force. I choose to be gentle. If I raise my voice, may it be only in praise. If I clench my fist, may it be only in prayer. If I make a demand, may it be only of myself."
> - Max Lucado

Tools to Become Set Free

In this chapter, we will discover **Tool #3 - FORGIVE**.

These tools will help you to become set free. Each tool is defined as the time comes. It is crucial to memorize these powerful tools and review them regularly in order to apply them to your daily life.

#1 - SEE: I must SEE the truth about what is in my heart so I am not defiled.

#2 - GIVE: I must GIVE my sin to God through repentance, knowing that Christ is waiting to take it. I must be sorry enough to change, and choose to go God's way over my own.

#3 - FORGIVE: I must FORGIVE as I am forgiven by Christ: Forgiving those who hurt, bruised, wronged, rejected, betrayed or harmed me, whether unintentionally or deliberately. I must ask God to forgive me for holding on to unforgiveness and know that He will.

#4 - FORGET: I must FORGET by no longer dwelling on the hurt or the painful reminders such as: phrases, smells, places, songs and comments. Instead, I am putting my mind on the higher calling that Christ has for me.

Be Healed and Set Free: Christ will heal me from my past, showing me the truth, so I can become a cleansed vessel, healed and set free.

This Week's Focus

Prayer: Ask God to help you SEE what's in your heart and GIVE Him the strongholds that our thinking and pride can cause.

By Memory: My challenge to you is to be able to recite the tool, definition and Bible verse from this chapter without looking. I know that by hiding these words of wisdom in your heart you are providing yourself with tools to truly be healed and set free. May we rise up to be women of the Word.

Tool #3 - FORGIVE: I must forgive as I am forgiven by Christ. Forgiving those who hurt, bruised, wronged, rejected, betrayed or harmed me, whether unintentionally or deliberately. I must ask God to forgive me for holding on to unforgiveness and know that He will.

Definition: To forgive means to stop feeling angry or resentful toward (someone) for an offense, flaw or mistake.

Bible Verse: "Bearing with one another, and forgiving one another, if anyone has a complaint against another; even as Christ forgave you, so you also must do" (Colossians 3: 13).

"And you shall know the truth, and the truth shall make you free" (John 8:32).

Many people over the years have asked me the same questions about forgiveness: How do you forgive a person who has passed on? A person you don't trust? A person who refuses to talk to you? These questions arise over and over from those seeking to forgive, but forgiveness is between us and God. The word "restoration" is defined as: the return of something to a former owner, place or condition. Doug Easterday points out the truth of God's promise to restore the fullness of our lives, no matter what has happened to you, through forgiveness.

Restoration Through Forgiveness

By Doug Easterday

We all have a past: a storehouse of good and bad memories that affect the way we live today. Even though I grew up in a godly home and had great parents, some painful things happened to me during my childhood years. I would love to just snap my fingers and *poof!*, all the painful memories would be gone, but I can't do that!

No matter what has happened to you in the past, God's goal is to bring you to a condition where the negative issues of the past no longer affect your present and future life in Him. In His Word, the Lord promises to restore the fullness of our lives. In Joel 2:25 (KJV) He says, "And I will restore to you the years that the locust hath eaten, the cankerworm and the caterpillar and the palmer worm, My great army which I sent among you."

Why did this scripture happen to list those four particular insects? Because if we were to release these insects on to a plant, all four working together would eat the leaves, branches, main stalk and finally the root. And what would be left? Absolutely nothing, the plant would be destroyed.

But God says He will restore to you the years that have been nibbled and eaten away, no matter what has happened to you! Even if you feel like you've been totally destroyed, God intends for you to be restored. But real hurts don't come out of the ground or the bushes, they come from other people. And deep hurts don't heal except through the process of forgiveness.

As I travel throughout the Body of Christ, I hear people saying, "I've forgiven, it's not a big issue for me anymore!" They want to pass forgiveness off as "no big deal," but they're not really understanding the significance God's Word gives to the issue of forgiveness. To God, it's a very big deal!

What Forgiveness is Not

First, let's talk about what forgiveness is not: Forgiveness is not pretending that you weren't hurt, or saying that what the person did wasn't wrong. Don't sweep the incident under the rug! Sometimes we feel that if we forgive, we're actually declaring that what the other person did wasn't so bad; as though you're saying, "It must have been my fault for being in the wrong place at the wrong time!"

For example, if I punched you in the nose, then later came back and said, "I'm really sorry," what would you say? Would you say, "It's okay"? If so, do you realize what you've just told me? You've just given me permission to do it again! You did say, "It's okay!" But what was okay? Was it okay to hit you? No! So when someone comes to you saying, "I'm sorry, I was wrong," and you respond back, "It's okay," I believe you're giving them permission to hurt you again, and that's giving them permission to sin. But we don't have the right to tell another person that it's okay to sin. The proper response is simply to say, "I forgive you."

Forgiveness doesn't mean you have to trust the person who hurt you. A young girl came to counsel with me awhile ago. She was very nervous, and it took 20 minutes for her to open up. She finally told me something she hadn't told another human being—that her father had raped her almost every day for the past four years.

Now, do you think that I should have encouraged her to forgive her father, *and* trust him? No! At that point, her father didn't deserve to be trusted. I'm not saying that she shouldn't ever trust her father again. As Christians, we need to allow those who have hurt us the chance to prove themselves trustworthy in the future. But forgiveness is a separate issue from trust, and we can completely forgive a person but not extend trust to them.

Trusting comes as we get to know someone and believe in their character. That's why I can trust God, because I am confident in His character! We develop trust for human beings only as they prove themselves trustworthy. When someone lashes out at you, your natural response will probably be anger, hurt and a lack of trust.

If forgiveness means that you have to make yourself totally vulnerable to that person, and leave yourself open for another emotional or verbal assault, you would be rational to not forgive. But if you can fully understand that "forgiveness" and "trust" are two separate issues, you'll see that forgiveness isn't beyond your grasp. Forgiveness is not relieving other people of their responsibility. We think, "They really hurt me! If I forgive them, they're going to walk away scot-free. They're not going to have to answer for their wrong-doings!"

But remember, God is completely capable of making sure that a person is held accountable. As you accept your attitude and the unforgiveness in your own heart, you allow God to work in a greater way than ever before!

- Forgiveness is not a feeling.
- Forgiveness is not pretending you weren't hurt.
- Forgiveness is not saying what the person did was okay.
- Forgiveness does not mean you have to trust someone again.
- Forgiveness is not relieving other people of their responsibility.

What Is Forgiveness?

Forgiveness is a decision we make to obey God. It is not a suggestion from the Lord, it's a commandment. When we forgive someone, we are being obedient to God. Forgiveness doesn't have to be a big public event, it takes place in your heart, just between you and God.

From "Restoration Through Forgiveness," published by Last Days Ministries, © 2007. Used by permission.

1. Are you ready to forgive those who have hurt you? Pray and tell Christ.

> "Even though you may not understand how God works, you know He does."
> - Max Lucado

Tammy's Reflections

Hide and Seek

As an only child, one of my favorite things to do was to go to my cousins' house. I can still remember playing hide and seek in the dark when I was seven years old. The excitement of the game left me breathless as I hurried to find the best hiding spot. I could feel my heart pound with anticipation at the thought of being caught at any moment. Alone in the dark I waited, when suddenly, I felt a hand on my shoulder. Expecting to find one of my cousins behind me, I was shocked to see my uncle standing there as if to say, "I got you."

His hands touched me in a way that felt uncomfortable, and I knew something was very wrong. Who would have thought my favorite childhood memory would become my worst nightmare? This incident was the beginning of a long pattern of sexual abuse by my uncle. Every time I was dropped off at my cousins' house, my uncle would come for me. I would try to get away from him, but he would always find me and take me to his "private" place.

Every night as my parents tucked me into bed, I longed to tell them what was happening. If only I could whisper in my mommy's ear, "Please don't take me back to that terrible place." But the thought of confessing was quickly overtaken by my uncle's voice echoing in my ears: "If you tell your parents, I will kill them." As my heart pounded, I would simply say, "Good night," and cry myself to sleep. I was left feeling dirty and unworthy of love. As I grew up, I went from lonely little girl to out-of-control teen, partying in a vain attempt to numb the pain.

Years later at a family wedding, my cousin was dancing with my two year old son, Caleb. I was full of joy while watching him, but when I saw my uncle walk toward him, my heart filled with rage as the memories of how my uncle had hurt me came rushing back. Paralyzed by fear, I watched as my uncle reached out to take Caleb. Turning to my father, I desperately choked out, "Go get Caleb." My parents grabbed him and we left the wedding.

God used this incident to trigger a chain of events that would change all our lives forever. We found out that every one of my cousins and all of the neighborhood kids had been sexually abused by my uncle. Seeking justice, we took it to court, and my uncle was sentenced to fifteen years in prison. But being abused had a far greater sentence for us, the victims. My cousins were destroyed by the trauma. Some of them turned to drugs, or even suicide in an attempt to numb the pain. And despite having justice, I was consumed by the memories. I felt insecure, vengeful, short-tempered and critical.

After living with these feelings for a long time, I finally decided to face the truth and stop giving God a false performance. I learned life-changing insights that healed and set me free from my past. Life is too short to let anger rule! No one needs to suffer in silence like I did for twenty years. Thankfully, God's Word heals! Jesus is near to the broken-hearted, and He will use the pain from our past to create a beautiful testimony that will glorify Him.

The Cross of Forgiveness

The cross exemplifies the love of God. From the cross, God provided forgiveness for people who were bound to fail, but who would return to Him someday to seek

His mercy and forgiveness. God sent His Son, Jesus, to be the sacrifice for our sins. He bore our sins on the cross: every sin, every evil thought, every wrong action. Because God is truth He cannot lie, and His Word continually tells us that He wants us to be in a trusting, loving relationship with Him.

"Thus God, determining to show more abundantly to the heirs of promise the immutability of His counsel, confirmed it by an oath, that by two immutable things, in which it is impossible for God to lie, we might have strong consolation, who have fled for refuge to lay hold of the hope set before us" (Hebrews 6:17-18).

2. Who did God offer forgiveness to?

Spiritual Warfare

The battles we face and the power of Satan are real. As Christians, we need to know that Satan will do whatever it takes to stop us from being healed and set free, especially when it comes to forgiveness. Satan hates what Jesus did on the cross, and would like nothing more than for us to think the cross has no power for forgiveness. But Satan is a liar. "He speaks from his own resources, for he is a liar; the father of lies" (John 8:44). Satan's highest priority is the destruction of your Christian life. As people in Christ, we need to resist the devil and his lies, and stand strong in the days to come, especially when it comes to the power of the cross for the forgiveness of sins!

Take a moment to pray before reading the following questions, and ask God to open your eyes to see the spiritual warfare happening in your life.

What the Enemy Knows About You

Do you know your own heart, weaknesses, insecurities and struggles? Answer the following questions about yourself in order to guard yourself from Satan's attacks.

3. He knows you. When do you get stirred up?

4. He knows your weaknesses. Recognize and write your weaknesses down.

5. He knows your fears and insecurities. What lies has Satan been whispering in your ears to activate your fears and insecurities?

6. He knows your struggles. What struggles tempt or lead you to failure?

Stories of Real People and a Real Savior

When I Was Just A Child

Teresa, Idaho

As a young girl, I was sexually molested by my father and then later by a friend's father. Thinking that was what men expected of me, I lost my virginity at age 14. I was ashamed of who I was. I would party and use drugs to block out my feelings. Then, when I was only 16, I found myself pregnant.

Although I decided to keep the baby, the father and I decided not to marry. For 18 years we lived together, barely able to hold on to each other because of the destruction we had brought into the relationship. He was very controlling, and I became an alcoholic and meth addict. My addiction led me to have an affair, which drove my oldest daughter to move out of our home when she was only 16.

My whole world was coming apart. Finally, realizing that I needed help, I committed myself into a rehab center. I gave my life to Jesus, accepting Christ as my Savior and believing that He died on the cross for me. I repented for my sins and received true forgiveness. Then, no longer willing to just live together, I married the father of my child. Praise God!

But although I knew God and my husband had forgiven me, I still felt ashamed of everything I had done. I had a hard time believing and accepting forgiveness from Christ for the sins I had committed against Him and others. But one day the Lord showed me the condition of my heart. He showed me that I was still sinning against Him by not accepting His forgiveness in my life. God reminded me that the old Teresa was gone, and the new Teresa was here to stay. Recognizing that I was indeed a new creation in Christ Jesus, I repented of my doubts.

At last, I let go of the shame, and by faith accepted the forgiveness Jesus offered. He has healed my heart and healed my marriage. I am no longer clothed in shame, because my Father in Heaven has made something beautiful out of my life.

Satan's Schemes

One of Satan's most effective tactics is to tempt you to forget that you have an enemy at all. When you fall for this lie, it leads you to embrace all the wrong answers. But no matter what kind of pleasure Satan offers you, his ultimate intention is to ruin you. Your destruction is his highest priority.

7. Do you know that Satan is cunning, tempting and deceitful? List three ways that he wants to keep you from obeying, trusting and following God.

    1. _____
    2. _____
    3. _____

8. Satan wants to "sift you as wheat" (Luke 22:31). Has he taken hold of you with temptations cleverly disguised as harmless pleasures? Summarize the temptations he throws at you:

___

9. Read James 4:7: "...Submit to God. Resist the devil and he will flee from you."

   How do you resist the devil?

___

10. Read Ephesians 6:13-17: "Therefore take up the whole armor of God, that you may be able to withstand in the evil day, and having done all, to stand. Stand therefore, having girded your waist with truth, having put on the breastplate of righteousness, and having shod your feet with the preparation of the gospel of peace; above all, taking the shield of faith with which you will be able to quench all the fiery darts of the wicked one. And take the helmet of salvation, and the sword of the Spirit, which is the word of God."

    How do you stand against the devil?

___

11. Bow your heart before the Lord and ask Him to reveal any sins in your life that might be separating you from Him. Then ask Him to forgive you and know that He will.

___

12. When we're hurt by others, we are faced with a choice of how to respond. Satan will always offer the wrong response. Look at the list below and circle the wrong responses that have crept into your life.
    - Denying or punishing myself
    - Turning to false gods or wrong attitudes
    - Feeling depressed or worthless
    - Blaming everyone else; being discontent with my life or my marriage
    - Getting even
    - Giving the cold shoulder
    - Pretending things don't bother me
    - Stuffing things deep into my heart and not accepting that they happened
    - Running to shopping fixes
    - Running to food fixes or starving myself
    - Running to parties or sex
    - Using illegal drugs or alcohol, or misusing medications
    - Longing for death
    - Thinking others don't like me; being self-absorbed

The Right Response

When hurt comes into our lives, a root of bitterness can grow from our broken heart, but how do we stop the root from growing and consuming us? The right response is to follow the truth, and the truth will set us free. Hebrews 4:12 says, "The word of God is living and powerful, and sharper than any two-edged sword..."

The right response is to get a sharp sword and cut the root of bitterness out of our lives. That sword is the Word of God! "Be filled with the knowledge of His will in all wisdom and spiritual understanding; that you may walk worthy of the Lord, fully pleasing Him, being fruitful in every good work and increasing in the knowledge of God" (Colossians 1:9-10).

13. Write down how you have applied the four tools to your heart in order to be filled with the knowledge of His will.

    I can now SEE...

    I have GIVEN...

    I have FORGIVEN...

    I desire to FORGET...

    I have been SET FREE from...

    Write down your thoughts:

Self-Preservation

Mary Katherine Kohl[2]

Many things have been done—or words were said
that pierced the heart—like a bullet of lead.
And though the event came—and soon was gone
the sting of it all—lingered on and on.

Dwelling on the past—though time has marched on
will make us miserable—no mood for a song.
Because peace and joy—Satan is stealing
thus, he alone prospers—if we hold an ill feeling.

We must forgive others—in a way that is right
leaving their flaws—for only God's sight.
Sometimes it's impossible—to humanly do
so we call on the Holy Spirit—to see us through.

When the Lord forgives us—our slate is wiped clean
God doesn't hold grudges—or see us as mean.
Yes, He gives us a chance—for a whole new start
He holds no memory—of our mistakes in His heart.

If we can't forgive—like the Lord intended
we have a miserable life—which can't be mended.
Because an unforgiving heart—is real devastation
and forgiving completely—is self-preservation.

This Week's Tool and Memory Verse

Tool #3 - FORGIVE: I must FORGIVE, as I am forgiven by Christ. Forgiving those who hurt, bruised, wronged, rejected, betrayed or harmed me, whether unintentionally or deliberately. I must ask God to forgive me for holding on to unforgiveness and know that He will.

"Bearing with one another, and forgiving one another, if anyone
has a complaint against another; even as Christ forgave you,
so you also must do" (Colossians 3:13).

Week 4: Day 2

Prayer: Bow your heart before the Lord in prayer prior to completing today's Bible study. Pray for the Lord to show you the truth about forgiveness.

"The thief does not come except to steal, and to kill, and to destroy. I have come that they may have life, and that they may have it more abundantly" (John 10:10).

Stories of Real People and a Real Savior

Cleaning Out the Junk Drawer

Debbie, Idaho

Can you imagine being a Christian for 20 years and not fully understanding the basic Christian principle of forgiveness? That was me! Most homes have a junk drawer: a drawer to throw in odds and ends such as screwdrivers, pencils, pens, and other items that don't have a home. I had been keeping a junk drawer in my heart ever since my stepfather had sexually abused me at a very young age. Throughout my life, I had learned to put broken trusts, painful memories and hurts that still lingered in the junk drawer of my heart.

I believed I was justified in my unforgiveness and that God understood. But as I did the *Healed and Set Free* Bible study, I was continually reminded in each chapter that I needed to see what was really going on in my heart and get real with the hurts that still lingered.

Now I have been SET FREE! God has shown me that forgiving somebody isn't saying that what they did was okay; it is never okay to hurt a child, for example. But when I opened the junk drawer of my heart to God, He shined His light in. I saw that I needed to clean out the drawer! It was a very humbling and healing experience!

When God forgives us, He's not saying that what we did was okay, He's saying that He sent Jesus to shed His blood and die for our sins—all of them. Abusing a child is a sin. Holding unforgiveness in your heart is a sin. Jesus died for all sins. *Healed and Set Free* gave me the tools to clean out the junk drawer of my heart. I now have a heart that has been healed and set free, and I know how to keep it that way.

> "This is what the past is for! Every experience God gives us, every person He puts in our lives, is the perfect preparation for the future that only He can see."
> - Corrie Ten Boom

Tammy's Reflections

A Weight Lifted

"If you are blessed with a naturally forgiving personality," writes Mary Hayes Grieco, "you shrug off your bad experiences and keep moving forward happily and purposefully, despite the hurts of the past. But if you, like many people, are the type of person who holds on to grudges, you [must] learn how to forgive."[3]

Forgiveness didn't come easily for me. I even asked, "Can you really forgive? Is forgiveness more than just a statement?" But I realized that when I constantly look at what's wrong or what someone did to hurt me, it's like wearing an itchy wool coat; it's dark, negative and heavy.

Why let unforgiveness or a grudge hold you back? It would be a shame to live even one day filled with hatred toward another person! Everyone is different. It might take a lifetime for an individual to heal. But we should believe in healing more than we believe in despair. Healing will come if your eyes are wide open to the truth of God's Word, and if you are willing to say, "I'm ready to change." Remember, forgiveness is a matter of the heart, which we do for our relationship with God, as well as for our own sake.

The journey of forgiveness is refreshing and freeing. It's like losing 100 pounds of unwanted fat. When we get down to business with God, and work to heal and bring closure to old wounds "we dissolve the stagnant weight of resentment," as Grieco says. It mends us, improves our relationships, restores our overall health and allows us to move forward with hope and a new outlook on life.

Everything may not be perfect, but friends, we need to learn how to be content and grateful in life. You may not have the perfect life, but who does? You can at least thank God that you've been given the very breath you breathe. God is working behind the scenes in our lives. We need to recognize that every day is a gift from Him! This is the life God has given me, and I'm going to make the most of it; how about you?

It's hard to say why we hold on to a problem for so long, or what makes us want to change it. One day you might just wake up and think, "I'm so tired of hating that person," or "I'm sick of letting that rejection keep me down!" But once you begin to work through the process of forgiveness, you'll feel as light as a feather. You'll wonder, "Why didn't I do this sooner? I didn't know life could be so beautiful!"

The good news is, there's nothing that's unforgiveable. There is no hurt too deep, no loss or betrayal or disappointment that is beyond healing. When we forgive, we are saying, "Even though this hurts and I'm unhappy, I am going to completely give the pain to God and move forward to a better life!" God has given us the permission to move forward. When you're willing, He will bring change to your life. No matter where you are now, you can be better! Start being grateful for what's right and good in your life. We can't make the mistake of sitting back and settling where we are. Take the time to practice the biblical tools in your everyday life of SEE, GIVE, FORGIVE, FORGET and BE SET FREE.

Don't Waste Your Pain: Use It

Tears can cleanse you, and pain can deepen your relationship with God, drawing you into His mercy and love. Draw near to God and He will draw near to you. Many brokenhearted people give up and walk away from Him. Don't let that be you! God's hand is there to set you free.

1. Read Ephesians 2:10: "For we are His workmanship, created in Christ Jesus for good works, which God prepared beforehand that we should walk in them."

   What are you to walk in according to Ephesians 2:10?

   _____
   _____
   _____
   _____
   _____

In His Hands: Joseph's Story

Joseph is one of the upstanding men of the Old Testament. His example for us is one of unwavering conviction and complete trust in God. Yet when we read about Joseph's story, just like when we reflect upon our own lives, it's easy to focus on the negative and unfair circumstances. I read a great devotional by The Active Word that shares a different perspective on Joseph's life. It's called "In His Hands."[4]

> "You meant evil against me; but God meant it for good, in order to bring it about as it is this day, to save many people alive" (Genesis 50:20).
>
> God is a great Redeemer. In His hands, bad is transformed into good. Just look at the life of Joseph in Genesis 37-50. As the obvious favorite of his father, Joseph is betrayed by his family; his older brothers plotted to get rid of him by selling him into slavery to a caravan of traders headed for Egypt. Then things only seemed to get worse. Joseph was sold to a man named Potiphar, whose wife tried to seduce him. When he resisted her advances, she accused him of attacking her and Joseph was sent to prison, where he remained in chains. At this point in the story, doesn't the crime Joseph's brothers committed against him appear purely wicked?
>
> But the story doesn't end there. As it turns out, Joseph interpreted a dream for a fellow prisoner, who eventually brought Joseph's ability to the attention of Pharaoh, who also had a disturbing dream. Joseph interpreted Pharaoh's dream, and got promoted to second in command over all Egypt. Because of his powerful position, Joseph was eventually able to save his family, including his brothers, from a life-threatening famine.
>
> Toward the end of his life, Joseph looked back at the bad that his brothers had done to him and said, "But God meant it for good." Satan meant all of this for evil. His intention was to destroy Joseph, but God used it for good. Joseph was willing to trust God and let Him work through his brokenness. He let his pain drive him into a deeper relationship with God.

Again, God is the Great Redeemer, and in His hands bad is transformed into good. When it comes to the things in your life that appear to be totally and utterly bad, remember there's a "But God..." that changes everything. In spite of how negative and unredeemable something looks, God is able to take that thing and turn it into something that's good for you.

You might say, "But I can't possibly imagine how _____ can be good for me!" Don't try to. Entrust that to the incredibly creative and redemptive power of God.

2. Write out Matthew 19:26 from page 303.

3. Read Romans 8:28: "And we know that all things work together for good to those who love God, to those who are called according to His purpose."

    Do you see how your hurts or failures can work together for good in the calling and the purpose that God has planned for your life? If so, how?

> "Forgiveness is not a one-time act, but rather a lifestyle that has to be maintained. The opposite of forgiveness is unforgiveness, and unforgiveness has two cousins. The first is resentment; the second is bitterness."
> -Doug Easterday

Week 4: Day 3

Prayer: Bow your heart before the Lord in prayer, asking Him to help you let go of the past and to examine your heart daily as you embrace His Word.

Learning God's Truth Through Tool #1

SEE the truth of the sins in your heart. Ask God to expose the root causes of sinful thoughts that could be springing up and defiling your heart. I had to face the truth in my heart. At first I tried to justify my feelings, but after many tears, lots of prayer and learning God's truth through His Word, I realized my sins of hatred and unforgiveness were no different than the sins my uncle had committed against me. SIN is SIN.

1. Have any of the following filled your heart? (Circle those that apply.)

    - Fear
    - Self-pity
    - Need for control
    - Hurt
    - Defensiveness
    - Doubt
    - Jealousy
    - Pride
    - Insecurity
    - Anxiety
    - Desire for revenge
    - Bitterness
    - Comparing myself to others

2. Read Hebrews 12:15 and 2 Corinthians 7:10:
    - "Looking carefully lest anyone fall short of the grace of God; lest any root of bitterness springing up cause trouble, and by this many become defiled" (Hebrews 12:15).
    - "For godly sorrow produces repentance leading to salvation, not to be regretted; but the sorrow of the world produces death" (2 Corinthians 7:10).

    Write down who you are bitter toward, and if you are harboring unforgiveness.

    _____

    _____

    _____

Learning God's Truth Through Tool #2

I had to GIVE my bitterness and hatred to Christ. This was the hardest part for me because I had built a thick wall of resentment around my heart. I knew the way I was living as a Christian was no longer acceptable, but with God's help, I began to GIVE my sinful burden to the Lord.

My heart began to heal when I asked for forgiveness. This wasn't a one-time thing, but the beginning of a painful journey. I needed to SEE the truth about what was in my heart and continue to GIVE it to Christ every time it tried to come back. I have no desire to let my ugly sinful nature take over, so I continue to apply Psalm 32:5 and James 5:16 in my life to this very day:

- "I acknowledged my sin to You, and my iniquity I have not hidden. I said, 'I will confess my transgressions to the Lord,' and You forgave the iniquity of my sin" (Psalm 32:5).

- "Confess your trespasses to one another, and pray for one another, that you may be healed. The effective, fervent prayer of a righteous man avails much" (James 5:16).

3. We need to become broken before God, opening our hearts to let the Healer set us free. Are you ready to give your bitterness, hatred and hurts to Jesus today? Yes or no?

4. Write out Psalm 32:5 from above.

Learning God's Truth Through Tool #3

I need to FORGIVE others as I am forgiven by Christ; forgiving those who hurt, bruised, wronged, rejected, betrayed or harmed me, whether unintentionally or deliberately. I must ask God to forgive me for harboring unforgiveness, and know that He will forgive me.

> Forgiveness is a decision. Even though some decisions can be very difficult, God has given us the ability to make them. Even if our emotions are screaming "No! No!" we're still capable of making a choice to forgive. It's not really accurate to say "I can't forgive." That's not true. What you're actually saying is, "I won't forgive." It's a choice. A difficult one? You bet. One you don't feel like making? Sure. But possible? Yes! It is possible to forgive, even though there is nothing within us that feels like forgiving. It's an act of our will—not our emotions.[5]

Doug Easterday's words, above, are true wisdom: We need to be sorry enough to change our thinking, and choose God's way over ours. The memories will still be there, but the feelings of hatred and emptiness will be gone. When I forgive from my heart, I don't even think about the memories anymore; it's not worth it! Remember, when you forgive, you set a captive free: yourself! Forget about the past. Choose to look forward, keeping your eyes on Jesus.

5. "Bearing with one another, and forgiving one another, if anyone has a complaint against another; even as Christ forgave you, so you also must do" (Colossians 3:13)

   Are you ready to forgive? Tell Christ about it, writing down your thoughts.

Learning God's Truth Through Tool #4

FORGET by no longer dwelling on your past hurts. I had to learn to forget and put the past behind me. This happened only after my heart was truly healed from unforgiveness, shame and anger. This is the easiest step to take for a fresh start, but you will need to be on your guard. If you are tempted to remember and dwell on past hurts, recognize it as an attack from the enemy. Instead, remember to forget. There is freedom for your heart and soul in forgetting the past and looking forward to the future. This tool will be covered in depth in chapter 7.

"Brethren, I do not count myself to have apprehended; but one thing I do, forgetting those things which are behind and reaching forward to those things which are ahead" (Philippians 3:13).

Living God's Truth

BE SET FREE, getting out of the chains that have kept you in bondage, and step into freedom by believing and trusting in God's true Word. Chapter 9 will cover the principles of living a life of freedom in-depth.

Read John 14:6 and John 8:32:

- "Jesus answered, 'I am the way, the truth, and the life'" (John 14:6).
- "And you shall know the truth, and the truth shall make you free" (John 8:32).

6. Use the space below to write your thoughts about forgiveness and the tools to **BE SET FREE!**

> "Friendly fellow believers will trip and fall, and end up landing on us, but if both parties put their pride aside and reconcile their differences, the bridge can be rebuilt with God's love, forgiveness and trust... Will we burn bridges and cut people out of our lives? Or will we follow Christ's example and 'live at peace with all men'? (Romans 12:18)."
> - Greg Laurie

Stories of Real People and a Real Savior

With a Gun to My Head, My Life Was Forever Changed

Loren, Pastor's Wife in Uganda

I was the youngest of three children, and I had two very loving and honest parents who were always doing something wonderful for our neighbors or community. My dad was a college professor and politician, named Teacher of the Year and Man of the Year. My mom was always even-keeled, never complaining about anything. People truly found strength in my parents, and although they weren't walking with the Lord, they were extremely Christlike in example and deed. They did, however, instill a concept in me which has taken many years to think about. They told me, "God helps those who help themselves." I was sure it was biblical, so I started being independent and helping God by being as self-sufficient as possible.

My college years came; I went off to Cal Poly, San Luis Obispo, and got involved immediately with Intervarsity. I led Bible studies in the dorms, trained students to lead, went on short-term missions, and tried to prove to everyone that I was a unique Christian who was totally sold out for God. Since I had grown up with such stability, it was easy for me to be a disciplined do-gooder. I had a hard time understanding why all Christians weren't as busy as I was. I was very independent (I never wanted a boyfriend); the one thing I never wanted anyone to think of me as was one of those sweet "only thinks of boyfriends and babies" type of girls. I wanted to be thought of as brilliant, independent, self-sufficient, fun and adventurous. I never wanted to lean too hard on God's grace. There was work to be done, and I certainly wasn't going to sit around and be idle. I was often frustrated and judgmental toward Christians who didn't seem to have it all together.

The Terror in Peru

God had other things to teach me: who He really is and His deep love for me. My junior year, since things seemed to be getting a little too easy at college, I decided to go abroad for a year of interchange. I went to a Catholic university in Peru, I took all my classes in Spanish, and I made sure to have all my credits transferred back so I wouldn't be missing a year. (I had to finish in four years because I was afraid of being looked at as a sloth.) I had really prayed about going, and to this day I know the Lord's hand was in it. Yet for reasons I hadn't planned, God was going to use my time in Peru to break my pride and teach me of His love.

My parents came for Christmas, and I traveled with them through South America. When I came back, there was still a month until school started. My other friends had left for the summer, and my Peruvian friends didn't travel like we did. Here I was, having lots of time to use wisely! I prayed a lot and faithfully read God's Word, but I felt useless just doing this; I wasn't ministering or talking to people about the Lord. So when some friends came back early and asked me to travel with them, of course, I said yes—I could witness to them! The three of us went to a famous city in Peru, where we visited some ruins. But my life was to be changed forever on our return journey. On the way back to school, three men with guns came up behind us and demanded all our money, jewelry, credit cards, etc. Then, with guns to our heads, they proceeded to rape us. It could have been much worse. They could have beaten us, brutally hurt us, or killed us.

When they finished, they told us to lie on our stomachs and not move or they would shoot. I thought about Heaven, and wondered what it was going to feel like to die with a bullet in my back. But then they left, and we made our way back to town where people taunted and made fun of us. They blamed us, and didn't help us, not even to let us use a phone. The police did find the attackers, but let them go for a bribe and told us laughingly that if we wanted them in jail, we'd have to go get them ourselves. Incredible! We were told by the program director not to tell a soul about what happened; he threatened us by saying that they'd take away our credits at school if we went home early or told what had happened. They blamed us, saying we must have been promiscuous. I didn't tell my parents, going instead to a secular counselor who told me to go have sex to get over the whole ordeal. I held it all in because "God helps those who help themselves."

The reason I tell you all this is because that year in Peru was probably the most life-changing incident in my life. When Moses killed the Egyptian, his life was changed forever, just as when Esther conceded to marry a king, or when David killed Goliath. It changed my personality, my career, and who I might have married. I didn't tell my parents because I wanted to get through this myself. I didn't want to be a crybaby about it. Again, "God helps those who help themselves."

I Was a Mess

When I came home, I became very withdrawn, depressed and introspective. I tried to tell friends about my experience in Peru, but people are busy, and no one had time to really listen. I became cynical, noticing that I didn't feel so independent anymore. So I desperately cried out to God. I needed someone to be there for me, and you know what? God heard me. Through the whole ordeal, I had an awesome sense that God cried with me. I was His child, and He was hurting with me. When we cry out to Him, He heals us. As Christians, we have that hope. God was with me the entire way. The experience was so incredibly humbling, I realized that I couldn't do it on MY OWN. I began to see why some people are the way they are regarding their weaknesses. I grew more compassionate as Christ had compassion on me. I saw that Christ came for the sick, not those who are well. Even though this was a rough time in my life, it was a sweet time in the Lord. I started to see God as my Father, not a partner in my Christian work.

My Wounds Were Healed

As my wounds were healed, I began plunging into ministry again. I met a wonderful Christian guy whom I married and had three kids with. When I had my first son, I was amazed at how dependent he was on me. It took me by surprise. Since then, I understand my relationship with God. It's been very humbling, setting aside my own desires for His glory, to do the mundane service of raising a family. Pain is relative; my experiences in Peru were no more difficult than the frustrations of everyday living. I'd have to say that serving my husband and my children has been difficult at times, but it has helped me understand my relationship with my Creator. He is our heavenly Father, and we are His children. I've learned what a joy it is to share my hard times with other believers and have them pray with me. I need others and God each and every second of my life. I don't have it all together, but praise God! He is able, more than able, to accomplish what concerns me today.

Week 4: Day 4

Prayer: Bow your heart before the Lord prior to completing the following study. Ask God to help you SEE what is keeping you from forgiving others.

Tammy's Reflections

Right Thinking Leads to Joyful Living

The crime of molestation sent my uncle to prison for fifteen years, but he wasn't the only one trapped in prison. Being molested put me in the bonds of bitterness and despair for twenty years. My uncle showed no remorse for his actions, and to this day he's a prisoner to his sin. But praise Jesus! He has shown me a better way. I am remorseful for my sins of hatred and unforgiveness. He has freed me from my bondage.

Forgiveness is a decision I made. Who made that decision? I did. Even God Himself couldn't make that decision for me. Only WE can decide to forgive. If we don't forgive, we have to live with the crippling consequences of our unforgiveness, stealing our joy and health, and weakening our relationship with Jesus.

Jesus Christ healed my bitterness toward my uncle, turning the unacceptable into compassion. He removed my hatred for my uncle, turning the unforgiveable into forgiveness. Jesus changed my desire for my uncle to burn in Hell forever into a prayer that he would inherit everlasting life. I still pray that one day my uncle will surrender his life to Christ.

Now, would I ever trust my uncle to be alone with a child? Never! It would be irresponsible. God tells us to use wisdom concerning those whose weaknesses can be harmful to others. But exercising discernment doesn't, and shouldn't, prevent us from forgiving. Although the memories will always be there, the emotional grief can be healed. I have been healed and set free by Jesus Christ. I am not to meditate on those memories anymore. I am to meditate on the purity of God's Word and to fill my heart and mind with His truth.

This Week's Tool and Memory Verse

Tool #3 - FORGIVE: I must FORGIVE, as I am forgiven by Christ. Forgiving those who hurt, bruised, wronged, rejected, betrayed or harmed me, whether unintentionally or deliberately. I must ask God to forgive me for holding on to unforgiveness and know that He will.

"Bearing with one another, and forgiving one another, if anyone has a complaint against another; even as Christ forgave you, so you also must do" (Colossians 3:13).

A Forgiving God

1. Read Psalm 103:3 and Micah 7:18-19:

   - "Who forgives all your iniquities, who heals all your diseases?" (Psalm 103:3).

   - "Who is a God like You, pardoning iniquity and passing over the transgression of the remnant of His heritage? He does not retain His anger forever, because He delights in mercy. He will again have compassion on us, and will subdue our iniquities. You will cast all our sins into the depths of the sea" (Micah 7:18-19).

   What do the verses above reveal about God and the forgiveness He extends to us?

   _____
   _____
   _____

2. Read Psalm 32:5, Psalm 65:3 and Psalm 86:5:

   - "I acknowledged my sin to You, and my iniquity I have not hidden. I said, 'I will confess my transgressions to the Lord,' and You forgave the iniquity of my sin" (Psalm 32:5).

   - "Iniquities prevail against me; as for our transgressions, You will provide atonement for them" (Psalm 65:3).

   - "For You, Lord, are good, and ready to forgive, and abundant in mercy to all those who call upon You" (Psalm 86:5).

   What does God do when we confess our sins?

   _____
   _____

3. Read 1 John 1:9, Acts 3:19 and Acts 10:43:

   - "If we confess our sins, He is faithful and just to forgive us our sins and to cleanse us from all unrighteousness" (1 John 1:9).

   - "Repent therefore and be converted, that your sins may be blotted out, so that times of refreshing may come from the presence of the Lord" (Acts 3:19).

   - "To Him all the prophets witness that, through His name, whoever believes in Him will receive remission of sins" (Acts 10:43).

   Who can receive God's forgiveness?

   _____
   _____
   _____
   _____

Forgive and Be Forgiven

Apply the following parable to your own experience by putting yourself in the place of the unforgiving servant. Your master is God. Your fellow servant is someone you have been unable to forgive.

4. Read Matthew 18:21-35 on page 302. From what debt has your Master released you? From what sin has He forgiven you?

5. Who is the person you can't forgive and why?

Continue to reflect on Matthew 18:21-35 as you answer the following questions:

6. In the parable, how did the servant treat his fellow servant?

7. What happened to the servant who did not forgive?

8. What happens when we are unwilling to forgive from our hearts?

Forgiving Others Even If They Aren't Sorry

It's difficult to forgive others when they aren't sorry for what they have done. You may want to set up conditions before you forgive someone for hurting you. You may want that person to show remorse or to confess guilt before you are willing to forgive. Examine your heart for a moment and ask yourself: Who am I really seeking to please? Am I seeking to please God, or am I more concerned with justifying my own negative thoughts and others' negative thoughts?

9. Complete the following statements:

- I will forgive the person who hurt me if… _____

- I will forgive my mother or stepmother if… _____

- I will forgive my father or stepfather if… _____

- I will forgive my sibling if… _____

- I will forgive my boyfriend or ex-boyfriend if… _____

- I will forgive my husband or ex-husband if… _____

- I will forgive my friend or ex-friend if… _____

- I will forgive the person involved in the abortion if… _____

- I will forgive my boss or co-worker if… _____

- I will forgive myself if… _____

10. How will Jesus treat you if you don't forgive your fellow servant?

11. Read Colossians 3:13: "Bearing with one another, and forgiving one another, if anyone has a complaint against another; even as Christ forgave you, so you also must do."

    What is the condition for forgiveness? How must we forgive?

> "For you were once darkness,
> but now you are light in the Lord.
> Walk as children of the light"
> (Ephesians 5:8).

12. Read Mark 11:25-26: "And whenever you stand praying, if you have anything against anyone, forgive him, that your Father in heaven may also forgive you your trespasses. But if you do not forgive, neither will your Father in heaven forgive your trespasses."

    Are you required to forgive others even if they aren't sorry for hurting you?

13. Read Matthew 5:23-24: "Therefore, if you bring your gift to the altar, and there remember that your brother has something against you, leave your gift there before the altar, and go your way. First be reconciled to your brother, and then come and offer your gift."

    If you know that someone has something against you, are you to wait for that person to come to you before asking for forgiveness?

14. Read Matthew 5:43-44: "You have heard that it was said, 'You shall love your neighbor and hate your enemy.' But I say to you, love your enemies, bless those who curse you, do good to those who hate you, and pray for those who spitefully use you and persecute you."

    If someone wants to burn the bridge and not reconcile, how can you apply Matthew 5:43-44 to your life?

15. Read Acts 7:59-60: "And they stoned Stephen as he was calling on God and saying, 'Lord Jesus, receive my spirit.' Then he knelt down and cried out with a loud voice, 'Lord, do not charge them with this sin.' And when he had said this, he fell asleep."

    Who was able to forgive others before he saw signs of repentance? What can we take away from this example?

16. Have those who brought heartache and pain in your life asked for forgiveness? Are you willing to forgive them even if they aren't sorry? Why or why not?

Stories of Real People and a Real Savior

Forgiveness

Norm, Idaho

My name is Norm and I am 45 years old. I accepted the Lord in July 1989. Since then, God has helped me to make many changes in my life; though it was a struggle, I have been set free from alcohol and smoking. James 4:8 says, "Draw near to God and He will draw near to you. Cleanse your hands, you sinners; and purify your hearts, you double-minded." I didn't want to be double-minded; I wanted light in every area of my life, so it was a blessing to be rid of these addictions that people could see on the outside.

But I still felt like something was missing, because there was more than just the things on the outside. On the inside, I was an angry man, frustrated with my wife and kids, and very unforgiving. I didn't think I had any problems with God, but in reality, I hadn't given Him everything. I had trust issues, which kept me from getting close to anyone; I held on to them so that if something happened, I would be prepared for it. The problem was that these issues were controlling my life.

At this point, I encouraged a friend of mine to spend time with my wife. That way I didn't have to worry about her being alone. I later found out that my wife was giving her emotions to him because I wasn't listening to her or trusting her. Unfortunately, I didn't understand what she was trying to tell me, and my marriage was about to end.

Then my wife heard about the *Healed and Set Free Bible Study*. We both decided to go through the study and try to save our marriage. During the study, I dug up many of my past hurts, mistrust and hurt feelings from my youth and a previous marriage. I also learned to forgive those who hurt me, and to forget the hurt done to me. I learned that I had to let God take control of my life, instead of trying to be in control.

Now that I am free from mistrust and anger, I can trust my wife. I don't sit and dwell on what she is doing or not doing. I feel peace where mistrust and anger lived before. Now my marriage is getting on the right track. My wife and I are talking and sharing our joys, hurts, disappointments and dreams with each other. We talk more now than we ever did in our previous 18 years of marriage: We can talk about our present and past hurts without becoming angry. We are now free in Christ!

"Is prayer your steering wheel or your spare tire?"
- Corrie Ten Boom

Week 4: Day 5

Prayer: Bow your heart before the Lord in prayer prior to completing today's Bible study. Thank the Lord that He is the Light in this dark and dying world, and for choosing to become light and truth to us personally.

Father, Forgive Them

God wants us to forgive, because He has forgiven us. He wants us to show mercy to others, because He has shown us His mercy. You may be suffering with the injuries of a broken heart or bruised feelings, but it's never too late to forgive.

Let's take a look at one of the most powerful yet heartbreaking moments surrounding the cross. Max Lucado asks, "What kind of people would mock a dying man?" Yet the criminal on the cross mocked Christ. "If You are the Christ, save Yourself and us!" (Luke 23:39). The passersby mocked the crucified Christ with insults that were meant to bruise and hurt. "We've broken the body, now let's break the spirit!"[6]

But Jesus does something extraordinary in this moment: He doesn't fight back. Despite the fact that He is all-powerful God, He didn't even threaten. He wouldn't let any guile be found in His mouth to say, "I'll get you." No such words were to be found on the lips of the Christ. Indeed, Christ, whose body was consumed with pain, lungs begging for air, could only speak with unconditional love, "Father, forgive them" (Luke 23:34).

Did you hear what Jesus said? He left us with His example. He "committed Himself to Him who judges righteously" (1 Peter 2:23). He didn't ask for an apology or seek revenge. He humbly begged for grace, "Father, forgive them, for they do not know what they do" (Luke 23:34).

The second part of Jesus' statement, "for they do not know what they do," allows us to see the heart of Christ, and look through His eyes. Our beaten Savior considered this crowd, insane with blood lust, not as murderers, but as confused and lost sheep, in need of a Shepherd. He didn't get angry, but saw that in their hearts, they didn't know what they were doing. Anger never does anyone any good. When we get angry at others or at God, it just causes us to become defiled. Look to Christ's example on the cross. If the Son sets you free, you are free indeed!

> "And we know that all things work together for good to those who love God, to those who are the called according to His purpose"
> (Romans 8:28).

1. Read Luke 6:35-36: "But love your enemies, do good, and lend, hoping for nothing in return; and your reward will be great, and you will be sons of the Most High. For He is kind to the unthankful and evil. Therefore be merciful, just as your Father also is merciful."

   What are the results of showing mercy to others?

   _____
   _____

2. Read James 2:13: "For judgment is without mercy to the one who has shown no mercy. Mercy triumphs over judgment."

   What are the consequences of not showing mercy to others?

   _____
   _____

3. Write down the definition of "judging" from page 301.

   _____
   _____

4. Read Romans 14:10 and 2 Corinthians 5:10:
   - "...Why do you judge your brother? Or why do you show contempt for your brother? For we shall all stand before the judgment seat of Christ" (Romans 14:10).
   - "For we must all appear before the judgment seat of Christ, that each one may receive the things done in the body, according to what he has done, whether good or bad" (2 Corinthians 5:10).

   Why are we not to judge our brother?

   _____
   _____

5. Read Matthew 7:1-2: "Judge not, that you be not judged. For with what judgment you judge, you will be judged; and with the measure you use, it will be measured back to you."

   How will we be judged if we judge others?

   _____
   _____
   _____

6. Read Matthew 7:3-5: "And why do you look at the speck in your brother's eye, but do not consider the plank in your own eye? Or how can you say to your brother, 'Let me remove the speck from your eye'; and 'look, a plank is in your own eye?' Hypocrite! First remove the plank from your own eye, and then you will see clearly to remove the speck from your brother's eye."

Taking the plank from our own eye includes looking at the ways we have hurt others. Ask God to show you the ways you have hurt others, and record what comes to mind. Ask Christ to forgive you and know that He will.

Our failures might include: gossiping, judging, verbal, physical or sexual abuse, outbursts of anger, unforgiveness, lying or stealing. Please circle those whom you have hurt:

- A brother or sister in Christ
- A family member
- A co-worker
- A friend
- An old classmate
- A neighbor

7. Read Hebrews 12:13-15: "...Make straight paths for your feet, so that what is lame may not be dislocated, but rather be healed. Pursue peace with all people, and holiness, without which no one will see the Lord: looking carefully lest anyone fall short of the grace of God; lest any root of bitterness springing up cause trouble, and by this many become defiled."

    You don't have to live your life damaged or destroyed because of your past failures or experiences. Do you desire to see the truth about what God says about forgiveness concerning your hurts and sins?

    _____
    _____

8. You can be freed from bondage by God's love, truth and forgiveness. You can grow into a deeper and sweeter relationship with Jesus Christ during this time. It's time for you to forgive and let go of the unacceptable sins from others and yourself. This is necessary for your healing.

    First: **SEE** what is in your heart.

    Second: **GIVE** the sin in repentance to the Lord.

    Third: **FORGIVE** those you're angry with.

    Fourth: **FORGET** by no longer dwelling on the past.

    You will **BE SET FREE** to enjoy a fresh, new beginning. You must now press on to a higher calling in Jesus Christ.

    Bow your heart before the Lord in brokenness, asking Him to reveal any sins in your heart that might be defiling you. Then ask Him to forgive you and know that He will. Write down your thoughts:

    _____
    _____
    _____
    _____

Forgiven Much, Love Much

Peace floods our hearts when we are forgiven. And when we forgive others, we replace anger and hatred with love and peace toward those who hurt us. The memories won't go away, but the feelings will. This is when we enjoy true freedom.

9. Read Luke 6:27-28 and 1 Peter 3:9:

    - "But I say to you who hear: Love your enemies, do good to those who hate you, bless those who curse you, and pray for those who spitefully use you" (Luke 6:27-28).

    - "Not returning evil for evil or reviling for reviling, but on the contrary blessing, knowing that you were called to this, that you may inherit a blessing" (1 Peter 3:9).

    How should we treat those who hurt us? How do you apply these verses to your life?

    _____

    _____

10. Read 1 Peter 3:10-12: "He who would love life and see good days, let him refrain his tongue from evil, and his lips from speaking deceit. Let him turn away from evil and do good; let him seek peace and pursue it. For the eyes of the Lord are on the righteous, and His ears are open to their prayers, but the face of the Lord is against those who do evil."

    Will God hear your prayers if you have unforgiveness in your heart?

    _____

    _____

11. Read 1 John 4:12: "No one has seen God at any time. If we love one another, God abides in us, and His love has been perfected in us."

    If we choose to love each other, what happens in our relationship with God?

    _____

    _____

12. Read Luke 23:34: "Father, forgive them, for they do not know what they do."

    Can you now forgive as Christ has forgiven you? Are you ready to forgive those who have hurt you? Why or why not?

    _____

    _____

Forgiving Others Without a Confrontation

I was convinced: If I could meet with the people who hurt me and tell them how much they had hurt me, then I could forgive. But it was a lie to think that I needed to have a meeting in order to forgive or heal. I never met face to face with my uncle or the guy who raped me. Instead, I met with God and took care of my unforgiveness and bitterness with Him. It is a matter of keeping my relationship right with God, regardless of the heart condition of those who hurt me.

13. When you forgive others, you are a witness to them of Christ's forgiveness. He died for all those who hurt you in the past, those who are hurting you now, and those who will hurt you in the future. Are you willing to say, "I am in Him, so I must forgive"? He suffered and died for you, so don't forget the price of your forgiveness. Release those who hurt you from judgment. Release yourself from the anger and bitterness. Come before God in broken sincerity. Write down your prayer:

Stories of Real People and a Real Savior

A Lesson in Forgiveness

A Letter from Cheryl

The chapter on forgiveness was a struggle for me. How could I forgive everyone who hurt me, especially my relatives? My husband and I were deeply hurt by his brother and sister-in-law. We were told we weren't welcome to live in their neighborhood when we were looking for a home. Their children were discouraged from playing with ours. It went on and on! We couldn't understand, and it hurt. Finally, we were so fed up we didn't speak to them for a year, moving across town to get away from them. We avoided family functions so we wouldn't run into them.

While in the forgiveness chapter, I prayed for the Lord to help me see all the people I was harboring anger against. I didn't want to include my in-laws, because I felt this anger was truly justified! I prayed and forgave everyone, except them. I couldn't move on to the next chapter; the Lord was ministering to my heart to repent and forgive my in-laws. His presence was so strong! I was broken by the weight of my guilt. So I obeyed the Lord: I wrote a letter of apology to my in-laws for not forgiving them. I couldn't take the silence or anger any longer. I gave the letter to my husband and asked him to read it. I told him this would mean no more resentment, anger or bickering with his brother; it would all come to a halt.

He didn't talk to me for an hour; it was the longest hour of my life! I prayed the Lord would open his heart so he could forgive too. He came upstairs and got on his coat, saying he was going to deliver the letter to his brother in person. I cried! I had obeyed the Lord and He opened the door! In the letter, I wrote that we needed a family hug. A few hours after my husband delivered the letter, his brother called and said they'd like to cash in on that hug. They came over, and through God's love another family was healed. Thank you, Lord, for ministering to my heart and teaching me how to truly forgive.

Prayer: Bow your heart before the Lord in prayer, asking Him to help you let go of the past and to examine your heart daily as you embrace His Word.

1. Look up Philippians 4:8 on page 303 and write it out here:

2. Write out two scriptures that particularly ministered to you from this chapter and use them to help you forgive the unacceptable things others have committed against you or unacceptable acts you have done.

    A.

    B.

3. Write a short paragraph summarizing what you have learned on the subject of forgiveness.

Stories of Real People and a Real Savior

Healing From Years of Fear and Trauma
By Cheryl, Minnesota

Proverbs 3:5-8 "Trust in the LORD with all your heart, and do not lean on your own understanding. In all your ways acknowledge him, and he will make straight your paths. Be not wise in your own eyes; fear the LORD, and turn away from evil. It will be healing to your flesh and refreshment to your bones."

I had been through a traumatic divorce and been deeply wounded from years of fear and abuse. I felt in my heart I had failed God and was left with a deep sense of shame and guilt that I could not admit to anyone. My learned response was to turn inward. Even though I pretended everything was fine on the outside my unspoken thoughts reflected a very troubled heart. I always seemed to be on the verge of panic and depression. I was not experiencing the abundant life that God tells me is available in John 10:10 (I came that they may have life, and may have it abundantly.) The life God had desired for me was being choked out by fear and unforgiveness.

I am so thankful that the Lord brought this beautiful Bible study into my life. When I went through "Healed and Set Free" for the first time, the scriptures I had read many times before suddenly came to life. I was able to forgive those that abused, rejected and hurt me. God redeemed the ashes of my life for beauty! I did not know at the time that I would face more heartbreaking losses in the future, but I was prepared because of the work God had done in my life. I am so thankful that God's healing touch is for the past, present and future.

No one can fully realize that it's possible to rise above the trials of life, until we feel God's supporting power beneath us. "I can do all things through Christ who strengthens me" (Philippians 4:13). It has been some 14 years since the Lord opened the door for me to lead the first "Healed and Set Free" Bible study in our community. Even today there are women desiring to attend the study because of the testimonies of those that have found freedom in Christ.

We can be free from the pains and shackles of the past! There is no greater gift than forgiveness of our sins through Jesus Christ. How beautiful it is when our Savior teaches us to forgive others as we have been forgiven. Praise the Lord for freedom!

Calvary Magazine reprint from interview with Cheryl:

> Cheryl had experienced serious trials in her 20s and 30s that had left her searching for more. A friend invited her to an evangelical church's women's tea. At the time, "I had nowhere to go, nowhere to turn," Cheryl noted. "So I went. I was saved there." Cheryl soon began attending Calvary Chapel Idaho Falls, where she was discipled for five years by the pastor's wife, Tammy Brown. Today Cheryl disciples ladies one-on-one.
>
> In 2009, Cheryl was invited to speak at a local Mothers of Preschoolers (MOPS) meeting. She shared how her life had been impacted by a Bible study called Healed and Set Free, by Tammy Brown and afterward a woman named Melissa Heglund indicated her desire to attend. Through Melissa's participation over the next few months, she came to Christ. *
>
> "In the Healed and Set Free course," Cheryl explained, "women hear the riches of the Gospel week after week. The theme is Christ and His forgiveness. So it teaches believers to forgive just as God has forgiven us through Christ, and it leads unbelievers to the cross."

*Melissa's story is located on page 72.

Tools to Become Healed and Set Free

To equip yourself in God's truth, look over the tools and verses that will be introduced in the coming weeks. Thinking about the past won't change it, but you can change your future by being set free from your past.

TOOL #1 - SEE: I must SEE the truth about what is in my heart so I am not defiled.

> **Definition**: To defile means to make filthy or dirty; to pollute.

> **Bible Verse**: "Looking carefully lest anyone fall short of the grace of God; lest any root of bitterness springing up cause trouble, and by this many become defiled" (Hebrews 12:15).

TOOL #2 - GIVE: I must GIVE my sin to God through repentance, knowing that Christ is waiting to take it. I must be sorry enough to change, and choose to go God's way over my own.

> **Definition**: To repent means to feel such sorrow for sin or fault as to be disposed to change one's life for the better; be penitent.

> **Bible Verse**: "For godly sorrow produces repentance leading to salvation, not to be regretted; but the sorrow of the world produces death" (2 Corinthians 7:10).

TOOL #3 - FORGIVE: I must FORGIVE as I am forgiven by Christ: Forgiving those who hurt, bruised, wronged, rejected, betrayed or harmed me, whether unintentionally or deliberately. I must ask God to forgive me for holding on to unforgiveness and know that He will.

> **Definition**: To forgive means to stop feeling angry or resentful toward someone for an offense, flaw or mistake.

> **Bible Verse**: "...Bearing with one another, and forgiving one another, if anyone has a complaint against another; even as Christ forgave you, so you also must do" (Colossians 3:13).

TOOL #4 - FORGET: I must FORGET by no longer dwelling on the hurt or the painful reminders, such as: phrases, smells, places, songs and comments. Instead, I am putting my mind on the higher calling that Christ has for me.

> **Definition**: To forget means to choose not to remember or notice, "forgive and forget".

> **Bible Verse**: "Brethren, I do not count myself to have apprehended; but one thing I do, forgetting those things which are behind and reaching forward to those things which are ahead" (Philippians 3:13).

Be Healed and Set Free: Christ will heal me from my past, showing me the truth, so I can become a cleansed vessel, healed and set free.

> **Definition**: To set free means to make free; set at liberty; release from bondage, imprisonment, or restraint.

> **Definition**: To heal means to make whole and healthy; to cure; to remedy or repair.

> **Bible Verse**: "And you shall know the truth, and the truth shall make you free" (John 8:32).

Conquering Depression

This Week's Focus

This week we sill be growing deeper in our understanding of the three tools we've learned so far: **Tool #1 - SEE**, **Tool #2 - GIVE**, and **Tool #3 - FORGIVE**. We will experience practical application of these tools to help on the journey to become healed and set free.

Tool #1 - SEE: I must SEE the truth about what is in my heart so I am not defiled (see Hebrews 12:15).

Tool #2 - GIVE: I must GIVE my sin to God through repentance, knowing that Christ is waiting to take it. I must be sorry enough to change, and choose to go God's way over my own (see 2 Corinthians 7:10).

Tool #3 - FORGIVE: I must forgive as I am forgiven by Christ. Forgiving those who hurt, bruised, wronged, rejected, betrayed or harmed me, whether unintentionally or deliberately. I must ask God to forgive me for holding on to unforgiveness and know that He will (see Colossians 3:13).

Prayer: Pray that the eyes of your heart may be enlightened so you may know the hope to which he has called you.

Week 5: Day 1

Prayer: Bow your heart before the Lord in prayer prior to completing today's study. Ask Him to help you focus your heart and mind on Him today.

What does the Bible say about depression? As Archibald Hart points out in his book *Dark Clouds, Silver Lining*, "Depression is the common lot of humanity, a normal reaction to life. Saints in both the Old and New Testaments experienced it."[1] Indeed, the Bible is scattered with references to saints who suffered from and conquered depression, and biblical "prescriptions" to alleviate its grip on our lives.

It's nice to know that we aren't alone, but we must also acknowledge that we don't always have to be depressed. We must focus our minds on God, maintaining our faith and trust in Him. Putting things in perspective is a necessary step toward resolving or avoiding depression. But how can we keep our spiritual life alive when we feel so low? Should we just abandon God to solve our problems alone? No! We should never abandon our spiritual life! In fact, just the opposite is true.

Satan would like us to believe that it is sinful and shameful to be depressed. He wants us to believe we can solve our problems in our own strength. He wants to prevent us from seeking God. He wants to isolate us by keeping us from fellowshipping with other Christians. He wants to prevent the spiritual growth and maturity that comes from pressing into the Lord in our time of need.

Don't allow the feelings of depression to keep you from dealing with its cause. You must recognize and fight the depression, seeing it as a symptom of something that's wrong and needs attention. Use the resources of Christ to SEE the problem and GIVE it to Him, asking for His help and healing. "The Lord is near to those who have a broken heart, and saves such as have a contrite spirit" (Psalm 34:18).

Stories of Real People and a Real Savior

Once I Forgave I Could Forget

Jonnie, Idaho

There was only one step before I would feel the rocks at the bottom of the cliff. Satan said, "DIE!" But Jesus said, "LIVE!" "Why are you cast down, oh my soul? And why are you disquieted within me? Hope in God; For I shall yet praise Him, the help of my countenance and my God" (Psalm 43:5). This scripture was the first seed planted in my heart. Having been raised in an alcoholic home, I had insecurities, self-pity and great fears. Only after I thought about taking my own life did I realize that the Lord was the only way to true healing. The first thing I had to do was give my pain to Jesus. The hardest part was surrendering my bitterness, the crusted protective coating I had put around my heart. But as I began to let go of the anger and hatred, I was able to forgive those who had harmed me. When I forgave I could forget, and God could bring true healing into my life.

Tools to Become Set Free

In this chapter, we will practice using the three tools we've learned so far: **Tool #1 - SEE, Tool #2 - GIVE** and **Tool #3 - FORGIVE**.

These tools will help you to become set free. Each tool is defined as the time comes. It is crucial to memorize these powerful tools and review them regularly in order to apply them to your daily life.

#1 - SEE: I must SEE the truth about what is in my heart so I am not defiled.

#2 - GIVE: I must GIVE my sin to God through repentance, knowing that Christ is waiting to take it. I must be sorry enough to change, and choose to go God's way over my own.

#3 - FORGIVE: I must FORGIVE as I am forgiven by Christ: Forgiving those who hurt, bruised, wronged, rejected, betrayed or harmed me, whether unintentionally or deliberately. I must ask God to forgive me for holding on to unforgiveness and know that He will.

#4 - FORGET: I must FORGET by no longer dwelling on the hurt or the painful reminders such as: phrases, smells, places, songs and comments. Instead, I am putting my mind on the higher calling that Christ has for me.

Be Healed and Set Free: Christ will heal me from my past, showing me the truth, so I can become a cleansed vessel, healed and set free.

This Week's Focus

Prayer: Pray that the eyes of your heart may be enlightened so you may know the hope to which he has called you.

By Memory: My challenge to you is to be able to recite the Bible verse from this chapter without looking. I know that by hiding these words of wisdom in your heart you are providing yourself with tools to truly be healed and set free. May we rise up to be women of the Word.

Tool #1 - SEE: I must SEE the truth about what is in my heart so I am not defiled (see Hebrews 12:15).

Tool #2 - GIVE: I must GIVE my sin to God through repentance, knowing that Christ is waiting to take it. I must be sorry enough to change, and choose to go God's way over my own (see 2 Corinthians 7:10).

Tool #3 - FORGIVE: I must forgive as I am forgiven by Christ. Forgiving those who hurt, bruised, wronged, rejected, betrayed or harmed me, whether unintentionally or deliberately. I must ask God to forgive me for holding on to unforgiveness and know that He will (see Colossians 3:13).

"And you shall know the truth, and the truth shall make you free" (John 8:32).

God's Love for You

You need to know without a doubt that the Father loves you. He gave you His love through Jesus Christ, and He has called you to be His workmanship, created in Christ Jesus as a vessel of His love. God wants to use your life in a special way, to comfort others as you have been comforted.

1. Read 2 Corinthians 5:17, Proverbs 17:22 and Jeremiah 29:11:

    - "Therefore, if anyone is in Christ, he is a new creation; old things have passed away; behold, all things have become new" (2 Corinthians 5:17).
    - "A merry heart does good, like medicine, but a broken spirit dries the bones" (Proverbs 17:22).
    - "For I know the thoughts that I think toward you, says the Lord, thoughts of peace and not of evil, to give you a future and a hope" (Jeremiah 29:11).

    What are Jesus' thoughts toward you?

    _____

    _____

2. Read Matthew 10:29-31: "Are not two sparrows sold for a copper coin? And not one of them falls to the ground apart from your Father's will. But the very hairs of your head are all numbered. Do not fear therefore; you are of more value than many sparrows."

    Do you know the number of hairs on your head? Who does? Do you believe there is anything too small or trivial to bring before God in prayer?

    _____

    _____

Understanding the Broken Spirit

The Bible is full of stories of people with broken hearts and broken spirits. Like them, depression, grief and sorrow can grip our hearts when things don't work out as we planned. A friend may talk behind our back, we may lose someone to death, or someone we love may walk away from Christ.

"Suffering comes to all of us, and no one can suffer for us," writes Dennis DeHaan. "However, we can be supported in those difficult times by the prayers and understanding of loved ones and friends."[2]

God created us and gave us our emotions. The Bible tells us we are to "rejoice with those who rejoice, and weep with those who weep" (Romans 12:15). It is when we are too proud to admit our needs to others that we are in the greatest danger.

3. Read Matthew 26:36-39: "Then Jesus came with them to a place called Gethsemane, and said to the disciples, 'Sit here while I go and pray over there.' And He took with Him Peter and the two sons of Zebedee, and He began to be sorrowful and deeply distressed. Then He said to them, 'My soul is exceedingly sorrowful, even to death. Stay here and watch with Me.' He went a little farther and fell on His face, and prayed, saying, 'O My Father, if it is possible, let this cup pass from Me; nevertheless, not as I will, but as You will.'"

   What two emotions flooded Jesus' heart and mind from Matthew 26 above?

   _____

   _____

4. Does it comfort you to know that even Jesus had times of sorrow and could be deeply distressed? If so, how?

   _____

   _____

   _____

5. Read Hebrews 4:15-16: "For we do not have a High Priest who cannot sympathize with our weakness, but was in all points tempted as we are, yet without sin. Let us therefore come boldly to the throne of grace, that we may obtain mercy and find grace to help in time of need."

   Does it comfort you to know that Christ understands your weaknesses and struggles and wants to help you in times of need? Why does Jesus understand?

   _____

   _____

   _____

6. How do we come boldly before His throne of grace?

   _____

   _____

7. Read Matthew 27:46 and Luke 22:41-45:
   - "My God, My God, why have You forsaken Me?" (Matthew 27:46).
   - "He knelt down and prayed, saying, 'Father, if it is Your will, take this cup away from Me; nevertheless not My will, but Yours, be done.' Then an angel appeared to Him from heaven, strengthening Him. And being in agony, He prayed more earnestly. Then His sweat became like great drops of blood falling down to the ground. When He rose up from prayer, and had come to His disciples, He found them sleeping from sorrow" (Luke 22:42-45).

   Jesus knew He was going to face the cross, where He would bear the sins of the world. This was the first and only time that Jesus would experience separation from His Father. Dying on the cross was the cup that He prayed to have taken from Him. In His darkest hour, Jesus, not wanting to be alone, asked for the presence and prayers of Peter, James and John. Although Jesus sought God in prayer, He also desired the prayers and support of His closest friends in His hour of crisis. Likewise, you are to seek God in prayer during your time of need, as well as seek out those who can pray with you and for you. Just as you need a friend, be willing to be a friend and look for opportunities to comfort and pray for others who are suffering.

What difficult circumstances have you asked God to remove from your life?

8. What do Christ Jesus' words, "Not My will, but Yours be done," mean to you in your difficult circumstances?

9. Was the cup removed from Jesus? What did Jesus do more earnestly?

10. Has God's answer in your circumstances been "yes," "no" or "wait"? Explain.

11. Do you believe that God's plans for you are good, even if you don't understand them at this moment?

12. What if Jesus had walked away from His cup and not submitted to God's will? What hope would we have for eternal life?

13. According to Luke 22, which friends did Jesus choose to have with Him during His greatest time of agony, and what did He ask of them?

14. Do you follow Jesus' example and call upon friends to pray with and for you, or do you isolate yourself from your friends? Explain.

15. Lamentations 3:49-54: "My eyes flow and do not cease, without interruption, till the Lord from heaven looks down and sees. My eyes bring suffering to my soul because of all the daughters of my city. My enemies without cause hunted me down like a bird. They silenced my life in the pit and threw stones at me. The waters flowed over my head; I said, 'I am cut off!'"

    Depression can come when we feel we have been cut off in some way. Have you ever been cut off in a relationship? Explain.

16. Read Job 16:16-22: "My face is flushed from weeping, and on my eyelids is the shadow of death; although no violence is in my hands, and my prayer is pure. O earth, do not cover my blood, and let my cry have no resting place! Surely even now my witness is in heaven, and my evidence is on high. My friends scorn me; My eyes pour out tears to God. Oh, that one might plead for a man with God, as a man pleads for his neighbor! For when a few years are finished, I shall go the way of no return."

    Have you ever had a friend criticize you? Explain how you can relate to what Job went through with his friends.

Week 5: Day 2

Prayer: Bow your heart before the Lord in prayer prior to completing today's study. Ask Him to help you focus your heart and mind on Him today.

Stories of Real People and a Real Savior

AIDS Rocked My World

A Changed Woman, Idaho

I had been physically and sexually abused for ten years before I met my husband. So from day one, I brought a lot of bitterness and unforgiveness into my marriage. I was very closed off because I didn't want to be vulnerable.

Not knowing where to turn for help, my husband eventually became fed up with me. One night while working out of town, he committed adultery. That night changed our lives forever: He contracted AIDS. Fear gripped my heart: fear of losing my husband, fear of being alone, fear of raising my children alone, fear of contracting AIDS myself.

At that point in our lives we realized something had to change. We both repented and gave our lives to Christ Jesus as our personal Savior. However, there were still a lot of burdens weighing down my heart. "Anxiety in the heart of man causes depression" (Proverbs 12:25).

I decided to take the *Healed and Set Free Bible Study*. Within the very first few weeks, I could feel the Lord lifting the burden from my heart as He began to show me my sin of unforgiveness.

"Bearing with one another, and forgiving one another, if anyone has a complaint against another; even as Christ forgave you, so you also must do. But above all these things put on love, which is the bond of perfection. And let the peace of God rule in your hearts, to which also you were called in one body; and be thankful" (Colossians 3:13-15).

When I read this verse, I understood. I was sinning by holding on to the hurts in my heart. God's truth was the only thing that was going to set me free from my past sin and hurt. I wanted to get real with Him. I could finally SEE that I was just as guilty as those who had hurt me, but now I could GIVE these sins to God. I allowed myself to FORGET the past and BE SET FREE by Jesus from the chains of fear, bitterness and unforgiveness.

This Bible study taught me to claim God's promises and hide them in my heart. Praise God! I have been healed and set free. God's mercy and love touched our marriage and our lives in a very real way. Now we are living each day for Jesus.

Warnings of a Heart Weighed Down

1. Read Luke 21:34: "But take heed to yourselves, lest your hearts be weighed down with carousing, drunkenness, and cares of this life, and that Day come on you unexpectedly."

    Are there any particular thoughts or questions concerning your experience that repeatedly plague your mind or cause your heart to be weighed down?

2. What will happen if you let these anxieties continue in your heart?

3. Write down the definition of "carousing" from page 301.

4. Are ungodly relationships in your life causing you to carouse around?

5. Does drunkenness numb or heal the pain? Does drinking solve problems or create more problems?

6. Have you had any cares of this life come upon you? Remembering chapter 4, are you seeking wrong answers to solve the cares of your life?

7. Read 1 Peter 5:7: "Casting all your care upon Him, for He cares for you."

    What does God want you to do with your anxieties?

8. Read Psalm 56:8: "You number my wanderings; put my tears into Your bottle; are they not in Your book?"

    What does God do with your tears? What does it mean to you that He cares this deeply about what's going on in your life, that your tears are precious to Him?

9. Read Psalm 18:6,16: "In my distress I called upon the Lord, and cried out to my God; He heard my voice from His temple, and my cry came before Him, even to His ears. He sent from above, He took me; He drew me out of many waters."

   What prayer of praise would you offer up to God concerning the truths you have learned from this study?

This Week's Memory Verse

"Anxiety in the heart of man causes depression, but a good word makes it glad. The righteous should choose his friends carefully, for the way of the wicked leads them astray" (Proverbs 12:25-26).

Week 5: Day 3

Prayer: Bow your heart before the Lord in prayer prior to completing today's Bible study. Ask Him to free you from the prison of depression.

The Prison of Depression

1. Read Psalm 107:13-14: "Then they cried out to the Lord in their trouble, and He saved them out of their distresses. He brought them out of darkness and the shadow of death, and broke their chains in pieces."

   What helped the prisoners in their deepest gloom? How did God respond to their change of heart?

2. Read Romans 6:17-18: "But God be thanked that though you were slaves of sin, yet you obeyed from the heart that form of doctrine to which you were delivered. And having been set free from sin, you became slaves of righteousness."

   What does it mean to obey God's Word from the heart, in peaceful as well as in struggling times?

3. What does it mean to be a slave to sin?

4. Read Galatians 5:1: "Stand fast therefore in the liberty by which Christ has made us free, and do not be entangled again with a yoke of bondage."

   Are you entangled with a yoke of bondage? Be specific.

Pray For Those Who Are Entangled

Prayer is one of our most powerful weapons as Christians. We never know the profound effect our prayers have in our lives and the lives of others, as God hears our petitions. I found this story about prayer from Elizabeth George's *A Woman After God's Own Heart*[3] truly inspiring:

> Jeanne Hendricks, wife of Dallas Theological Seminary professor Howard Hendricks, spent a season in intense prayer for one of her children. During his late adolescence, her son went through what Jeanne called a "blackout" period. He was unenthusiastic, moody and depressed, communicating only with single-syllable responses. "This was one of the most traumatic times of my life," Jeanne admits. "He was so far from the Lord and from us. I felt like the devil himself was out to get my child. I prayed as I never had before." Mrs. Hendricks shared that during the half-year when this situation continued, she covenanted with God to give up her noon meal. As she fasted each day, she prayed for her son for one hour until God broke through to him.

5. Do you know someone who needs you to pray for them? Pray for them now.

Conquering the Cycle of Depression

When we are depressed, we suffer from "ingrown eyeballs," where our eyes are turned inward, and we focus on our own problems and on ourselves. The more we focus inward, the worse we feel, and the harder it is to take the necessary steps to see the truth and allow the Lord's love and grace to flow into our lives.

6. Read Hebrews 12:1-2: "Therefore, we also, since we are surrounded by so great a cloud of witnesses, let us lay aside every weight, and the sin which so easily ensnares us, and let us run with endurance the race that is set before us, looking unto Jesus, the author and finisher of our faith, who for the joy that was set before Him endured the cross, despising the shame, and has sat down at the right hand of the throne of God."

   What advice does Hebrews 12 give on how to break the cycle of depression? Where should your eyes be focused? Explain.

7. We must remember: Satan has come to "kill, steal and destroy." When he shoots his fiery darts your way, you mustn't look back, but look inside your heart, checking for things that defile. What reminders from your past such as places, songs or smells does Satan throw in your face to catch you off guard, ensnare or weigh you down? What four steps must you take to be set free?

8. Read Ephesians 4:22-24: "That you put off, concerning your former conduct, the old man which grows corrupt according to the deceitful lusts, and be renewed in the spirit of your mind, and that you put on the new man which was created according to God, in true righteousness and holiness."

    What former conduct have you put off by being renewed in your mind?

    _____

    _____

9. Concerning your present conduct, what has the Holy Spirit been showing you that needs to be put off?

    _____

    _____

10. Read Ephesians 5:8: "For you were once darkness, but now you are light in the Lord. Walk as children of light..."

    To "walk as children of light" means God's light is within us. We can't hide from God, and we shouldn't hide God from others. Are you witnessing and sharing Christ with others?

    _____

    _____

11. "All things are naked and open to the eyes of Him to whom we must give account" (Hebrews 4:13).

    Do your acquaintances know you are a Christian?

    _____

    _____

12. How do pride or fear keep you from pleasing God by pleasing others instead?

    _____

    _____

13. Was Jesus concerned about pleasing man or God?

    _____

    _____

14. Read 2 Corinthians 3:18: "But we all, with unveiled face, beholding as in a mirror the glory of the Lord, are being transformed into the same image from glory to glory, just as by the Spirit of the Lord."

    Write down and share ways you could be reflecting God's glory to others.

    _____

    _____

Stories of Real People and a Real Savior

All Mama's Unhappiness Is Because of Daddy

Gina, Idaho

It was Monday, June 13, 1994. It had been a painful couple of months as we sold our new home in Boise, made major job changes, and condensed a large three bedroom home into a small two bedroom apartment in Twin Falls. My husband of six years chose this time to inform me that he thought it would be best if he didn't live with his wife and baby. He suggested that we start dating again, and he didn't mean each other. In a matter of seconds, my life and my son's life changed forever. I could write a book on all the anger, bitterness, fear, hatred, devastation and loneliness I experienced. The reality of divorce is sin. And sin, whether we ourselves transgress or someone else transgresses against us, produces absolutely nothing good, unless we can forgive, forget and be healed and set free.

I came to the first session of a confidential Bible study not knowing exactly what was in store for me. I was nervous and knew nothing about the other women in the study. They were all so put together. They were smiling, they knew each other, and they certainly loved the Lord. Why had I come? Tammy handed out booklets as we introduced ourselves and discussed the importance of confidentiality. She put my mind at ease by making it clear that we didn't have to share anything, read or pray aloud if we didn't want to, or if we felt uncomfortable in any way.

"Well, I don't need healing," I thought, "The divorce was four years ago." I had coped well and did what I had to do. But of course, I blamed my ex-husband for everything. If he hadn't committed adultery with "that woman," I wouldn't be in this situation; my son would have a father at home, and we could be a normal family. Someday I planned to tell my son what a terrible dad he had, and that all of mama's unhappiness was because of daddy. I didn't need healing. My ex-husband just needed to stay as far away as possible from me and my son.

I read the first chapter. Honesty with myself was my goal. My first studies were somewhat difficult and uncomfortable. I had answered "yes" to all the questions! Where did these questions come from? As I read and answered honestly, my heart was softened. I was broken as emotions flooded over me. I believe to this day that, as I sat alone in my bedroom one night, God revealed to me the issues about my past. He was with me and would remain with me no matter what happened.

I began reading, praying and learning about how much He really did love me. However, being a selfish sinner, I wanted the Lord all to myself. I didn't want Him to love my ex-husband or "that woman." After all, they were the ones who had sinned. I continued to pray that they would get what was coming to them—Hell.

As our group met, we shared more about each other and our life experiences, and I began to love these women. I was never so humbled in all my life as I was during the "session of confession," as I call it! I listened to these women talk about hurts and express emotions so powerful that I couldn't hold back the tears. The compassion and empathy I felt for these suffering women was too close to my own painful memories. We were finally discussing these "never-talked-about" subjects! We women in Christ were doing just as He instructed us to do. We were being obedient in our walks. However ugly the past was, together we brought our darkness into the light. We confessed the sin and let the healing begin!

The Lord made it very clear that I needed to forgive many people for many things, so I could be forgiven and go on with what was really important—Him! Just when I thought it was getting easier, it got much harder to obey. Forgive my ex? Forgive the woman who slept with my husband? Forgive the man who molested me as a young girl? Forgive the men who used or abused me in other relationships? Yet, time and time again, scriptures about "forgiving so as to be forgiven" kept coming back to me. "For if you forgive men their trespasses, your heavenly Father will also forgive you. But if you do not forgive men their trespasses, neither will your Father forgive your trespasses" (Matthew 6:14-15).

Many nights, I prayed for them. At first, halfheartedly, "Oh, yeah, and I pray for… Amen." Gradually, my heart became filled with God and His love. I see it everywhere! My prayers are now for their salvation! Only by the power of His Holy Spirit would I ever be able to forgive and pray for someone who caused so much pain in my life. PRAISE THE LORD!

I am living proof that God does heal. He does answer our prayers. I also know my future is so much more critical than my past, so I will not dwell on things that no longer exist. My ex-husband and I no longer raise our voices at each other in anger. We both make sacrifices for our son. I even find myself smiling when I answer the door to greet him, and often thank him for his efforts toward our son. I will never tell Steven what a terrible daddy he has or that our lives are bad because of his father's sins; those are lies! I have and will tell him only the truth. I love him so very much and there is nothing I would ever change about my life, good or bad, because I have such a precious gift!

I hear other women talking poorly about their ex-husbands, using colorful language and harsh wishes, often demeaning them in front of their own children. I know their pain; only recently have I been able to see the fruit of my own healing. I was privileged to share the peace of the Lord with another young woman who was divorced recently. She asked me, "How do you cope with it?" It was a blessing to see God use my past experience to bless someone else!

> HEALING... it's what God does.
> Invigorating others about His healing power in our lives...
> it's what He longs for us to do.

Week 5: Day 4

Prayer: Bow your heart before the Lord in prayer prior to completing today's Bible study. Thank Him for the abundant life He offers to you.

The Power of Praise

It isn't always easy to praise the Lord, we often have to overcome our own feelings to do so. After all, we have very real trials to face every day of our lives. So how do we find the strength to celebrate our lives? This devotional, "The Power of Praise" by The Active Word[4] offers some insight into living a life of joyful praise, even when things are hard.

> "Deliver me from my enemies, O my God; defend me from those who rise up against me" (Psalm 59:1).

> For a number of years, David lived under the constant shadow of his enemies. He was a fugitive on the run, and just about every indistinct figure on the horizon held the threatening prospect of being an adversary sent to kill him. But with the threat of enemies all around, David discovered something that gave him the ability to prevail over his persecutors:

> "But I will sing of Your power; yes, I will sing aloud of Your mercy in the morning" (Psalm 59:16).

> As day breaks, David envisions his enemies all around him. He unsheathes a weapon... and he sings. He sings? What kind of weapon is that? But this is no ordinary song that David sings. He opens his mouth and sings praises *to* God, praises *of* God and praises *for* God. It connected him to the Lord and sheltered and protected David as he dwelled in God's presence. And because this praise carries that kind of a connection, it's powerful. So powerful, in fact, that it can win any war or overcome any adversary.

> Praise and worship are some of the most reliable and formidable weapons in your spiritual arsenal. When you're feeling overwhelmed and dismayed, worship God and see what happens. If you're ensnared by depression, doubt or discouragement, open your mouth to praise the Lord and watch what takes place. You will always emerge stronger and better off.

> There is power in praise. David knew it, and we need to know it—not as theory but as a reality in our daily walk. You are the only One worthy of our worship, O Lord, and we purpose in our hearts to position ourselves to praise You in all occasions.

The Power of the Word

Truly, no matter what we face in our lives, we are not without blessings. After all, the Lord has given us the richest, sweetest and most wonderful gift of all: eternal life! Find things in your life to be thankful for and freely offer praise to the Lord! As 1 Thessalonians 5:18 says, "In everything give thanks; for this is the will of God in Christ Jesus for you."

Colossians 2:6-7 says, "As you therefore have received Christ Jesus the Lord, so walk in Him, rooted and built up in Him and established in the faith, as you have been taught, abounding in it with thanksgiving." Are you abounding in thanksgiving? Remember that no matter what, you have blessings in your life to praise Him for! Thank Him for the very breath you breathe. Thank Him for a new day. Thank Him for giving you eternal life in Christ Jesus. Pray and meditate on these scriptures to help you develop a thankful heart:

Job 10:8,12: "Your hands have made me and fashioned me, an intricate unity... You have granted me life and favor, and Your care has preserved my spirit."

Psalm 8:4-6: "What is man that You are mindful of him, and the son of man that You visit him? For You have made him a little lower than the angels, and You have crowned him with glory and honor. You have made him to have dominion over the works of Your hands; You have put all things under his feet."

2 Corinthians 8:9: "For you know the grace of our Lord Jesus Christ, that though He was rich, yet for your sakes He became poor, that you through His poverty might become rich."

Colossians 1:12: "Giving thanks to the Father who has qualified us to be partakers of the inheritance of the saints in the light."

2 Peter 1:3-4: "His divine power has given to us all things that pertain to life and godliness, through the knowledge of Him who called us by glory and virtue, by which have been given to us exceedingly great and precious promises, that through these you may be partakers of the divine nature, having escaped the corruption that is in the world through lust."

Ephesians 1:3,7-9: "Blessed be the God and Father of our Lord Jesus Christ, who has blessed us with every spiritual blessing in the heavenly places in Christ... We have redemption through His blood, the forgiveness of sins, according to the riches of His grace which He made to abound toward us in all wisdom and prudence, having made known to us the mystery of His will, according to His good pleasure..."

1. After reading the above scriptures, what are some things you can be thankful for? List them here, giving thanks to Him who gives all blessings!

The Dash

Linda Ellis[5]

I read of a man who stood to speak at the funeral of a friend.
He referred to the dates on her tombstone, from the beginning… to the end.

He noted that first came the date of her birth,
and spoke of the following date with tears,
but he said what mattered most of all was the dash between those years.

For that dash represents all the time that she spent alive on earth.
And now only those who loved her know what that little line is worth.

For it matters not, how much we own, the cars… the house… the cash.
What matters is how we live and love and how we spend our dash.

So, think about this long and hard. Are there things you'd like to change?
For you never know how much time is left that can still be rearranged.

If we could just slow down enough to consider what's true and real
and always try to understand the way other people feel.

And be less quick to anger and show appreciation more
and love the people in our lives like we've never loved before.

If we treat each other with respect and more often wear a smile,
remembering that this special dash might only last a little while.

So, when your eulogy is being read, with your life's actions to rehash…
would you be proud of the things they say about how you spent YOUR dash?

2. What would be your answer to the last line of "The Dash"? Would you be proud of the things said about you in your eulogy? Are there things you'd like to change? If so, what? List some things you can do now to start making the most of your "dash." You never know how much time you have left!

Stories of Real People and a Real Savior

I Was Crying Out for a Reason to Live

Karen, Minnesota

I have always believed in my head that God is the Wonderful Counselor, but as I prayed over the past few years for healing from my painful emotional baggage, He didn't seem to hear or respond. I was at the point of seeking professional counseling, disappearing for a few weeks, or both, when this study was offered at my church in Minnesota. I immediately knew when I heard the title, *Healed and Set Free*, that this was God's answer for me. So I signed up.

How do I communicate the total unhappiness and effort that living was for me? I'd wake up anticipating each day, looking forward to things I liked to do. But guess what? I didn't like to do anything anymore. I just did things out of habit. It was all an effort; I was so sad. I really didn't want to live like this—to waste my life. I was at the bottom of a dark, distrustful hole for several years, which had just gotten larger and deeper.

I hung on to every little real and imagined hurt and stuffed it deep inside, feeling justified, but stuck in a horrible nightmare. I was doubtful, because of the patterns and habits that had already been established, but I wanted a new perspective.

This Bible study has truly been a great healing experience for me. As I wrote down my heart, shared my frustrations and prayed for a work to be done, the garbage just faded away. I really can't remember some of the things that I thought were so big before. I am just so grateful to God for healing and leading me and for the enthusiasm He has restored in me for life and serving others. I see so many who need this study that I'm praying about becoming a leader so that no one misses out. I'd like everyone to experience the abundant Christian life.

This Week's Memory Verse

"Anxiety in the heart of man causes depression, but a good word makes it glad. The righteous should choose his friends carefully, for the way of the wicked leads them astray" (Proverbs 12:25-26).

The Power of the Tongue

Words can either bring life or death to us and others; they have a profound effect on our emotions and the emotions of others. Let's look at one area that is very powerful and affects everyone in our lives. Our example and action in this area is vital, and reflects our heart toward others.

3. Read Proverbs 18:21: "Death and life are in the power of the tongue."

   What does criticizing or gossiping do to a relationship?

   _____

   _____

   _____

4. Read Proverbs 15:28: "The heart of the righteous studies how to answer, but the mouth of the wicked pours forth evil."

   What practical steps can you take to avoid criticizing or gossiping?

   _____

   _____

   _____

5. Read 1 Thessalonians 5:11 and Hebrews 3:13:

   - "Therefore, comfort each other and edify one another, just as you also are doing" (1 Thessalonians 5:11).

   - "But exhort one another daily, while it is called 'Today,' lest any of you be hardened through the deceitfulness of sin" (Hebrews 4:13).

   What does the Bible instruct us to do for one another?

   _____

   _____

6. Read Lamentations 3:21-26: "This I recall to my mind, therefore I have hope. Through the Lord's mercies we are not consumed, because His compassions fail not. They are new every morning; great is Your faithfulness. 'The Lord is my portion,' says my soul, 'therefore I hope in Him!' The Lord is good to those who wait for Him, to the soul who seeks Him. It is good that one should hope and wait quietly for the salvation of the Lord."

   What does it mean to you that Christ's compassions never fail?

   _____

   _____

   _____

   _____

7. What is new every morning according to Lamentations 3?

8. According to Lamentations, what does it mean for you to give others new mercies when they fail you?

9. Has anger, lack of patience or faith, a sharp tongue or the wrong attitude been a part of your life this week? If so, how?

10. Read Psalm 34:13-14: "Keep your tongue from evil, and your lips from speaking deceit. Depart from evil and do good; seek peace and pursue it."

    You are responsible for your own choices and actions in seeking to keep your relationship right with God. Write down a time when you made the right choice to obey God's Word in a difficult situation. What was the outcome?

11. Write down a time when you made the wrong choice and followed after your own desires and ways. What was the outcome?

> "Search me, O God, and know my heart; try me, and know my anxieties; and see if there is any wicked way in me, and lead me in the way everlasting" (Psalm 139:23-24).

Stories of Real People and a Real Savior

Breaking the Horrible Habit of Gossip

Jenny, Idaho

When I took the *Healed and Set Free* study, one of the things I really wanted to do was to stop gossiping, because I knew that it wasn't what God wanted for my life. It made me feel bad about myself, even though I gossiped to make myself feel better. Throughout this study, I knew that I needed God's help and forgiveness to stop this horrible habit. During one of our study sessions, Tammy told us that in the past, she too had struggled with gossiping. She shared how God had shown her a practical way to stop: When she thought about gossiping, she imagined there was a baby monitor turned on, and the person she was gossiping about had the other monitor and could hear everything she said! I decided to try, with God's help, to stop gossiping. I wrote "baby monitor" in big letters on a card with a check mark for each hour of the day so that I could track my progress. As the days went by, I saw that I was progressing toward my goal of a gossip-free day. Seeing my progress gave me the incentive to stick with it. I'm not perfect, but am working to break the habit. With God's help, I know I can do it!

Understanding Emotions During a Woman's Cycle

Perhaps you have another issue bringing you down emotionally: As Kathy Babbitt writes, "Our emotions and life circumstances aren't the only things that affect our outlook on life. As women, we also deal with hormonal ups and downs. The difference in estrogen levels in a woman's body during various times of the month correlates to a predictable pattern of behaviors and emotions."[6] Here is a breakdown from Kathy of how our emotions tend to fluctuate during our cycle:

- The first week of a woman's cycle, she is outgoing, ambitious and self-confident: Life is peaceful.

- The second week she is hopeful, easy-going, and has an inner strength and sense of well being: Life is fun.

- The third week she lacks coordination, longs for peace, is impatient, gloomy and depressed: Life is sad.

- The fourth week she is irritable, touchy, sexually withdrawn and lacks self-confidence: Life is war.

Mark your calendar to help you be more aware of what will be going on from week to week. This will help you understand your mood swings and allow you to see what may be causing you to be depressed, gloomy, irritable, withdrawn or have a lack of patience at certain times of the month, and to not take it too seriously!

12. What have you noticed about your cycle and how it affects your moods?

Week 5: Day 5

Prayer: Bow your heart before the Lord in prayer prior to completing today's Bible study. Ask Him to let you SEE and GIVE Him what may be leading to depression in your life.

Guilt Leads to Depression

Guilt comes as a result of breaking one of God's laws. When guilt remains in your heart, it will lead to depression. If you have broken one of God's laws, He desires for you to come to Him in confession and repentance. When you confess your sin, Christ is faithful to cover your sin with His blood and extend His forgiveness to you. This is Christ's example for you to follow. In Christ, you can be forgiven and set free from your guilt. In Christ's strength, you can refuse to hold grudges, and forgive others as you have been forgiven.

Ignoring Sin

If you choose to ignore your sin, you have not removed your guilt. By holding grudges, you add to your sin and guilt. By refusing to forgive, you are refusing to be forgiven. If you haven't gotten rid of the sin, you haven't gotten rid of the guilt or shame. You can choose to have Christ set you free from your sin and guilt, or you can ignore it and be in bondage to bitterness, depression and unforgiveness. God can use guilt for your good by encouraging you to SEE what is in your heart and GIVE it in confession to Him. Ignoring your guilt will affect your relationship with God. It will cause you to become entangled in a web of self-condemnation, self-pity or self-justification as you are inwardly overcome by guilt, anxiety and increasing depression. God has provided a way to conquer depression and become healed and set free. "For whoever desires to save his life will lose it, but whoever loses his life for My sake will find it" (Matthew 16:25).

1. Read Matthew 26:33-35: "Peter answered and said to Him, 'Even if all are made to stumble because of You, I will never be made to stumble.' Jesus said to him, 'Assuredly, I say to you that this night, before the rooster crows, you will deny Me three times.' Peter said to Him, 'Even if I have to die with You, I will not deny You!' And so said all the disciples."

   What was Peter confident he would never do? In the end, what did he do?

   _____

   _____

2. Read Romans 7:19: "For the good that I will to do, I do not do, but the evil I will not to do, that I practice."

   Have you ever said, "I will never do that," then found yourself doing exactly what you said you would never do? If so, when and how?

   _____

   _____

3. Refer to Matthew 26:33-35 from the previous page. Would identifying with Peter give you a heart of compassion toward the shortcomings and failures of others? If so, how?

4. Have you ever stumbled and gossiped, held a grudge, failed to show mercy, used drugs, alcohol, filthy language, sharp words or had angry outbursts? What happens to your heart and emotions when you stumble and do something you know is wrong?

5. Read 2 Corinthians 7:9-10: "Now I rejoice, not that you were made sorry, but that your sorrow led to repentance. For you were made sorry in a godly manner, that you might suffer loss from us in nothing. For godly sorrow produces repentance leading to salvation, not to be regretted; but the sorrow of the world produces death."

    What does godly sorrow produce? What does the sorrow of the world produce?

6. Write down the definition of "repent" from page 301.

7. Read Jeremiah 2:22: "'For though you wash yourself with lye, and use much soap, yet your iniquity is marked before Me,' says the Lord God."

    In this example, what attempt is made to conceal guilt?

8. Read Hebrews 10:19-22: "Therefore, brethren, having boldness to enter the Holiest by the blood of Jesus, by a new and living way which He consecrated for us, through the veil, that is, His flesh, and having a High Priest over the house of God, let us draw near with a true heart in full assurance of faith, having our hearts sprinkled from an evil conscience and our bodies washed with pure water."

    How are you to draw near to God? How do you have your heart sprinkled from an evil conscience?

9. Read Titus 3:5: "Not by works of righteousness which we have done, but according to His mercy He saved us, through the washing of regeneration and renewing of the Holy Spirit."

    Are you saved by your works of righteousness, or according to God's mercy?

10. Read Revelation 1:5: "From Jesus Christ, the faithful witness, the firstborn from the dead, and the ruler over the kings of the earth. To Him who loved us and washed us from our sins in His own blood."

    Who loves you and washes away your sins with His own blood?

    _____

    _____

11. Read Psalm 32:5: "I acknowledged my sin to You, and my iniquity I have not hidden. I said, 'I will confess my transgressions to the Lord,' and You forgave the iniquity of my sin."

    What do you need to do to be forgiven?

    _____

    _____

Shame From the Past

When we have a painful past, we may blame ourselves for having this wound. We may experience shame, discouragement and despair.

12. Read Isaiah 54:4-8: "'Do not fear, for you will not be ashamed; neither be disgraced, for you will not be put to shame; for you will forget the shame of your youth, and will not remember the reproach of your widowhood anymore. For your Maker is your husband, the Lord of hosts is His name; and your Redeemer is the Holy One of Israel; He is called the God of the whole earth. For the Lord has called you like a woman forsaken and grieved in spirit, like a youthful wife when you were refused,' says your God. 'For a mere moment I have forsaken you, but with great mercies I will gather you. With a little wrath I hid My face from you for a moment; but with everlasting kindness I will have mercy on you,' says the Lord, your Redeemer."

    What sins or shame from your past lingers in your heart?

    _____

    _____

    _____

> To walk in God's will means to spend time daily in His Word, discovering His will, and then obeying what He has told us.

13. What attitude should you have about the shame of your past according to Isaiah 54:4-8 from the previous page?

14. How does God gather you?

15. Read 2 Corinthians 4:2: "But we have renounced the hidden things of shame, not walking in craftiness nor handling the Word of God deceitfully, but by manifestation of the truth commending ourselves to every man's conscience in the sight of God."

    Is there hidden shame in your life today? Are you ready to walk away from it and commit yourself to the truth? Write down the hidden shame you need to give over to Christ. Take the step to let the old go and the new come! You no longer need to wear the clothes of shame. Christ died for all the shame from your past. Can you believe that His death on the cross was enough for you to begin to wear the clothes of purity? Write down your thoughts.

Stories of Real People and a Real Savior

I Am a Completely Different Person

Sheila, Minnesota

I don't know an eighth of the things that the Lord has shown and done in me through the *Healed and Set Free Bible Study*. What I do know is that I am a completely different person than I was three months ago.

I am a victim of rape. I went for counseling before my daughter was born, and at the time thought it helped, but it didn't truly heal me. I have applied the tools: SEE, GIVE, FORGIVE and FORGET to my life. Christ has taken the wrong and sinful feelings away. I can now say, "He has healed me!" I am no longer a slave to sin.

Chapter Review

Prayer: Bow your heart before the Lord in prayer, asking Him to help you let go of the past and to examine your heart daily as you embrace His Word.

1. Look up Philippians 4:8 on page 303 and write it out here:

2. Write out two scriptures that particularly ministered to you from this chapter and use them to help you forgive the unacceptable things others have done to you or unacceptable acts you have done.

   A.

   B.

3. Write a short paragraph summarizing what you have learned on the subject of forgiveness.

Stories of Real People and a Real Savior

From a Walking Disaster to a Woman Who is Thriving
By Chrissy, Pastor's wife of the Latino Ministry, Calvary Chapel Boise, ID

I grew up in a very dysfunctional family. Both my parents were drug addicts, and my dad spent most of my life in prison. Because of this lifestyle, I grew up seeing and experiencing violence, neglect, rejection from society, sexual abuse and rape.

By the age of 16, I had gotten pregnant, married, and was on a path to start a family of my own. The day I found out I was pregnant, I swore that I would never take my children through all the pain and suffering that my parents took me through.

Within the first few years of my marriage, my husband and I were walking disasters, hurting each other and our two beautiful daughters along the way. I got to a point where I felt angry, hopeless and helpless. I ran to the only thing I knew to ease the pain: I abandoned my family and ran to drugs and alcohol.

Through this chapter in our life, my husband found the Lord and started praying for me. I was lost, ashamed and broken. Yet God in His mercy saved me, forgave me, and restored my marriage. I had been living in the bondage of my past hurts and actions for so long, but now I was forgiven.

Healed and Set Free taught me how to see what was in my own heart that was defiling and corrupting me and how to give it to God in repentance. But the tool that truly did it for me was forgiving—just as I had been forgiven.

I was able to forgive the people who hurt me as a child and took my innocence from me; I was able to forgive my parents for taking me through and allowing all those things to happen to me; I was able to forgive my husband for how he hurt me, and myself for all the horrible things I had done.

Now I am a woman who is healed and set free. It is amazing to see how God can use such horrible things for good. My husband is now the Latino Ministry Pastor in Boise, Idaho, and I work alongside him serving the women in our church body.

The Lord has used our lives to minister to the many hurting and broken people and marriages that we encounter. I thank You, Jesus, for using Tammy to bring this study to my life.

Tools to Become Healed and Set Free

To equip yourself in God's truth, look over the tools and verses that will be introduced in the coming weeks. Thinking about the past won't change it, but you can change your future by being set free from your past.

TOOL #1 - SEE: I must SEE the truth about what is in my heart so I am not defiled.

> **Definition**: To defile means to make filthy or dirty; to pollute.
>
> **Bible Verse**: "Looking carefully lest anyone fall short of the grace of God; lest any root of bitterness springing up cause trouble, and by this many become defiled" (Hebrews 12:15).

TOOL #2 - GIVE: I must GIVE my sin to God through repentance, knowing that Christ is waiting to take it. I must be sorry enough to change, and choose to go God's way over my own.

> **Definition**: To repent means to feel such sorrow for sin or fault as to be disposed to change one's life for the better; be penitent.
>
> **Bible Verse**: "For godly sorrow produces repentance leading to salvation, not to be regretted; but the sorrow of the world produces death" (2 Corinthians 7:10).

TOOL #3 - FORGIVE: I must FORGIVE as I am forgiven by Christ: Forgiving those who hurt, bruised, wronged, rejected, betrayed or harmed me, whether unintentionally or deliberately. I must ask God to forgive me for holding on to unforgiveness and know that He will.

> **Definition**: To forgive means to stop feeling angry or resentful toward someone for an offense, flaw or mistake.
>
> **Bible Verse**: "...Bearing with one another, and forgiving one another, if anyone has a complaint against another; even as Christ forgave you, so you also must do" (Colossians 3:13).

TOOL #4 - FORGET: I must FORGET by no longer dwelling on the hurt or the painful reminders, such as: phrases, smells, places, songs and comments. Instead, I am putting my mind on the higher calling that Christ has for me.

> **Definition**: To forget means to choose not to remember or notice, "forgive and forget".
>
> **Bible Verse**: "Brethren, I do not count myself to have apprehended; but one thing I do, forgetting those things which are behind and reaching forward to those things which are ahead" (Philippians 3:13).

Be Healed and Set Free: Christ will heal me from my past, showing me the truth, so I can become a cleansed vessel, healed and set free.

> **Definition**: To set free means to make free; set at liberty; release from bondage, imprisonment, or restraint.
>
> **Definition**: To heal means to make whole and healthy; to cure; to remedy or repair.
>
> **Bible Verse**: "And you shall know the truth, and the truth shall make you free" (John 8:32).

Body Image

This week we will grow deeper in our understanding of **Tool #1 - SEE**, **Tool #2 - GIVE** and **Tool #3 - FORGIVE** and they apply to our lives in the area of body image.

Tool #1 - SEE: I must SEE the truth about what is in my heart, so I am not defiled (see Hebrews 12:15).

Tool #2 - GIVE: I must GIVE my sin to God through repentance, knowing that Christ is waiting to take it. I must be sorry enough to change, and choose to go God's way over my own (see 2 Corinthians 7:10).

Tool #3 - FORGIVE: I must forgive as I am forgiven by Christ. Forgiving those who hurt, bruised, wronged, rejected, betrayed or harmed me, whether unintentionally or deliberately. I must ask God to forgive me for holding on to unforgiveness and know that He will (see Colossians 3:13).

Prayer: Ask God to help you be willing to SEE what's in your heart and to GIVE Him the strongholds that our thinking and pride can cause. Continue to ask God to fill you with the knowledge of His will through all the wisdom and understanding that the Spirit gives.

Week 6: Day 1

Prayer: Bow your heart before the Lord prior to completing today's study. Ask for help to be honest with God and yourself about your relationship with food.

God is intimately involved with every aspect of our lives, minds, bodies and souls. To be obsessed with our bodies or food is to live in bondage. When there is a stronghold in our lives, we are working against ourselves and against God's design for us. We are His workmanship created in Christ Jesus.

SEE the Stronghold

You can make the choice to change and enter into a life of self-control with God's help. To do this, it is necessary to:

- **SEE** the stronghold in your life.
- **GIVE** it over to God, ask for His help and His strength to change.
- **FORGIVE** as Christ has forgiven you.
- **FORGET** the lies you have believed.
- **BE SET FREE** by God's truth as you stand firm in your new choices.

GIVE the Stronghold to God

The battle to break strongholds requires that we get up each day and pray for God to kill our flesh, our own will, our own thinking and our own pride. We must pray for His will and His Word to be lived out in our lives, day by day. Satan is your adversary, a very real and crafty enemy who has targeted you and is using food or pride as his weapon of destruction.

Stories of Real People and a Real Savior

A Secret My Husband Didn't Know About

A Sister in Christ Walking in the Truth

I had been praying for God to give me someone to go to for help. I had kept my secret hidden deep inside, even from my husband. I almost shared it with a sister in Christ, but then couldn't work up the courage. Then one day, Tammy called me out of the blue and the desire to share my secret with her was so strong that I knew it was time. I told her I was bulimic, and that I was really struggling. I started the *Healed and Set Free* Bible study to end the slavery of this sin. The study brought out many issues from my past that I had never fully dealt with. One of those issues was being molested as a child. In the weeks of doing the study, God has shown me so much in my life. Sin is sin is sin, no matter what. I couldn't do it alone. I needed God to help me. We need to SEE, GIVE, FORGIVE, FORGET and BE SET FREE.

Tools to Become Set Free

In this chapter, we will practice using the three tools we've learned so far: **Tool #1 - SEE**, **Tool #2 - GIVE** and **Tool #3 - FORGIVE**.

These tools will help you to become set free. Each tool is defined as the time comes. It is crucial to memorize these powerful tools and review them regularly in order to apply them to your daily life.

#1 - SEE: I must SEE the truth about what is in my heart so I am not defiled.

#2 - GIVE: I must GIVE my sin to God through repentance, knowing that Christ is waiting to take it. I must be sorry enough to change, and choose to go God's way over my own.

#3 - FORGIVE: I must FORGIVE as I am forgiven by Christ: Forgiving those who hurt, bruised, wronged, rejected, betrayed or harmed me, whether unintentionally or deliberately. I must ask God to forgive me for holding on to unforgiveness and know that He will.

#4 - FORGET: I must FORGET by no longer dwelling on the hurt or the painful reminders such as: phrases, smells, places, songs and comments. Instead, I am putting my mind on the higher calling that Christ has for me.

Be Healed and Set Free: Christ will heal me from my past, showing me the truth, so I can become a cleansed vessel, healed and set free.

This Week's Focus

Prayer: Ask God to help you be willing to SEE what's in your heart and to GIVE Him the strongholds that our thinking and pride can cause. Continue to ask God to fill you with the knowledge of His will through all the wisdom and understanding that the Spirit gives.

By Memory: My challenge to you is to be able to recite the tools you've learned so far without looking. I know that by hiding these words of wisdom in your heart you are providing yourself with tools to truly be healed and set free. May we rise up to be women of the Word.

Tool #1 - SEE: I must SEE the truth about what is in my heart, so I am not defiled (see Hebrews 12:15).

Tool #2 - GIVE: I must GIVE my sin to God through repentance, knowing that Christ is waiting to take it. I must be sorry enough to change, and choose to go God's way over my own (see 2 Corinthians 7:10).

Tool #3 - FORGIVE: I must forgive as I am forgiven by Christ. Forgiving those who hurt, bruised, wronged, rejected, betrayed or harmed me, whether unintentionally or deliberately. I must ask God to forgive me for holding on to unforgiveness and know that He will (see Colossians 3:13).

"And you shall know the truth, and the truth shall make you free" (John 8:32).

Bulimia Could Have Taken My Life

By the time I reached my senior year of high school, my life was out of control. I had given my life to Christ, but was still doing anything and everything that felt good to me at the time—partying, lying and gossiping. Jesus Christ was my Savior, but He was not the Lord, King or Master of my life. I wasn't serving Him with joyful obedience. I wasn't in the Bible feeding my spirit. I was consumed by the world's ways, going down a dead-end street.

My food issues all started with a friend of mine bragging about how she could eat as much as a horse and never gain weight. All she had to do was vomit up her food after eating and take laxatives to stay thin. Right then the thought was placed in my mind, and I decided to give it a try. Unfortunately, I didn't realize the deadly consequences.

I would take in large amounts of food, then vomit at least five times a day just to stay thin. I was filled with pride and wanted to be perfect. I was consumed with "self," what people thought of me and how they looked at me. I wanted to control my weight and my life. In reality, my struggle with bulimia was controlling me. My mind became sick; I thought I was fat when I was actually very thin.

Closing Off My Heart to God

I was determined to build walls around myself, retreating to the safety of my own world. I closed my heart to God and went my own way. I continued to struggle with bulimia, pride and self-image. I partied hard, and in turn, my heart became hard. When I looked in the mirror, my face was lifeless. I looked like I had cut my lifeline. I looked like I was dying. In fact, I had cut my lifeline: I had cut God out of my life.

Even though I had moved away from God, He still remained loving and faithful to me. All I had to do was reach up, take His hand and unconditionally trust Him. The Holy Spirit was tugging on my heart. I'm not sure when or how it happened, but it did happen. I realized I was sinning in my thoughts about the importance of self. God wasn't "God" in my life. My thinness was my god. My self-image was my god. I wasn't reaching to God for comfort when I was discouraged, stressed or lonely. I was reaching to food for comfort.

He is a Jealous God

Often times, things become more important to us than God. But God will have nothing before Him in our hearts: not our husbands, children, careers, homes, bodies or ministries.

Psalm 73:25 tells us that there should be nothing upon earth we desire more than God. If we have put anything before Him in our hearts, we will never be able to completely give Him our lives, something will always be standing in the way.

Changing My Life

I knew I needed to make a change in my life, my thoughts and my eating habits. It was time to stop my bulimic lifestyle and start having self-control. In fact, if I wouldn't have stopped, I might not be here today. I am thankful that God has healed my mind from the sin of bulimia. I have asked for forgiveness, confessed my sin with my mouth, and been set free by God. It's just a matter of having the right perspective on food.

Today when I sit down to eat, I don't feel guilty or worry if I'm going to get heavy. I feed my body the food it needs to stay alive, and when I'm full, I stop eating. I know it sounds too easy, but it really is that simple. It is a matter of choice at every meal, a matter of applying self-control as a fruit of the Spirit.

"But the fruit of the Spirit is love, joy, peace, longsuffering, kindness, goodness, faithfulness, gentleness, self-control. Against such there is no law. And those who are Christ's have crucified the flesh with its passions and desires. If we live in the Spirit, let us also walk in the Spirit" (Galatians 5:22-25).

Seeing Ourselves How God Sees Us

I recently read an interview with famous female singer and Dove Award Vocalist of the Year, Natalie Grant. She shared how Jesus healed the pain in her life caused by "self" and bulimia. For her, it happened one day while she was kneeling at her toilet. She had never heard God speak audibly. But on this day, she felt like the Holy Spirit was saying, "My grace is enough. My grace is enough" (2 Corinthians 12:9).

The scripture began to minister to her heart. She remembers looking at the toilet and saying, "I am kneeling to the wrong god. I'm kneeling to the god of myself, because I want to make myself feel better and feel accepted, and to look a certain way. I'm kneeling to the wrong god, and this will destroy my life!"[1]

She continued, "I wish I could tell you that I just popped up from the toilet, stopped making myself throw up and never did it again. I didn't. It was a long process of discovering what it means to see myself like God sees me."

Natalie said a scripture that really helped her was 1 Peter 5:10-12: "But may the God of all grace, who called us to His eternal glory by Christ Jesus, after you have suffered a while, perfect, establish, strengthen and settle you."

> "I will praise You, for I am fearfully and wonderfully made;
> Marvelous are Your works, and that my soul knows very well"
> (Psalm 139:14).

Week 6: Day 2

Prayer: Bow your heart before the Lord prior to completing today's Bible study. Ask God to enable you to praise Him for the way He has created you, for you are "fearfully and wonderfully made" (Psalm 139:14).

Eating Disorders: More Than Just a Teen Problem

Historically, eating disorder research has focused on teens and young women. But in 2012, a ground-breaking study by the International Journal of Eating Disorders found that 13% of women 50 and older struggle with an eating disorder. The researchers conducted an online survey of 1,849 women from across the nation to find out how older women felt about their bodies, and how prevalent eating disorders are. This first-of-its-kind study looked specifically at older women (the average age in the study was 59), and found that not only are eating disorders common among older women, but 62% of those surveyed said their weight or shape has damaged their lives, 79% said their weight or shape affected their self-perception. Common eating disorders include: purging, binge eating and excessive dieting or exercising. The study noted, "The disorders have serious physical as well as emotional consequences."[2]

Study Results

- 41% weighed themselves daily, and 36% spent at least half of the past five years dieting. Such behaviors and attitudes put women at higher risk for full-blown eating disorders.

- The most common symptom was binge eating. Bingeing differs from overeating in that one eats large amounts of food in a short time and then throws it up. On top of making you feel bad about yourself, binge-eating causes swings in blood pressure and glucose levels and can lead to obesity.

- More than half of the women in the study (56%) were obese or overweight. 42% were normal weight and 2% were underweight.

A Bombardment of Messages

The issues that drive women to an eating disorder are complex, but one reason is very clear, as Janice Bremis, executive director of the Eating Disorders Resource Center notes: "We have that constant bombardment of messages to look perfect, to be skinny and to be in control. It's on television, in magazines, and women wonder 'How can I ever be perfect like that?'"

The report found purging and binge-eating to be the most common disorders among those 50 and older. Eight percent said they purged, that is, eliminated food by vomiting (or other means). Binge-eating, which the study defined as eating a large amount and feeling out of control, was a disorder that 3.5% of those surveyed struggled with.

Eating disorders are sinful, causing us to be consumed with "self," and take our eyes off the things of the Lord. But they also have real health risks: cardiovascular, gastrointestinal and musculoskeletal issues, obesity, cancer, or even death.

So what are the triggers of mid- to late-life eating disorders? The most common answers women gave were divorce, loss, children leaving or returning home, taking care of children and parents. It's during these seasons of stress that "food can be seen as a way to regulate moods," the study authors said.

Facing Reality

Terri Schiavo's story is a recent example of the horrors that surround eating disorders. Terri's struggles began long before the legal battle over whether she would live or die. As USA Today reported, "Before Terri Schiavo was [a] severely brain-damaged patient... she was a young woman who desperately wanted to be thin. The Schiavos' lawyer said her 1990 collapse was caused by a potassium imbalance brought on by an eating disorder. Keeping the weight off was a struggle for [her], and years later—after her heart stopped briefly, cutting off oxygen to the brain—a malpractice case brought against a doctor on her behalf would reveal she had been trying to survive on liquids and was making herself throw up after meals."[3]

Finding Answers

Stop confusing what you look like with who you are. Some, but not all, in the study above acknowledged having had an eating disorder when they were young. But regardless of age, we must let go of the ideas we have about "self." We have to let go of our ideas about how we should look, or the number on the scale.

Focus your energy on eating healthy and getting regular exercise. Focus on how God sees you. We need to head in that direction.

1. Write a brief description of how you currently view yourself. What do you think about this reflection of your self-image in light of what you've just read?

> This is not a game; this is spiritual warfare, and you are going to have to war in the Spirit as Satan launches his attacks on your very life.

2. Read Matthew 12:50: "For whoever does the will of My Father in heaven is My brother and sister and mother."

   Sit down and go over the reasons why you eat and what you feel during and after eating, then you can pinpoint areas where problems exist for you. If you are eating for any reason other than a normal feeling of hunger, food has an inappropriate place in your life. You need to find out why so that you can SEE, GIVE, FORGIVE, FORGET and BE SET FREE. The following yes or no questions are designed to help you take a closer look at the place you give food in your life.

   - Do you starve yourself?

   - Do you eat uncontrollably until you become physically ill?

   - Do you have episodes where you eat an enormous amount of food in a short period of time?

   - Do you make yourself vomit to get rid food you've eaten?

   - Is it hard to eat normal meals without bingeing and purging?

   - Do you use laxatives to control your weight or get rid of food?

   - Do you spit your food out after chewing to avoid digesting it?

   - Do you eat because you are bored, angry or upset?

   - Do you exercise excessively?

   - Do you use enemas regularly to control your weight?

   - Have you become preoccupied with what you eat?

   - Are you unwilling to gain weight in order to stop any faulty eating patterns you might have?

   - Do you eat to relieve stress or to comfort yourself if you are depressed?

   - Is it hard for you to stop eating when you are full?

   - Do you feel eating is a sin or feel guilty for eating?

   - Have others made fun of you because of your weight?

   - Do you compare your weight or size with that of other women?

   - Do you believe that by not eating you are more in control than someone who overeats?

Strongholds and Self-Control

Self-control is the ability from the Holy Spirit to say "no" to what is wrong and say "yes" to what is right. Take each day one step at a time. Face the truth about any weaknesses in your life. Ask for God's strength to apply self-control in this area.

Do you remember the "Falling Down" story (chapter 3, page 91)? As you begin to practice self-control and take steps to change your eating habits, you may fall down and get up and fall down and get up again. Praise Jesus for the times you are up! Praise Jesus that His mercies are new every morning as you pick yourself up and begin again to fuel your body in a wise and healthy manner. The more you practice self-control, the easier it will become to choose to follow the Spirit and not the flesh.

3. Do you desire to embrace or reject self-control in this area of your life?

4. Read 2 Peter 1:3-9 on page 304.
    How can you have self-control in your life?

5. Do you look at your eating disorder with a heart to change and become more obedient? Pray and ask the Holy Spirit to show you practical steps to begin this change. Write down the steps you will take, then share these steps with someone who can help you get out of this bondage.

> Ignorant disobedience is when you don't know what you are doing is sinful. Willful disobedience is when you know what you are doing is sinful and you continue to sin.

Week 6: Day 3

Prayer: Bow your heart before the Lord in prayer prior to completing today's Bible study. Ask God to help you embrace what He wants to teach you.

The Dead-End Reality of Eating Disorders

Those in bondage to eating disorders can experience freedom. God's healing is always available to those who desire recovery, but there is a difference between surviving and living.

This part of the study offers you hope. Not just to survive, but to live an abundant life, free from the bondage of an eating disorder. It is a journey, which means leaving one place and moving toward another. A journey requires change, and change can be very unsettling.

Your eating disorder on the other hand is a predictable and comfortable behavior that has been with you for a long time. If you are focused on the uncomfortable nature of change, you need to look ahead at the dead-end reality of an eating disorder. Change and movement are scary and challenging, but you wouldn't have picked up this study and gotten this far if you didn't know the way you are living is no longer acceptable.

It's time to get real with God. He's not looking for a performance, just an honest and open heart. It's my prayer that as you meditate on the following scriptures, you will let God in. Look at the truth of what is going on in your heart. As a child of God, realize that God is truth, and only the truth can set you free!

What is Anorexia?

Anorexia Nervosa is an eating disorder in which a person's preoccupation with dieting and being thin causes excessive weight loss and self-starvation. It sometimes leads to other symptoms like hypothermia, amenorrhea or hyperactivity. Hypothermia can accompany anorexia because, as the body's natural fat stores, which provide insulation and warmth, are depleted, the body becomes cold all the time. Loss of fat stores may also result in amenorrhea, the absence of a period. Those who struggle with anorexia sometimes become hyperactive in an attempt to burn as many calories as possible to lose weight.[4]

An innocent diet may be the start of anorexia: Weight loss often evolves into problems, such as excessive weight loss or restricted eating. People commonly lose their appetites due to anxiety, irritation, anger or fear, but with anorexia a person still has an appetite, they just refuse to eat.

An anorexic person feels fat and wants to hide their "ugly" body, even though they may be disturbingly thin. People who struggle with anorexia sometimes have rituals they go through before they eat, like cutting all their food into tiny pieces, or weighing every piece of food before eating it. Anorexic people often feel that their weight is the only part of their life they can control, yet they don't see that they may literally be starving themselves to death. Truly, anorexia, if not treated, is starving yourself to death, all because the person has an obsessive phobia of being fat. Maintaining a healthy body weight is normal, but starving oneself to be "thin" is an obsession. Sadly, it's estimated that more than 60% of all who are anorexic are also bulimic. In most cases, both anorexia and bulimia begin near puberty.

If you are anorexic, it will be easy for you to deceive yourself. The only protection against this deception is total honesty on your part, and if necessary, the wise counsel and help of those who truly love you.

1. Are you being honest with yourself about your body and food issues?

___

Warning Signs of Anorexia

2. Circle or mark the warning signs below that describe you. Be totally honest with yourself so that you won't be deceived. I struggle with:

   - Intense fear of gaining weight or of getting fat
   - Unnatural or obsessive preoccupation with food, dieting and weight
   - Eating only small amounts of fruits or vegetables, sometimes only coffee
   - Eating sprees, usually at night, then forcing myself to vomit
   - Distorted perspective of how my body actually looks
   - Feeling fat even after losing weight
   - Continuing to diet when I am already too thin
   - Denying hunger
   - Avoidance of social situations where food is present
   - Preferring to eat alone
   - Difficulty making friends or meeting strangers
   - No longer having monthly menstrual periods
   - Weakness, fatigue, depression or lack of energy
   - Exercising compulsively
   - Decreased coordination
   - Inability to concentrate
   - Indecisiveness
   - Mood swings, irritability or depression

3. Could you share the answers that you have circled with someone you are accountable to during your healing of anorexia?

___

4. Do you worry that you will get fat as part of recovery? Are you avoiding dealing with your anorexia because you don't want to gain weight as a result?

___

Our Christ-Centered Values

You must reject the false values of society and accept your own worth, based on who you are as a person in Christ and not on what your body looks like. You'll find that you must exercise the fruit of the Spirit of self-control in your life. No, you don't have to get heavy to get well. Your identity is in Christ, not in your weight. It's a matter of the choices you make at mealtimes. Food is just the fuel for your body. Food is not your enemy, and food is not your companion!

Definition of Bulimia

Bulimia is an eating disorder that involves bingeing and purging. Bingeing is when a person eats large amounts of food in a short period of time. This type of eating is not normal. A person struggling with bulimia will purge the food eaten through vomiting, abusing laxatives or diuretics, taking excessive enemas or exercising obsessively. Some use a combination of all four methods.[5]

Sustained bulimia severely damages the body. Side effects include: memory impairment, blackouts, a feeling of psychological abnormality, numbness or even a ruptured stomach. Repetitive vomiting can erode the esophagus and larynx, causing inflammation, tearing or bleeding; can cause facial glands to become swollen; and cause tooth decay. Excessive laxative use leaches the body of essential nutrients, like potassium, which regulates heartbeat, and may lead to a rapid or irregular heartbeat. Bulimia may also cause irregular or absent menstrual cycles.

People who struggle with bulimia fear they won't be able to stop eating voluntarily and fear losing all control. They binge or purge in secret. When around others, they either don't eat or drastically reduce their food intake. They insist that they are dieting to lose a few pounds, but since they usually maintain a normal or above normal body weight, they can hide their problem for years. Some with bulimia also struggle with drug and alcohol addiction, compulsive theft, clinical depression, anxiety or obsessive-compulsive disorder.

With both bulimia and anorexia, food replaces other people, and even God, as a source of comfort and companionship. When you withdraw from others, Satan has you right where he wants you—isolated. Purging is the most common warning sign of bulimia. This eating disorder can accelerate quickly and early recognition is a must in order to prevent serious physical consequences.

5. Read 1 Corinthians 10:12-13: "Therefore let him who thinks he stands take heed lest he fall. No temptation has overtaken you except such as in common to man; but God is faithful, who will not allow you to be tempted beyond what you are able, but with the temptation will also make the way of escape, that you may be able to bear it."

    Write down verses that speak to you on pieces of paper. Place them in your bathroom or kitchen and take time this week to really meditate on them.

Warning Signs of Bulimia

6. Circle or mark the following warning signs that describe you. Be totally honest with yourself so that you won't be deceived. Do you:

    - Binge and/or purge
    - Hide stashes of food such as chips or candy
    - Eat in secret
    - Disappear to the bathroom for long periods of time after eating
    - Avoid social situations where food will be present
    - Experience withdrawal from normal activities
    - Have a distorted body image
    - Fear becoming fat
    - Deny your hunger
    - Exercise compulsively
    - Use laxatives or diet pills
    - Experience physical changes (including dehydration)
    - Have bloodshot eyes from vomiting
    - Have abrasions/discoloration on the back of hands from induced vomiting
    - Have swollen salivary glands
    - Have an irregular or rapid heartbeat
    - Have tooth decay
    - Experience menstrual irregularities
    - Have mood swings, depression and/or irritability

7. Could you share the answers that you have circled with someone you are accountable to during your healing of bulimia? Yes or no?

This Week's Memory Verse

"Stand fast therefore in the liberty by which Christ has made us free, and do not be entangled again with a yoke of bondage"
(Galatians 5:1).

Warning Signs of Compulsive Overeating

8. Circle or mark the warning signs below that describe you.
    - You have lost all hope of ever being anything but fat.
    - You have concluded that life's greatest pleasure is food.
    - Your most important goal is getting the next food fix.
    - You can't stop eating because food is your only source of comfort.
    - Your eating is out of control.
    - You hide food, stashing it around the house.
    - You eat in secret.
    - You make jokes about your eating habits.

9. Could you share the answers you have circled with the one person you are accountable to during your healing from compulsive overeating? Yes or no?

Self-Control is Fruitful

10. Galatians 5:22-25: "But the fruit of the Spirit is love, joy, peace, longsuffering, kindness, goodness, faithfulness, gentleness, self-control. Against such there is no law. And those who are Christ's have crucified the flesh with its passions and desires. If we live in the Spirit, let us also walk in the Spirit."

    Write down the description of the fruit of the Spirit from Galatians 5:22-23:

    _____

    _____

11. How can you apply "self-control" from Galatians 5:23?

    _____

    _____

12. Finish the statements that apply to you by inserting "self-control."
    - If I want to overeat at meals or during the day, I can remember the fruit of the Spirit of _____ to stop eating once I'm full.
    - If I find myself wanting to vomit after meals, I can remember the fruit of the Spirit of _____, and not vomit after meals.
    - If I have a desire to starve myself, I can remember the fruit of the Spirit of _____ and not let food control me by eating when I'm hungry.

> A compulsive overeater is more intimate with food than people.
> Be totally honest with yourself so you won't be deceived.

13. Read Matthew 6:25: "Therefore I say to you, do not worry about your life, what you will eat or what you will drink; nor about your body, what you will put on. Is not life more than food and the body more than clothing?"

    With Matthew 6:25 in mind, is life more than just food?

14. Is it sinful to eat when you are hungry and your body needs fuel?

15. "Food is my enemy" because…

16. "Food is my friend" because…

17. Why do we need to eat?

18. A balanced perspective is that food is fuel for the body. Is this your perspective?

19. Have you been blinded by things controlling your life? Explain.

Practical Steps to Flee the Bondage

Galatians 5:1 says: "Stand fast therefore in the liberty by which Christ has made us free, and do not be entangled again with a yoke of bondage."

- Pray daily for the Spirit to help you make the right choices about food.
- Learn to listen to your body. When you're hungry, eat till you're full, then stop eating, even if there is still food left on your plate.
- Tell a Christian you're close to—a husband, friend or family member — about the struggles you face with food. Make Jesus the focus of every conversation to break away from the bondage.
- Place scripture in the bathroom, kitchen and bedroom to strengthen you in your choices and decisions when you are weak.

Self-Control Questions to Ask Yourself

20. Ask yourself the following questions before eating:

    - Why am I eating?
    - Am I hungry?
    - Am I angry?
    - Am I frustrated?
    - Am I nourishing my body?
    - Am I eating just to fuel my body?
    - Am I still eating when my hunger is satisfied? Why?
    - Am I going to stop eating when my hunger is satisfied? Why?
    - Why do I need to eat each day to keep living?

21. Self-control is a part of God's will for each of us. Are you going to follow your own desires or seek God's desires for you? Your will or God's will? Explain.

_____
_____
_____
_____
_____
_____

> "Charm is deceitful and beauty is passing,
> but a woman who fears the Lord, she shall be praised"
> (Proverbs 31:30).

Week 6: Day 4

Prayer: Bow your heart before the Lord in prayer prior to completing today's Bible study. Ask Him to strengthen you as you apply His Word to your life.

Strive to Satisfy

Some people continually act on impulse, grabbing at whatever seems attractive at the time. If you strive to satisfy your impulses, you will defeat yourself and the bondage will continue.

1. Read Matthew 7:24-25: "Therefore whoever hears these sayings of Mine, and does them, I will liken him to a wise man who built his house on the rock: and the rain descended, the floods came, and the winds blew and beat on that house; and it did not fall, for it was founded on the rock."

    What does it mean to build your house on the rock?

2. What trial or struggles in your life have led you to problems with food?

3. Describe a time that you made a choice by faith to apply God's Word to your difficult circumstance.

4. What was the outcome?

5. Do you sense that your outlook on eating is stable or healthy? Explain.

6. What is it about your eating that is "up and down"?

   _____

   _____

7. When you sense yourself becoming unstable, reach out to a godly source to establish accountability. Name a godly person that fits this role. Schedule a meeting with this person to share your struggle or stronghold, then ask that person to be a safeguard when you are weak.

   Name of confidant: _____

Learning From the Mistakes of Others

8. Read Proverbs 2:10-12: "When wisdom enters your heart, and knowledge is pleasant to your soul, discretion will preserve you; understanding will keep you, to deliver you from the way of evil..."

   Find someone who has faced and gained wisdom from the same struggles. Talk with them about the choices that led them into bondage. What wise choices did they eventually make, and how did those choices end their life in bondage?

   Write down the questions you would ask them:

   _____

   _____

   _____

   _____

   _____

   _____

   _____

   _____

   _____

God's Thinking vs. Our Thinking

For every negative thing we say to ourselves, God has a positive answer. Let's look at the things we say and how God responds:

We say: "It's impossible!"
God says: "All things are possible in Me" (Luke 18:27).

We say: "I'm too tired."
God says: "I will give you rest" (Matthew 11:28-30).

We say: "Nobody really loves me."
God says: "I love you" (John 3:16, John 13:34).

We say: "I can't go on."
God says: "My grace is sufficient" (2 Corinthians 12:9).

We say: "I can't figure things out."
God says: "I will direct your steps" (Proverbs 3:5-6).

We say: "I can't do it."
God says: "You can do all things through Me" (Philippians 4:13).

We say: "I'm not able."
God says: "I am able" (2 Corinthians 9:8).

We say: "It's not worth it."
God says: "It will be worth it" (Roman 8:28).

We say: "I can't forgive myself."
God says: "I FORGIVE YOU" (1 John 1:9, Romans 8:1).

We say: "I can't manage."
God says: "I will supply all your needs" (Philippians 4:19).

We say: "I'm afraid."
God says: "I have not given you a spirit of fear" (2 Timothy 1:7).

We say: "I'm always worried and frustrated."
God says: "Cast all your cares on me" (1 Peter 5:7).

We say: "I don't have enough faith."
God says: "I've given everyone a measure of faith" (Romans 12:3).

We say: "I'm not smart enough."
God says: "I will give you wisdom" (1 Corinthians 1:30).

We say: "I feel all alone."
God says: "I will never leave you or forsake you" (Hebrews 13:5).

9.   Write down your thoughts after reading this section.

_____

_____

_____

Drawn Away by Desire

As long as we are in these bodies, we will never stop sinning, but there is a difference between being a sinner and living in a pattern of habitual sin, as Greg Laurie explains in this devotional "Drawn Away by Desire."[6]

> We have all seen the bumper sticker that reads, "Lead me not into temptation, I can find it myself." Jesus knows that we are easily tempted, so He taught us to pray, "Do not lead us into temptation, but deliver us from the evil one" (Matthew 6:13). What does this actually mean? Is this implying that God would lead us into a situation in which we would be tempted? Or worse yet, that God Himself would tempt us? Certainly not. God does not tempt us.
>
> The Bible says, "Let no one say when he is tempted, 'I am tempted by God' for God cannot be tempted by evil, nor does He Himself tempt anyone. But each one is tempted when he is drawn away by his own desires and enticed. Then, when desire has conceived, it gives birth to sin; and sin, when it is full-grown, brings forth death" (James 1:13–15).
>
> In this petition from the Lord's prayer, we are asking God to guide us so we do not get outside His will and place ourselves in the way of temptation. We are essentially praying, "Lord, don't let me be tempted above my capacity to resist. Lord, give me common sense. Help me to see the pitfalls. Help me to see the traps. Help me to see the areas where I am vulnerable and avoid them!" When we pray like this, God will be faithful to help us escape temptation.

In this devotion called "Excess Baggage,"[7] Greg goes on to further explain how not only must we rid our lives of sin, but of anything that hinders us spiritually.

> "Let us lay aside every weight, and the sin which so easily ensnares us, and let us run with endurance the race that is set before us" (Hebrews 12:1).
>
> I am the kind of person who likes to drag a lot of stuff with me when I travel. I have been traveling for many years, yet I still overpack. I want to bring everything I own. But excess baggage makes traveling complicated.
>
> In the same way, when you are running the race of life, you need to run light. Sometimes we drag along lots of excess weight. The Bible says to strip off every weight that slows us down, especially sin that hinders our progress.
>
> Sin is sin, and there are certain things that are non-negotiable to which we must hold fast. There might be a weight in your life that may not necessarily be a weight in someone else's life. There may be something you are doing that is impeding your spiritual progress which doesn't have an effect in someone else's life.
>
> Periodically, I need to take stock of my life as a Christian and look at the things I am doing with my time. I need to ask myself the question, "Is it a wing or a weight? Is it speeding me on my way spiritually, or is it slowing me down? Is it increasing my spiritual appetite, or is it dulling it?"
>
> How often do we do things that aren't really important, but seem important at the time? We need to ask if we need to do those things. Are they slowing us down? We have to lay aside the weight that hinders our progress.

Be Yourself

The world is always trying to press us into its mold. The world points its finger saying, "You have to be young, you have to be thin, you have to be rich, and you have to be perfect to be worthy." Remember God's love for you is absolutely steadfast, unlike human love. He doesn't give or take away His love based on our appearance or performance. The Word says that you don't have to be any of those things. Trust God and be yourself. God wants you to be yourself and to make yourself available to Him so He can work in and through you, for your good and for His glory.

- **SEE** the stronghold as sin.
- **GIVE** the sin to God in confession.
- **FORGIVE** as Christ has forgiven you.
- **FORGET** the lies of Satan and the world telling you to overeat, starve or vomit.

BE SET FREE by God's truth and His love for you, enabling you to be yourself. We need to make a conscious decision in order to change. Our aim is to develop godly habits that result in godly living.

10. Read 1 John 3:1: "Behold what manner of love the Father has bestowed on us, that we should be called children of God! Therefore the world does not know us, because it did not know Him."

    How can you apply your desire to be obedient in the area of eating habits?

    _____

    _____

11. Which of the following influence your choices and actions?
    (Circle those that apply.)

    - Fear
    - Anxiety
    - Need to control
    - Insecurities
    - Hurt
    - Guilt
    - Pride
    - Resentment
    - Bitterness
    - Doubt
    - Negative thoughts
    - Defensiveness

12. What happens when these thoughts influence our choices? What scriptures could you use to replace these thoughts?

    _____

    _____

    _____

    _____

13. Does food control you, or do you control food?

    _____

    _____

14. Are overeating, starving yourself, or making yourself vomit part of God's plan for you in the area of self-control?

15. If you are ready to change, write out how you plan to apply self-control and change your eating habits in order to change your life.

16. What people or activities make you feel the need to consume large amounts of food, or no food at all, to feel happy?

17. Look up 1 Peter 4:2 on page 304 and fill in the blanks below.

    "That he no longer should live the rest of his time in the flesh for the lusts of men, but for the _____ _____ _____."

18. In the past, I learned that I needed to be thin in order to be happy through the following people and things:

19. I have decided to make my happiness and acceptance come from the truth of God's Word. I plan to do that in the following ways:

20. Strongholds are hard to break. Sometimes it's a second-by-second choice. Is there one person in your life that you can talk to and work with in order to break this stronghold? Name the person and make plans to tell them this week.

Week 6: Day 5

Prayer: Bow your heart before the Lord in prayer prior to completing today's Bible study. Ask Him to shine His light into the darkness so you can **SEE**, **GIVE**, **FORGIVE**, **FORGET** and **BE SET FREE**.

Happiness Should Not Be Based on the Opinions of Others

Some of the values you hold right now may be those of your culture. Be aware of how much these cultural expectations may be influencing and defining your expectations for personal happiness. Your personal happiness should not be based on the opinions of others. When your heart is surrendered to God, you will experience true joy.

1. Psalm 139:14 says: "I will praise You, for I am fearfully and wonderfully made; marvelous are Your works, and that my soul knows very well."

   Take time this week to meditate on Psalm 139:14 and write it down.

2. Read Proverbs 14:30 and Galatians 5:26:

   "A sound heart is life to the body, but envy is rottenness to the bones" (Proverbs 14:30).

   "Let us not become conceited, provoking one another, envying one another" (Galatians 5:26)

   Do you envy other women? Explain.

   _____
   _____
   _____

3. Summarize in one sentence why you have believed it is most important to be thin.

   _____
   _____

What is True Beauty?

We've all heard the expression, "You need to get a life." Spiritual growth happens when you determine that being useful to God is more important than being noticed by people. Physical appearances can tempt you to live for the wrong reasons. We are all uniquely made: some naturally thin, some with a medium or large frame, some short, others very tall. Size doesn't determine worth or beauty.

When you allow a stronghold to keep you down, it may keep you from reaching out. Let every part of your life be in Christ: Anchor yourself to the great "I AM" and you will be free to become who God intended you to be: whole, true and at peace.

"And the people said to Joshua, 'The Lord our God we will serve, and His voice we will obey'" (Joshua 24:24).

4. Read 2 Corinthians 4:16-18: "Therefore we do not lose heart. Even though our outward man is perishing, yet the inward man is being renewed day by day. For our light affliction, which is but for a moment, is working for us a far more exceeding and eternal weight of glory, while we do not look at the things which are seen, but at the things which are not seen. For the things which are seen are temporary, but the things which are not seen are eternal."

   Can you accept that the body is perishing? Write down the evidence of how you see this happening.

5. In what way is your spirit being renewed day by day?

6. What's more important to you: the outward or the inward? Explain.

7. Where will you choose to turn when there are disappointments or heartaches? Will you choose the things which are seen or unseen? Temporary or eternal? Flesh or Spirit? God's will or your will? What will you choose?

8. Memorize scripture that brings comfort when you feel out of control with overeating or starving yourself. Remember this week's memory verse, as well! Write out these scriptures and hide them in your heart as a tool for strength.

The Value of Relationships

Close relationships are necessary and vital part of our lives. If someone we love is having a difficult time, if they're stressed or have too many pressures, we'd most likely ask, "What can I do for you?" Jesus does the same for us, as James MacDonald explains in his devotional "Relationship Building."[8]

> One of the most touching stories in all the Bible is the exchange between Jesus and the man who has come to be known as Blind Bartimaeus. It's "classic Jesus": "So Jesus answered and said to him, 'What do you want Me to do for you?'" (Mark 10:51). As the Lord makes His way through the city of Jericho, a blind beggar named Bartimaeus hears that He is within walking distance. The commotion of the crowd grows louder and louder as they pass by him. It's Jesus! And before the opportunity slips through his fingers, the blind man cries out, "Jesus, Son of David, have mercy on me!"
>
> His cries are barely audible above the clamor of the multitude. Then someone takes notice of him, then another person and another. He keeps

calling out into the black void before him. "Jesus, Son of David, have mercy on me!" Before long the crowd starts telling him to be quiet, that Jesus is too busy to bother with him.

But then Jesus does what nobody expects: He stops in His tracks and asks for blind Bartimaeus to be brought to Him. Face to face, Jesus asks him, "What do you want Me to do for you?"

At first, the question seems somewhat foolish. "Isn't it obvious? Here I am, blind and calling out to you! Do you think healing me might have something to do with it?" But as always, there's a deeper issue attached to Jesus' question. The reason He asked this question was to give Bartimaeus the opportunity to confess and state his request. "That I may receive my sight," says Bartimaeus.

More than anything else, Jesus wants to build a relationship with us. A big part of that is when we express and confess the desires of our heart to Him. Regardless of how obvious our requests may be, He wants us to share them with Him.

9. Discuss what you would say if Jesus asked you what you want Him to do for you. Share your answer and the reason why you would make this request.

10. Look up Mark 10:46–52 on page 304. What impresses you about verses 49–50? What does blind Bartimaeus do once he is healed? What does this passage say to you about Jesus' compassion for people?

11. Decide to pray for those who long to be healed. Ask God to touch those who are in physical and spiritual need.

Stories of Real People and a Real Savior

Shackles of Anger and Bulimia

A Brand New Woman

I can't express the hatred and anger I held in a dark hole in my heart toward my brothers. I have four older brothers; three out of the four abused me sexually. It started when I was quite young, five or six years old. My oldest brother is 10 years older than I am. He would take me into the back bathroom when my parents were gone and pay me pennies to do things to him and allow him to do things to me. I knew it was wrong, but I truly trusted him, especially because he said it was okay. Small incidents (if any sexual abuse is small) went on with my second brother.

The youngest of my brothers forced intercourse on me. I remember fearing that I was pregnant by him when I was only in the fifth or sixth grade. I would do hurtful things to my body to make sure the baby wouldn't survive, just in case I was pregnant. But for some reason I still trusted my brother; I knew it was wrong, yet I thought it was normal or okay all at the same time.

I had to face my brothers every day. Even after they moved out, we would still have many family get-togethers. In order to survive, I tucked all my hatred, anger and fear down deep in my heart. I never dealt with these feelings, but I knew they were there because of the way I treated my husband. I would lash out in anger at him for no reason. I thought sex was dirty and only for the pleasure of the man. My husband didn't understand why I hated sex and hated being intimate with him. I didn't know about God's perfect plan for intimacy in marriage. Another way this abuse affected my adult life was through an eating disorder. I am bulimic, which I thought was just a sickness like alcoholism. I felt this was the only area of my life that I could control. I would eat nothing or eat a lot and then throw it up, feeling like I was in control.

A few years after I was married, my husband received Christ. A few months later, I too received Christ. Our relationship did a complete U-turn, but I knew that the deep dark holes in my heart were still there. Years passed, and I thought, "This is me," that the anger toward my husband and children was there to stay.

I started the *Healed and Set Free Bible Study* for my eating disorder. I also thought I might get something out of it with regard to my brothers' abuse. A lot of emotional issues started coming out as I began the study. Through this study, I found out that I wasn't in control of my eating, instead my eating was in control of me. I also found out that being bulimic is giving in to the flesh, and that I was sinning every time I threw up.

The deep dark holes in my heart were exposing themselves. I had told myself that I would never forgive my brothers for what they had done to me. For all I knew, they had long forgotten about any of it, but I was still angry, still remembering, still carrying around all the baggage.

One day during the study, I shared my memory of the pennies and how much it had affected me, when another woman in the study said she had the same experience. All my emotions came flooding back; I was crying uncontrollably. Tammy Brown stopped the study, and we prayed and prayed as I gave the hurt and fear over to Christ, asking for help and strength to be set free from my past hurts. I was finding out that I couldn't do it without God's help.

I think the turning point for me was when one of the women in the *Healed and Set Free* Bible study shared what God had shown her—that sin is sin is sin. I knew what my brothers did wasn't okay, that it was sin. I also learned I was sinning just as much as my brothers did by not forgiving them when God wanted me to forgive them. I was sinning by being bulimic. I now know that I can control this through prayer and asking God daily to kill my flesh.

After completing the Bible study, I prayed in my heart for forgiveness toward my brothers. I knew God was healing my heart, because my hatred turned into compassion. God put their lives and their families' lives on my heart. I prayed for their salvation and that I would be able to share God's Word with them. I wanted to show them how God had changed my life and my heart.

Just three weeks after I finished *Healed and Set Free*, my brother received Christ and God completely restored our relationship. If I had been asked five years ago if I would ever have compassion on my brothers, I would have said, "NEVER!" But through God's Word and being in prayer with Him, He has allowed me to leave all my pain at the foot of the cross and to use my experiences to minister to others.

My marriage and relationship with my family isn't perfect, but I continue to seek God for the strength to love my husband and children the way He desires. God has changed my life and my heart, and I have been healed and set free.

A Fresh Start

It's easy to get discouraged as we fall, get up, fall and get up again. But I am encouraged by the words of Greg Laurie in his devotional, "A Fresh Start."[9]

> A man was reading the newspaper and was shocked to find his name listed in the obituaries. He called the newspaper, outraged that they had made such a mistake. "This is terrible," he screamed, "How could you do this to me?" He stormed down to their office, screaming and yelling, and demanded to see the editor. After some time the editor grew frustrated and said, "Look, buddy! Cheer up. I'll put your name in the birth column tomorrow and you can have a fresh start."
>
> You may laugh at that story, but wouldn't it be great to start over again? In reality, as a Christian you can have a fresh start. There are opportunities ahead of you, and you decide which course you are going to take.
>
> Jeremiah 6:16 says, "Thus says the Lord: 'Stand in the ways and see, and ask for the old paths, where the good way is, and walk in it; then you will find rest for your souls…'" You decide which path you are going to walk in. You decide what your priorities will be and what direction you will take. Those are decisions each of us will make each day. Every day is a new day, choose the good way and walk in it. Only there will you find peace.

Caught Up in God's Love

We are Christians caught up in the love of God that surrounds us every day. As we serve Him in the area of our calling and enjoy the gifts of life, there is neither room nor time for living destructively. Every part of our lives: our style, direction, eating, thinking, let it all be in Christ.

"He has shown you, O man, what is good; and what does the Lord require of you but to do justly, to love mercy, and to walk humbly with your God" (Micah 6:8).

12. Write down three things that you struggle with concerning your eating habits.

   1. _____

   2. _____

   3. _____

Love

"If I can speak eloquently and sing like an angel, but don't love others, I sound like a sounding brass or prolonged clanging noise. If I'm very bright and considered brilliant, and can answer all of the hardest Bible questions or understand cutting-edge computer systems, but don't love others, I am nothing. What is love?"[10]

- Love will stand in line and wait its turn.
- Love is friendly and looks for the good in others.
- Love doesn't always demand its own way.
- Love doesn't envy another's better fortune.
- Love is polite, even when the other person is rude.
- Love doesn't get angry over the small things.
- Love doesn't remember reasons to hold a grudge.
- Love doesn't delight when someone else fails, but delights in the truth.
- Love always protects others, especially those who are made fun of or teased.
- Love always believes the best about others.
- Love hopes all things and endures all things.

13. Read 1 Peter 5:6-7: "Therefore humble yourselves under the mighty hand of God, that He may exalt you in due time, casting all your care upon Him, for He cares for you."

    Have you cast the cares of your heart upon the God who loves you?

14. Name what you want to change about your eating habits. On a daily basis, ask God to help you to break any strongholds in your life.

15. Do you think it is God's business how you eat? Explain.

16. Read 2 Peter 1:9: "For he who lacks these things is shortsighted, even to blindness, and has forgotten that he was cleansed from his old sins."

    What have you been cleansed from?

From Bondage to Freedom

Bring your life under the submission of Christ. Ask God to show you the lies about yourself in which you have been programmed over the years, and upon which you are basing your identity. Choose to give these over to God and replace them with His truth. God does answer prayers, not always in the way we envision the answer, but according to His will.

17. Read Hebrews 12:11-12: "Now no chastening seems to be joyful for the present, but painful; nevertheless, afterward it yields the peaceable fruit of righteousness to those who have been trained by it. Therefore strengthen the hands which hang down, and the feeble knees."

    Say the following prayer out loud, sending your petition to Him:

    Dear God,

    Thank you for loving me unconditionally. Thank you for being intimately involved
    with every aspect of my life. Thank you for wanting to heal me. As I continue this journey of self-control, please give me insight and understanding concerning my eating disorder, or my wrong thinking about food and my body. Bring your Word to my mind to give me the strength, courage and power to change. Be with me in a special way, as I desire to be healed and set free from this idol in my life.

    Signed: _____

    Date: _____

This Week's Memory Verse

"Stand fast therefore in the liberty by which Christ has made us free, and do not be entangled again with a yoke of bondage" (Galatians 5:1).

You may need to reread this chapter, meditating on the truth of God's Word to free you from the stronghold of your eating habits. Make a conscious decision to change. Our aim is to develop godly habits that will result in godly living.

"Behold what manner of love the Father has bestowed on us, that we should be called children of God! Therefore the world does not know us, because it did not know Him" (1 John 3:1).

- **SEE** the stronghold in your life.
- **GIVE** it over to God, ask for His help and His strength to change.
- **FORGIVE** as Christ has forgiven you.
- **FORGET** the lies you have believed.
- **BE SET FREE** by God's truth as you stand firm in your new choices.

1. What have you learned about self-control?

2. What have you learned about the strongholds pertaining to bulimia, anorexia or compulsive eating?

3. What encouraged you about God's plans for eating to live, not living to eat?

4. What do you need to do with your thoughts in order to be obedient to Christ with your eating habits?

5. Does God look at the outward appearance or the inward heart?

6. What challenged you about this chapter?

7. In what specific ways will you open your heart to let the Healer set you free from the bondage in your life?

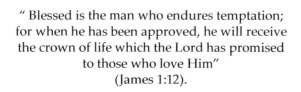

" Blessed is the man who endures temptation;
for when he has been approved, he will receive
the crown of life which the Lord has promised
to those who love Him"
(James 1:12).

Stories of Real People and a Real Savior

God Brought Me Out of the Fog
By Susan, Idaho

I was born with a blood disorder and an immune dysfunction that caused me to have severe medical problems all my life. I have struggled since childhood with feelings of inadequacy: I felt I wasn't pretty enough, not slim enough, not doing things correctly or well enough, not being a good enough friend, etc. To compensate for these feelings, beginning in my early teens, I became the "go to" person for everyone and everything. I thought I had to be a woman who could work full time, manage the company, handle the children and husband, run the household, and still be ready to do anything else. I could always be counted on to do a good job no matter what it was, but I ended up controlling all situations (emotional, physical, material) for family, friends, work, etc. What an exhausting way to live! I wondered if people liked me for me, or if they were just pretending to like me so I'd continue doing everything for them.

In 2001, I suffered the murders of my father and my daughter. I immediately tried to make sure my mom, who witnessed the murders, and the rest of my four children were all handling things. I never dealt with my own feelings or grief. A few years later, my husband was diagnosed with several neurological conditions, two of which are terminal. Again, I jumped into taking him to doctors, clinics, etc., while still working, and not dealing with these life changes. In the midst of all this, I struggled with the feeling that I was not where I was supposed to be or doing what I was supposed to be doing, but I had no clue how to change it.

In the summer of 2005, my husband started taking interest in another woman. His doctors had told us this would probably happen due to behavioral and personality changes caused by his condition. But I was in "in sickness and in health," and he convinced me he wasn't interested in anyone else, he just wanted to move out of state before he got too much worse so he could enjoy what years he had left.

We came to look for a home in Idaho Falls, and I knew as soon as I put my feet on the ground that this is where God wanted me. We moved into our house in June 2006. In the first week, my husband's phone calls to and from his "friend" were 30 per day; she was his first call each morning and his last call every night. We filed for divorce in November. He purchased a house a mile down the road from me and moved his "friend" in.

With all these issues and my difficult health situation, I eventually developed chronic fatigue and Epstein Barr. My white and red blood cells were never anywhere near the normal ranges. My doctor advised me to change my lifestyle and go to therapy or I would probably die before I was 50! Not having dealt with these issues before—my health, my divorce, grief, the emotions—I spent the next few years in a fog.

Fortunately, I met several outstanding people in those years, and I got back to my relationship with the Lord! Last summer, I attended my first Healed and Set Free class, and I was blessed to have Vicki McKinney as my facilitator. Boy, I didn't realize how much work was ahead! I had to pray consistently for weeks to even begin giving up control of everything. I stuck to seeing what was in my heart and forgiving myself and others. Then I could give it to God and forget it! Learning to pray, listen to God, and use the tools made such a profound difference that I signed up again! I wanted to be sure I was on the right track. I felt freed by the knowledge that God loves me. Yes, just the way I am. I don't have to be the best or the one in control. Once I really understood this concept, the peace and acceptance were absolute!

Now I use the Healed and Set Free tools almost daily as memories or new situations come up. As soon as something creeps in, I immediately banish Satan and the thoughts and turn to God. I used to wish for peace in my soul, never knowing how to get it. But now I have peace in my relationship with God, and I can just enjoy being a mom and grandma. And I thank Tammy Brown for sharing her story and developing this phenomenal tool called Healed and Set Free!

Tools to Become Healed and Set Free

To equip yourself in God's truth, look over the tools and verses that will be introduced in the coming weeks. Thinking about the past won't change it, but you can change your future by being set free from your past.

TOOL #1 - SEE: I must SEE the truth about what is in my heart so I am not defiled.

Definition: To defile means to make filthy or dirty; to pollute.

Bible Verse: "Looking carefully lest anyone fall short of the grace of God; lest any root of bitterness springing up cause trouble, and by this many become defiled" (Hebrews 12:15).

TOOL #2 - GIVE: I must GIVE my sin to God through repentance, knowing that Christ is waiting to take it. I must be sorry enough to change, and choose to go God's way over my own.

Definition: To repent means to feel such sorrow for sin or fault as to be disposed to change one's life for the better; be penitent.

Bible Verse: "For godly sorrow produces repentance leading to salvation, not to be regretted; but the sorrow of the world produces death" (2 Corinthians 7:10).

TOOL #3 - FORGIVE: I must FORGIVE as I am forgiven by Christ: Forgiving those who hurt, bruised, wronged, rejected, betrayed or harmed me, whether unintentionally or deliberately. I must ask God to forgive me for holding on to unforgiveness and know that He will.

Definition: To forgive means to stop feeling angry or resentful toward someone for an offense, flaw or mistake.

Bible Verse: "...Bearing with one another, and forgiving one another, if anyone has a complaint against another; even as Christ forgave you, so you also must do" (Colossians 3:13).

TOOL #4 - FORGET: I must FORGET by no longer dwelling on the hurt or the painful reminders, such as: phrases, smells, places, songs and comments. Instead, I am putting my mind on the higher calling that Christ has for me.

Definition: To forget means to choose not to remember or notice, "forgive and forget".

Bible Verse: "Brethren, I do not count myself to have apprehended; but one thing I do, forgetting those things which are behind and reaching forward to those things which are ahead" (Philippians 3:13).

Be Healed and Set Free: Christ will heal me from my past, showing me the truth, so I can become a cleansed vessel, healed and set free.

Definition: To set free means to make free; set at liberty; release from bondage, imprisonment, or restraint.

Definition: To heal means to make whole and healthy; to cure; to remedy or repair.

Bible Verse: "And you shall know the truth, and the truth shall make you free" (John 8:32).

Chapter 7

Remembering to Forget

This Week's Focus

This week we will be learning **Tool #4 - FORGET** . Once we've seen the truth, given it to God and forgiven those involved, then we are truly free to move on and forget those things which are behind us.

Tool #4 - FORGET: I must FORGET by no longer dwelling on the hurt or the painful reminders such as: phrases, smells, places, songs and comments. Instead, I am putting my mind on the higher calling that Christ has for me.

Definition: To forget means to cease remembering or noticing.

Bible Verse: "Brethren, I do not count myself to have apprehended; but one thing I do, forgetting those things which are behind and reaching forward to those things which are ahead" (Philippians 3: 13).

Prayer: Ask God to help you to move forward by letting go of past grudges or personal failure, and apply the fourth tool to your life from Philippians 3:13-14.

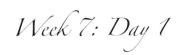

Prayer: Bow your heart in prayer before the Lord prior to completing today's Bible study. Ask God to show you how to "remember to forget" the suffering and trials of the past.

The past teaches us about God, life and ourselves. But many times we have a hard time having the right perspective when looking at the past. We focus on the heartache and pain instead of focusing on the lessons we have learned and the disguised blessings we received through the trial.

To forget means to stop dwelling on the past or letting it rule and cripple our lives. It means to move forward from the past into the new life that God has for us. In other words: remember to forget. My own experience with forgetting the past led me to Philippians 3:13: "Brethren, I do not count myself to have apprehended; but one thing I do, forgetting those things which are behind and reaching forward to those things which are ahead." After giving my sin of selfishness, pride and unforgiveness to Christ, I began moving ahead, putting my focus on Jesus and not on the things behind me.

This is what being set free is all about: you SEE, GIVE, FORGIVE and FORGET! There may be things in your past that you are ashamed of or that haunt you—memories or sins—but remember, if you have handed them over to God in confession and faith, He has put them away and forgotten them "as far as the east is from the west" (Psalm 103:12).

Forgetting in the Present Tense

Note that the word "forget" is in the present tense. Forgetting is not an act that's done once and for all. The apostle Paul, the author of Philippians, didn't want his past mistakes or hurts to keep him from moving on, and neither should we. Like Paul, we must keep forgetting the things that have hurt us or held us back.

Again and again, I have told myself, "No, Tam, that is in the past. That is over, it's no longer real; don't dwell on it or let it hold you back. Forget the things that keep you from moving forward in your faith and spiritual growth." Now I look to the past only to remember God's role in solving the problems and pains of yesterday. I remember His gracious provision, His presence, His faithfulness, His compassion and His healing.

Looking to the past for lessons God has taught us will help us to remember the importance of getting real with Him. We must SEE, GIVE, FORGIVE and FORGET the pain and resentment, then be set free.

God wants us to move on from the suffering of the past. He doesn't want the circumstances and situations of life to weigh us down. With any suffering you've experienced, whether two minutes or twenty years ago, whether it resulted from someone's passing comment or an intentional sin against you, you can move on and be SET FREE!

Tools to Become Set Free

In this chapter, we will continue to use **Tool #1 - SEE, Tool #2 - GIVE** and **Tool #3 - FORGIVE**, as well as introducing **Tool #4 - FORGET**.

These tools will help you to become set free. Each tool is defined as the time comes. It is crucial to memorize these powerful tools and review them regularly in order to apply them to your daily life.

#1 - SEE: I must SEE the truth about what is in my heart so I am not defiled.

#2 - GIVE: I must GIVE my sin to God through repentance, knowing that Christ is waiting to take it. I must be sorry enough to change, and choose to go God's way over my own.

#3 - FORGIVE: I must FORGIVE as I am forgiven by Christ: Forgiving those who hurt, bruised, wronged, rejected, betrayed or harmed me, whether unintentionally or deliberately. I must ask God to forgive me for holding on to unforgiveness and know that He will.

#4 - FORGET: I must FORGET by no longer dwelling on the hurt or the painful reminders such as: phrases, smells, places, songs and comments. Instead, I am putting my mind on the higher calling that Christ has for me.

Be Healed and Set Free: Christ will heal me from my past, showing me the truth, so I can become a cleansed vessel, healed and set free.

This Week's Focus

Prayer: Ask God to help you to move forward by letting go of past grudges or personal failure, and apply the fourth tool to your life from Philippians 3:13-14.

By Memory: My challenge to you is to be able to recite the tool, definition and Bible verse from this chapter without looking. I know that by hiding these words of wisdom in your heart you are providing yourself with tools to truly be healed and set free. May we rise up to be women of the Word.

Tool #4 - FORGET: I must FORGET by no longer dwelling on the hurt or the painful reminders such as: phrases, smells, places, songs and comments. Instead, I am putting my mind on the higher calling that Christ has for me.

Definition: To forget means to cease remembering or noticing.

Bible Verse: "Brethren, I do not count myself to have apprehended; but one thing I do, forgetting those things which are behind and reaching forward to those things which are ahead" (Philippians 3: 13).

"And you shall know the truth, and the truth shall make you free" (John 8:32).

God's Remedy Is the Same

We live in a fallen world and innocent people suffer when others sin. What we must remember is that if we are harboring resentment, bitterness or hatred toward those that hurt us, we are no different than the ones who hurt us.

1. Write down the definition of the word "remedy" from page 301.

2. Read Philippians 3:13-14: "Brethren, I do not count myself to have apprehended; but one thing I do, forgetting those things which are behind and reaching forward to those things which are ahead, I press toward the goal for the prize of the upward call of God in Christ Jesus."

   Does God want you to mull over the past according to Philippians 3:13-14?

3. According to Philippians 3 above, what are we to press toward?

4. Read Titus 3:3: "For we ourselves were also once foolish, disobedient, deceived, serving various lusts and pleasures, living in malice and envy, hateful and hating one another."

   If hate and envy consume a person, what's happening to their life according to Titus 3:3?

5. Read Philippians 4:8: "Finally, brethren, whatever things are true, whatever things are noble, whatever things are just, whatever things are pure, whatever things are lovely, whatever things are of good report, if there is any virtue and if there is anything praiseworthy; meditate on these things."

   What are we to meditate on as we look toward Christ?

6. Read 2 Timothy 1:7: "For God has not given us a spirit of fear, but of power and of love and of a sound mind."

   What has God not given us?

Stories of Real People and a Real Savior

The Smell of Terror and Distress

Cheryl, Idaho

For the first ten years of my marriage, I changed the sheets on our bed almost every day. The smell of even slightly dirty sheets made me feel irritable and upset. I couldn't sleep unless the sheets were fresh and clean. I carried this behavior into the rest of my house as well. My husband felt like I was compulsive about clean sheets. I knew he was right, but I couldn't understand why I was so compulsive, and I certainly didn't know how to change my behavior.

As a child, I couldn't walk past my abusive father's bedroom without breathing in the horrible smell of body odor. My father rarely bathed, and his bed sheets were a smelly reflection of his personal behaviors. Sometimes the smell would take over the entire house, and there were times when I just couldn't breathe. I was surrounded by violence and what I called "the smell of violence."

During the course of my *Healed and Set Free* Bible study, I learned that the slightest smell of uncleanness reminded me of my abusive father, and was robbing me of my peace. If my home wasn't clean (including the smell), I felt unsafe and insecure. Bad smells triggered feelings of terror and distress that I had felt while living with my father. As a result, I would clean my house with strong cleaners and burn candles to keep the feelings and "smell" of terror at bay. The problem was that this was Satan's way of keeping me in the chains of fear!

I prayed a great deal, asking Jesus to help me let go of the feelings associated with smells. And for the first time in my life, I started to understand that although my abusive dad was my earthly dad, God was the Father of my home, and I didn't have to fear my earthly father any longer.

Praying and asking Jesus to heal me really helped me get past the idea that everything had to "come up smelling like roses" in my home. I started putting some new behaviors into practice: Instead of washing the sheets daily, I only washed them once a week.

It was hard at first, I would crawl into bed with my husband and imagine the smell was there just because I knew the sheets weren't fresh. Sometimes I concentrated on my husband's yummy smelling cologne to distract me; sometimes I would just lie there praying for Jesus to calm my mind and help me go to sleep without fear. After a while, I could crawl into bed without thinking about the sheets!

I still love to burn candles and have a clean home, but not because I'm wrapped up in the fear of that smell, but just because I love to burn candles and have a clean home—simple as that. I learned that Jesus, my Healer, wanted to release me from my past and He has! Thank You, Jesus, for giving me freedom from the oppressiveness of smells through Your healing power!

> Thinking about the past will never change the past.
> But you can change your future and be set free from your past.

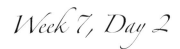

Prayer: Bow your heart before the Lord in prayer prior to completing today's Bible Study. Ask Him to give you insight into your perspective.

Changing Your Outlook

Perspective is all about how we choose to see things. Changing our perspective calls for a willingness to SEE things differently.

1. Read Psalm 84:11: "For the Lord God is a sun and shield; the Lord will give grace and glory; no good thing will He withhold from those who walk uprightly."

   Write down four blessings that you see in your life.

   1.
   2.
   3.
   4.

Forgiveness in Action

2. Bow your heart before the Lord in prayer. Ask God to help you begin to forget. If you have forgiven those who hurt you, put this forgiveness into action. Write down the reasons why you have chosen to forgive those who hurt you.

Tammy's Reflections

He Stood There Glaring

Several years ago, we took a trip to our hometown. We met our family at the fair to hang out, go on rides and eat fair food. Then out of the blue I saw him: the brother of the guy who raped me. My heart started pounding as he walked closer. All I could do was focus on my little girl's smile and pretend he wasn't there, but when I looked up, he was standing right next to me!

I could tell by the look on his face that he had already come to his own conclusions about me. I thought to myself, "If only you knew the real story, you wouldn't be looking at me that way." I couldn't believe it! I was in the process of writing the *Healed and Set Free Bible Study*, and leading two separate classes through the study, when BAM! An attack from the enemy! He was trying a new angle to drag me back into the shame and anger from my past.

Flashbacks

I had given everything to God and had forgiven the guy who raped me, but in that moment I started to hold a grudge against his brother. Flashbacks of that year of terror came flooding back, and I became withdrawn for about ten minutes. It was obvious that I needed to deal with my bad feelings right then and there. By faith, I chose to GIVE my feelings to God. I didn't let the enemy get ahold of me, and I wasn't going to let the past wreck my day. I had to get real with God right there at the state fair. I used the four steps of SEE, GIVE, FORGIVE and FORGET, and I was SET FREE!

Healed and Set Free

I had to SEE my own sin of resentment toward the man who was judging me. I had to GIVE it over, in the silence of my mind, in repentance to Christ. I had to FORGIVE him for his judgmental attitude against me. I had to FORGET about his hurtful glare, and look instead toward Christ, who SET ME FREE. I went on to enjoy my day with a peaceful mind.

We simply have to be willing to make the choice to set ourselves aside and do what God desires in our lives; to let go and let God move in those moments when our past comes to haunt us.

How to Clear Your Conscience

Greg Laurie made a great analogy in his devotion titled "How to Clear Your Conscience."[1] He points to 1 Timothy 1:19: "Cling to your faith in Christ, and keep your conscience clear. For some people have deliberately violated their consciences; as a result, their faith has been shipwrecked." He says:

> Imagine for a moment there is a bad smell in your house. As you wander around trying to find the source of it, it gets stronger and stronger. Then you open your closet door, and there it is: a dead rat you have caught in a trap. What should you do to get rid of the smell? You get rid of the rat. It's that simple. When the rat is gone, the smell goes with it.
>
> As we walk through life, our conscience can trouble us and guilt can overwhelm us. We don't get rid of the guilt by ignoring it, we must get

to the source. What is your conscience saying? What is the guilt pointing to? It is pointing to sin. The way to get rid of guilt is to get rid of what produced it, which is sin. So confess your sin. Hebrews 10:22 says, "Let us go right into the presence of God with sincere hearts fully trusting Him. For our guilty consciences have been sprinkled with Christ's blood to make us clean, and our bodies have been washed with pure water."

We might come up with new terms for our sin, "a mistake" or "a little shortcoming," but God still calls it sin. So why don't we call it the same thing? We are reminded in 1 John 1:9, "If we confess our sins to Him, He is faithful and just to forgive us our sins and to cleanse us from all unrighteousness." Only Jesus Christ can forgive sin and recalibrate the conscience. He died on Calvary's cross and He shed His blood for you. So face your sin. Call it what it is and stop making excuses for it.

3. What are we enabling Satan to do when we focus on our past?

4. Read Proverbs 5:21-22, John 8:34 and Ephesians 4:29-30:

- "For the ways of man are before the eyes of the Lord, and He ponders all his paths. His own iniquities entrap the wicked man, and he is caught in the cords of his sin" (Proverbs 5:21-22).

- "Jesus answered them, 'Most assuredly, I say to you, whoever commits sin is a slave of sin'" (John 8:34).

- "Let no corrupt word proceed out of your mouth, but what is good for necessary edification, that it may impart grace to the hearers. And do not grieve the Holy Spirit of God, by whom you were sealed for the day of redemption" (Ephesians 4:29-30).

What happens when we dwell on negative thoughts from our past?

5. What scriptures could you memorize to help you "remember to forget" if bad thoughts or emotions come in?

6. Read Romans 5:5: "Now hope does not disappoint, because the love of God has been poured out in our hearts by the Holy Spirit who was given to us."

Who gives you the love you need to love others?

Right Thinking Leads to Joyful Living

Some things just have to be nailed to the cross and given to Christ once and for all. Don't examine the list anymore. Jesus wants to do a new work in your life, and you need to let Him. It's time to get on with your life and tackle the opportunities and challenges that lie ahead. Remember to forget what lies behind and look ahead, walking forward in the wisdom and power of God.

Stories of Real People and a Real Savior

Open Wounds

Cei Cee

In the shadows of my hidden pain poured teardrops from my heart,
Flowing over open wounds that were ripping me apart.
I couldn't ever seem to shake the captivity of my past.
I stood within the darkened shadows from the turmoil that they'd cast.

So I took my heart to Jesus, I laid it at His throne.
I knew He was my only hope for it wasn't healing on its own.
Lord, my heart's been wounded many times, some scars have eased the pain,
But it's these open wounds that seem to cause the turmoil once again.

I can sense the roots of bitterness spreading throughout my life.
Anger is consuming me causing resentment, hurt and strife.
I don't want my life to be this way, I need healing so I can live.
God tenderly held me close to Him and said, "Child, you must forgive."

I found my tears came pouring forth, "Lord, that's so hard to do."
He handed me back my heart and said, "And here's my gift to you:
Forgiveness will heal the very wounds that plague your inner soul.
You'll find a life worth living, your heart will then be whole."

I knew He was right as He took my sin and hurled it far from me.
My thoughts were cleansed; I was healed with a peace that set me free.
I also knew down deep inside I'd been given a brand new start,
For as a reminder, with His own blood, He autographed my heart.

I Learned to Forgive

A Letter from Kim

Working through my issues, being able to GIVE them to Jesus, and being free from my past hurts has given me great peace. Knowing that our loving God desires us to cleanse our hearts daily so the enemy doesn't creep back in has been another great lesson.

It has been a life-changing experience, knowing that people will disappoint us and that we need to forgive daily, and daily seek His forgiveness for ourselves. The application of His mighty Word has been a blessing to me and many others.

> We don't have to lose our bearings in the fog of human opinion.
> That is why we need to read through the Bible
> verse by verse, chapter by chapter.

Week 7, Day 3

Prayer: Bow your heart before the Lord in prayer prior to completing today's Bible study. Ask Christ to show you what you have been set free from.

It's Time to Forget

Once you get real with God, letting Him bring peace to your heart, the emotions connected to your pain are no longer bitter but full of forgiveness and compassion. Forgiving and taking on the heart and attitude of our Lord and Savior Jesus Christ allows us to fall back into His strong arms of grace. FORGET and enjoy the abundant life He intended His children to live.

- "For I have satiated the weary soul, and I have replenished every sorrowful soul" (Jeremiah 31:25).
- "He heals the brokenhearted and binds up their wounds" (Psalm 147:3).

Forget the Past

The first time I read Philippians 3:13-14, I realized God was giving me permission to move from the past toward Christ Jesus. This was the first scripture I memorized in my walk with Jesus. Without a doubt, memorizing scriptures is the most important part of hiding His Word in our hearts. Greg Laurie offers God's truth from this verse in his devotional, "Forget the Past."[2]

> Everyone who has run a race knows that you break your stride by looking over your shoulder to see how your opponents are doing. Many races have been lost when the leader looks back. When you see that finish line, you are supposed to give it everything you have, because sometimes it is mere inches that separate one runner from another. You must stay focused. This is the idea behind Paul's statement in Philippians 3:13: "Brethren, I do not count myself to have apprehended; but one thing I do, forgetting those things which are behind and reaching forward to those things which are ahead." Paul was saying, "Look ahead! Don't look behind you."
>
> When God says, "I am He who blots out your transgressions for My own sake; and I will not remember your sins" (Isaiah 43:25), He is not predicting a lapse in His memory. He's saying, "I am not going to hold your sin against you, because my Son has paid for it at the cross." Therefore, we need to do what God does: forget our past. We need to learn from our mistakes and remember the bitter lessons we have learned. However, we no longer need to be controlled by our past. That is what Paul meant by "forgetting those things which are behind." Think about the horrible things Paul did before coming to Christ: He was responsible for the death of Stephen. He had to carry that burden in his conscience until his final day. He knew he was responsible for some terrible things, but he was able to put his past in the past, and we need to do the same.

The Pep Talks that Make a Difference

"Therefore we also, since we are surrounded by so great a cloud of witnesses, let us lay aside every weight, and the sin which so easily ensnares us, and let us run with endurance the race that is set before us" (Hebrews 12:1).

More than once does Paul compare the Christian life to running a race. When I was growing up, running was a big part of my life, and I had lots of ribbons to show for it, many for first place. Every now and then I would even break school records in the 50- and 100-meter sprint. I remember the thrill and support of my parents and friends cheering me on. My dad's pep talk before each race prepared me to run with purpose. He'd say, "Remember, never look over your shoulder, Tam, it will slow you down. Keep your eyes on the finish line." There is a temptation to look over your shoulder and see where other runners are, but those pep talks kept me looking forward. Before the race even started I purposed in my heart not to look back, no matter how bad the temptation. This contributed to my wins.

Living the Christian life is *not* a 100-meter sprint, it's a long-distance run. God is cheering us on, and by keeping our eyes on the finish line, we are letting go of the weights from our past. I am running this race for Jesus, and I know there is a reward in Heaven waiting for me. My reward will be based on how faithful I am to what God has called me to do; your reward will be based on how faithful you are to what God has called you to do. We mustn't run the race for other people, for prestige or attention. We all should be running for Jesus. Are you running for Jesus, yourself or someone else? That is a question we all must answer!

Paul presents his motivation in Philippians 3:10: "That I may know Him and the power of His resurrection, and the fellowship of His sufferings, being conformed to His death..." Paul's saying, "This is why I'm doing it: my purpose is to know Jesus Christ." And that is what should matter to you and me on this journey.

1. What have you been trying to improve in your own strength, rather than simply laying down your will and emotions to be God's instrument? Pray for Him to show you what you need to surrender. Write down your thoughts.

2. Do you want God to use you? Pray and ask Him how you can be used by Him. Write down ways you can serve God, then take it prayer and put it into action.

Making Christ Lord

Before you accepted Christ, you were a slave to sin. However, when you began to follow Christ and step out in faith, making Jesus the Lord of your life, you became a slave to God.

It's easy to get our priorities mixed up, and trying to get back on track can be hard. The first step is wanting to do God's will. He will help you make the right choices, even though they may be hard choices.

Is God speaking to you right now about how you are living your life? Is time with God the first thing you seek each day?

3. Read Psalm 63:1: "David cried out to God in the wilderness: 'O God, You are my God; early will I seek You; my soul thirsts for You; my flesh longs for You in a dry and thirsty land where there is no water.'"

    Are you making the most of your free time, being filled with God's Word so you can serve Him and His people? Are other people encouraged by you, receiving the outpouring of God's Spirit that dwells in you? Yes or no?

The Devil, Your Flesh and the World

Three enemies prevent you from walking in forgiveness: the devil, your flesh and the world. Perhaps God's most precious gift to the believer is His provision for forgiveness and reconciliation. For Jesus reconciled all things through His blood. There is no need to continue to dwell in the past. God wants you to walk in His forgiveness—accept it as a gift.

4. Are there any ways that you have been punishing yourself? When you desire to punish yourself, it's like saying that the sacrifice of God's Son was not enough to cover your sins. Explain your desire to punish yourself:

    _____

    _____

    _____

5. Is there anything else God could have done to cover your sins and the sins of those who hurt you? Write down your thoughts:

    _____

    _____

6. "There is therefore now no condemnation to those who are in Christ Jesus, who do not walk according to the flesh, but according to the Spirit. For the law of the Spirit of life in Christ Jesus has made me free from the law of sin and death" (Romans 8:1-2).

    Do you feel condemnation from your past? If so, what must you do to be free from condemnation?

    _____

    _____

    _____

7. Read Colossians 1:19-20 and 2 Corinthians 5:18-19 below:

    - "For it pleased the Father that in Him all the fullness should dwell and by Him to reconcile all things to Himself, by Him, whether things on earth or things in heaven having made peace through the blood of His cross" (Colossians 1:19-20).

    - "Now all things are of God, who has reconciled us to Himself through Jesus Christ, and has given us the ministry of reconciliation that is, that God was in Christ reconciling the world to Himself, not imputing their trespasses to them, and has committed to us the word of reconciliation" (2 Corinthians 5:18-19).

    Are you reconciled in your heart toward the person or people who hurt you? If so, how have you put this into action in your heart?

    _____
    _____
    _____

8. In the space below, describe your heart toward _____ when you first started *Healed and Set Free*. What is your attitude toward this person now?

    _____
    _____

9. In which areas of your life are you still struggling to apply the four tools?

    _____
    _____
    _____

10. Are you ready to walk in God's ways? Are you really ready to change? If you are, just watch what God will do.

    What specific steps can you take this week to experience victory?

    _____
    _____
    _____

This Week's Tool and Memory Verse

Tool #4 - FORGET: I must FORGET by no longer dwelling on the hurt or the painful reminders such as: phrases, smells, places, songs and comments. Instead, I am putting my mind on the higher calling that Christ has for me.

"Brethren, I do not count myself to have apprehended; but one thing I do, forgetting those things which are behind and reaching forward to those things which are ahead" (Philippians 3:13).

Week 7, Day 4

Prayer: Bow your heart before the Lord in prayer prior to completing today's Bible study. Ask God to help, by the power of the Holy Spirit, to give you a heart of reconciliation to walk in His forgiveness.

Tammy's Reflections

I Got the Drift

I live in Idaho, where the winters bring tons of snow and the blowing winds cause large snowdrifts. One winter afternoon, I was headed into town for a few appointments. There was a very narrow path to get out of the driveway: it had been cleared by the snowplow the day before, causing snowdrifts on both sides of the drive. As I drove forward, I started thinking about a pole that was sticking up to mark an underground tank, wondering if the snow plow driver had knocked it over. My curiosity got the best of me: I quickly looked back to see if the pole was anywhere in sight, taking my attention off my narrow path, on to what was behind me. The next thing I knew, I came to an abrupt stop, smashing right into a snowdrift!

As I worked my van back and forth trying to get it unstuck, God spoke to my heart. He told me the truth of what I had been doing for years. I was always looking back and mulling over my past hurts: memories, words hurled at me that hurt my feelings, physical attacks, betrayals, sexual abuse and past failures.

I finally "got the drift": I was stuck in the past. I couldn't continue to move forward, because my focus was on what was behind me. Looking behind to live in the past was robbing me of looking forward and living the life that was in front of me.

God has set a straight and narrow path before us: "Enter by the narrow gate; for wide is the gate and broad is the way that leads to destruction, and there are many who go in by it. Because narrow is the gate and difficult is the way which leads to life, and there are few who find it" (Matthew 7:13-14). You can't change the way you think in your own power. When you're weak and overwhelmed, you need to draw near to God and spend time getting to know Him in His Word. God is faithful to His Word, which transforms how you think and will strengthen you.

The Race We Must Run

In the devotional "The Race We Must Run,"[3] Greg Laurie explains how important it is to keep the proper perspective and press on toward Jesus.

> I heard a story about one man's New Year's resolutions. One year his resolution was, "I will not get upset when Sam and Charlie make jokes about me being bald." The next year his resolution was, "I won't get annoyed when Charlie and Sam kid me about my hairpiece." A year later: "I will not lose my temper when Charlie and Sam laugh at me for wearing a girdle." The following year he made one last New Year's resolution, "I will not speak to Charlie and Sam anymore."

The story is funny, but true: We adjust our resolutions and thinking with the passing of time, don't we? But instead of resolutions, we need a spiritual solution anchored in God's Word. In Philippians 3:7-8, the apostle Paul identified what really matters in life. He helps us to understand what our priorities ought to be: "But what things were gain to me, these I have counted loss for Christ. Yet indeed I also count all things loss for the excellence of the knowledge of Christ Jesus my Lord, for whom I have suffered the loss of all things, and count them as rubbish, that I may gain Christ."

Next, he shared what he really wanted in life: "Brethren, I do not count myself to have apprehended; but one thing I do, forgetting those things which are behind and reaching forward to those things which are ahead, I press toward the goal for the prize of the upward call of God in Christ Jesus" (Philippians 3:13–14).

On more than one occasion, Paul compared the Christian life to running a race. But again, we need to realize that it is a long-distance run. Consequently, there are some principles we need to remember as we run:

First, we must pace ourselves. It's not all that significant if you hold first place for nine out of ten laps. What matters is the tenth lap. That's why David said, "Create in me a clean heart, O God, and renew a steadfast spirit within me" (Psalm 51:10). "Steadfast" could also be translated "consistent." David was saying, "Give me consistency. Help me to stick with this."

Secondly, we must play by the rules, or we will be disqualified. In an athletic event, you have to play by the rules; you can't make up your own. In the race of life, we have a rule book called the Bible, and if we are going to run well, we need to play by the rules God's given us in scripture.

Remember, too, that we must get rid of any extra weight or sin that would slow us down. We need to run light. Periodically, we need to take stock of our lives as Christians and ask ourselves, "Is this a wing or a weight? Is this helping me on my way spiritually or slowing me down?"

We must also run with the right motive. Paul said, "I also count all things loss for the excellence of the knowledge of Christ Jesus my Lord" (Philippians 3:8). If you are a Christian just because you want to impress someone, then you are not going to make it in this race. You must run for the Lord Himself. It is what will give you the strength to keep going when things get hard—and they will get hard.

Don't look back. Remember, "Forgetting those things which are behind" (Philippians 3:13). If you look to see what other runners are doing, you will break your stride and ultimately lose the race. And finally, press on, even when it's hard. Paul said, "I press toward the goal" (Philippians 3:14). The word "press" comes from the Greek *agonizo*, which points to strong exertion. There are times in our lives when it gets hard. But it is then that we learn what it means to walk by faith and not by feelings.

1. Write down the definition of "restitution" from page 301.

2. Read Hebrews 9:14-15: "How much more shall the blood of Christ, who through the eternal Spirit offered Himself without spot to God, cleanse your conscience from dead works to serve the living God? And for this reason He is the Mediator of the new covenant, by means of death, for the redemption of the transgressions under the first covenant, that those who are called may receive the promise of the eternal inheritance."

   From what has God cleansed your conscience?

3. What is God's plan for you after you have cleansed your conscience before Him? Explain.

4. What are some things from your past that you are ready to forget? Explain.

5. Share a situation when you had no love for another person, but had to put your own interests aside so that God could love them through you.

Stories of Real People and a Real Savior

Stability Restored

Becky, Idaho

I had a very safe, protected upbringing. My father, who was a pastor, was a very compassionate, gentle, honest and sincere man. I didn't realize how naïve and idealistic I was as I went into life on my own. In my mid-twenties I married a man who was a missionary/pastor.

My daughter was 8 months old when his unreasonable fits of anger and abuse began. He didn't drink, but he was what I call a "dry alcoholic." His drugs of choice were control over me through fear and the adrenaline rush he got from being abusive. There was nothing in my background to prepare me for a pastor/husband who was abusive. I knew if I tried to tell anyone what I was going through, they wouldn't believe me.

By the time our daughter was 18 months old, I'd had a miscarriage and was severely depressed. In an attempt to save our marriage, we attended a Marriage Encounter weekend. I went into it very hopeful, but my husband refused to participate. He spent all our alone communication times watching TV.

Throughout our 18 years of marriage, I was diagnosed with anxiety/panic disorder and was in and out of mental hospitals and women's shelters trying to deal with the abuse, the miscarriage and my husband's pornography addiction. Toward the end there was even an incident involving a knife where the cops were called. Although I had left several times due to the abuse, I was still fighting to save my marriage, praying that my husband would join me in marital counseling.

I got so depressed that I tried to kill myself; not because I wanted to die, but because my life seemed so impossible and I just wanted to be with Jesus. I ended up in a mental hospital for about two months.

When I got out, I knew I had to find a place where I would have the support of Christian women to whom I could entrust the truth of all I'd been through. As a result of a series of closed doors, God led me to Calvary Chapel of Idaho Falls. The first two times I attended a ladies' event, I remember breaking down in tears and feeling so grateful to be surrounded by godly women who prayed for me.

Though my marriage has ended, God has restored my relationships with my children and family. The healing in my life and the stability I now experience is so dramatic it is breathtaking. My medical personnel have repeatedly said they can't believe someone who spent over two months hospitalized so recently could be doing so well.

I am now doing *Healed and Set Free* in a one-on-one study and have just begun helping with a *Healed and Set Free* Bible study at the jail. The verse that has helped me the most is 1 Peter 3:9, "Not returning evil for evil or reviling for reviling, but on the contrary blessing, knowing that you were called to this, that you may inherit a blessing." I don't know what my future holds, but I know God is going to use all I have been through to be a blessing both to myself and to others.

His Love at Work in Our Lives

6. Read Matthew 10:37-39: "He who loves father or mother more than Me is not worthy of Me. And he who loves son or daughter more than Me is not worthy of Me. And he who does not take his cross and follow after Me is not worthy of Me. He who finds his life will lose it, and he who loses his life for My sake will find it."

   Do you love God enough that you are willing to die to your own past, your fears and doubts, in order for His light to shine through you? Yes or no? Express your feelings:

7. Read Philippians 2:5-9: "Let this mind be in you which was also in Christ Jesus, who, being in the form of God, did not consider it robbery to be equal with God, but made Himself of no reputation, taking the form of a bondservant, and coming in the likeness of men. And being found in appearance as a man, He humbled Himself and became obedient to the point of death, even the death of the cross. Therefore God also has highly exalted Him and given Him the name, which is above every name."

   Why do we need to set ourselves aside and become open vessels?

8. How can your life glorify God? Explain.

9. Read 1 John 4:10: "In this is love, not that we loved God, but that He loved us and sent His Son to be the propitiation for our sins."

   How does God desire for His love to work in your life?

10. Read Philippians 2:3-4: "Let nothing be done through selfish ambition or conceit, but in lowliness of mind let each esteem others better than himself. Let each of you look out not only for his own interests, but also for the interests of others."

    What practical ways can we love others on a daily basis?

    _____
    _____
    _____

11. As you move from the past into your present, write down some of the changes you see in yourself this week:

    _____
    _____
    _____
    _____
    _____
    _____
    _____
    _____
    _____

> Re-order your life in the light of God's Word. It doesn't matter if you're a business woman, a stay-at-home mom or a pastor's wife. It doesn't matter if you have been a Christian for five minutes or 55 years, these tools will enrich your life day by day to become healed and set free from life's hurts.

Prayer: Bow your heart before the Lord in prayer prior to completing today's Bible study. Ask Christ to work His unconditional love in your life.

How Not to Win the Spiritual Race

"Samuel said to Saul, 'You have done foolishly. You have not kept the commandment of the Lord your God, which He commanded you. For now the Lord would have established your kingdom over Israel forever'" (1 Samuel 13:13). Using this verse, Greg Laurie[4] again sheds light on how we are—or are not—to run the spiritual race:

> When we put our faith in Jesus, we are enrolled in a spiritual race, where we must play by the rules or we'll be disqualified. Samuel tells the story of King Saul, a man who didn't play by the rules. He began in victory and ended in humiliating defeat. He lost his character, power, crown, and in the end, his very life. Based on Saul's life, here are a few principles on how not to run the spiritual race:
>
> - **Ignore the Little Things**: Saul's failure was not immediate, but then pride turned into envy, and he ignored what God had plainly told him to do. Likewise, it is not for us to pick and choose what parts of the Bible we like and don't like. We are to obey God even in the smallest matters, because "small" sins turn into big sins. They certainly did for Saul.
>
> - **Never Take Responsibility for Your Actions**: More than once Saul blamed others for *his* bad choices. In 1 Samuel 13, when Saul is facing battle, he admits to Samuel, "I said, 'The Philistines will now come down on me at Gilgal, and I have not made supplication to the Lord.' Therefore I felt compelled, and offered a burnt offering." But Saul just wanted to save face. He forgot that no matter what, God knows the truth.
>
> - **Don't Get Mad, Get Even**: Saul's animosity destroyed him. He turned away from God, and he was jealous as God anointed and began using David. David, who God called "a man after My own heart" (Acts 13:22), would take Saul's place as king of Israel. Understand that God chooses whom He will choose. Don't let hatred destroy you like it did Saul!
>
> God has given you potential, talents and gifts like he did Saul. It is up to us to run the race well and play by the rules. Don't be disqualified. Don't be prideful. Don't play the fool. Don't crash and burn. God has a plan for you.

This Week's Tool and Memory Verse

Tool #4 - FORGET: I must FORGET by no longer dwelling on the hurt or the painful reminders such as: phrases, smells, places, songs and comments. Instead, I am putting my mind on the higher calling that Christ has for me.

> "Brethren, I do not count myself to have apprehended; but one thing I do, forgetting those things which are behind and reaching forward to those things which are ahead" (Philippians 3:13).

1. In what areas of your life do you naturally ignore "the little sins"? List 4 here:

   1. _____

   2. _____

   3. _____

   4. _____

2. Write down a personal experience when you ignored a little sin which turned into a big sin.

3. Don't let jealousy or hatred destroy you like it did Saul. God chooses whom He will. Have you been expressing jealousy toward anyone? If so, who?

What Do You Give to God: Tokens or Your Best?

If you have children, have you truly dedicated them to Him, giving Him authority over their lives to shape them and send them on His chosen course? What about your own life? Does the Lord have a little of your life, half of your life or your whole life? All you are, all you have, all you hope?

Until He does, you will suffer spiritual barrenness. Don't accept it! You will be ready for the impossible when your heart truly cries out, "I surrender all."

A New Creation in Jesus

4. Remember, if you are in Christ, you are a new creation. The following verses give a description of who you are in Him.

   - "But you are a chosen generation, a royal priesthood, a holy nation, His own special people, that you may proclaim the praises of Him who called you out of darkness into His marvelous light" (1 Peter 2:9).
   - "Beloved, I beg you as sojourners and pilgrims, abstain from fleshly lusts which war against the soul" (1 Peter 2:11).

   Write down who you are in Christ, and what these scriptures mean to you.

Letting Past Hurts Work for Good

Elizabeth George offers some great wisdom in *Loving God with All Your Mind*[5] on what to do in those times when we find ourselves looking back:

> Our Heavenly Father does indeed use our past. The great truth of Romans 8:28-29 is God's promise that any and all events in the past will be used for good purposes to make you more like Christ. He will redeem even the worst, the most painful, and the most perplexing aspects of your past and use them ALL for good. I have seen God redeem suffering and terrible trials in many people's lives. In fact, some of the most gentle, peaceful and gracious people are those who have known the most pain. God has used their experiences to make them more like Him, and He is truly glorified in their lives.
>
> The next time you catch yourself saying or thinking, "If only" in regard to the past, I encourage you to pause and ponder God's sovereignty, knowledge and presence in that past situation. Refuse to allow yourself to get bogged down thinking about something that is no longer real. Instead, draw near to God by thanking Him for His continual presence with you throughout time, and thank Him for His promise to redeem the hard times of the past. God's grace and God's healing powers are wide, deep and marvelous.

Can God Bring Good out of Bad?

Again, I am thankful for the wise words of Greg Laurie in his insightful devotional "Can God bring good out of bad?"[6] I encourage you to ponder Greg's words as we bring the "Remembering to Forget" chapter to a close.

> In this life, there is no way to avoid suffering; it is inevitable. No one gets a free pass. The fact of the matter is, you are either coming out of a storm or headed into another. It's just a matter of time.
>
> What you want to do is get ready now, then you will have a solid biblical foundation so you can properly process and respond to these challenges. As Randy Alcorn says in his book *If God is Good*, "Most of us don't give focused thought to evil and suffering until we experience them. This forces us to formulate perspective on the fly, at a time when our thinking is muddled and we're exhausted and consumed by pressing issues. People who have 'been there' will attest that it's far better to think through suffering in advance."
>
> In other words, be prepared ahead of time! But we would rather not, because the topic of suffering is difficult and uncomfortable. In fact, suffering is something we all want to avoid, if possible. If you are flying and you see a storm, you try to fly around it, not into it. But here's the reality: sometimes you simply can't fly around. Your life can be going reasonably well one moment, and then change in a flash.
>
> But Paul reminds us that we should "let the word of Christ dwell in you richly in all wisdom, teaching and admonishing one another in psalms and hymns and spiritual songs, singing with grace in your hearts to the Lord" (Colossians 3:16).

Here is one of the "good things" that comes out of crisis and suffering: You turn to God with a dependence like you never had before, like a child running to his mom or dad and burying his face in their shoulder. And do you know what? God is there waiting for you with the strength, peace and love you need. Not necessarily with all the answers you may want, but He is there.

One of the things you should treasure in the midst of suffering is knowing God is present. Your faith begins to grow stronger: Faith does not grow through ease and comfort. It grows through challenge, conflict and difficulty. Faith is like a muscle in that it gets stronger through use, not neglect. If you do not use your "faith muscle," it can atrophy. We have a choice in life—use it or lose it!

The Bible reminds us, "Consider it a sheer gift, friends, when tests and challenges come at you from all sides. You know that under pressure, your faith-life is forced into the open and shows its true colors. So don't try to get out of anything prematurely. Let it do its work so you become mature and well-developed, not deficient in any way" (James 1:2-4, The Message).

5. Can you name an instance when God used a seemingly bad situation for something good? Share your thoughts.

> "One vital ingredient in our relationship with Jesus is our willingness to be honest with Him and to get real with God on a daily basis."
> - Clair Cloninger, *When God Shines Through*

Review this chapter, "Remembering to Forget." Reflect on the truths you learned.

1. Rewrite the scriptures that accompany the first three tools to freedom:

    - **SEE**: Asking God to expose the root cause of my sinful thought and actions, so I'm not defiled, and I don't defile others (Hebrews 12:15).

    - **GIVE**: I must be sorry enough to change and choose to go God's way over my own way (2 Corinthians 7:10).

    - **FORGIVE**: I must forgive as Christ has forgiven me (Colossians 3:13).

2. In what specific way will you apply God's truth to you life?

Stories of Real People and a Real Savior

Whole From Years of Self Destruction
By Tami, Idaho

I was dying, emotionally and physically. That's when I believe Jesus rescued me. Self-destruction was the consummation of my being. Ruled by drugs, alcohol and sexual immorality, I was a liar and a thief. The decaying effects of rage, resentment and selfishness were seeping from my pores and into every aspect of my life. I was a woman who, with my own hands, had torn down every relationship in my life.

Raised in a home of raging alcoholics, I learned from an early age not to trust people. I learned that I could not depend on anyone to care more for me than I did myself. I was taught that I would have to love myself before anyone else would ever love me. I knew that I would have to value myself more than everyone else in order to gain respect from others. Demanding honor and loyalty from all, I was loyal to no one but myself. I respected no authority and allowed no interpretation of love to infiltrate my self-absorption. I would not be moved, shaken or changed for any person, commanding that others "love me for who I was." However, in completion of the passive-aggressive cycle I had created, I was clingy and needy, terrified of not being loved, hanging on to destructive relationships long after I had completely sabotaged them. I was convinced that the hole I felt deep inside could be filled with the love and adoration of "the right man."

Believing that the God of my youth was not real, I created my own god: I believed (my) god knew I was "a good person" and would "take care of me." I compared myself to others, who seemed conveniently to be living a more demented lifestyle than myself. I believed all others were living in self-righteousness. I was not aware of any other God.

But then I came to the end of myself. I knew I was dying. I knew I had become insane; after years of drug and alcohol abuse and being told I was crazy, finally I too was convinced. I checked myself into a mental hospital, and shortly after my stay, I found myself concocting the details of my suicide. I was dying. I was done. Broken and emotionally helpless, I cried out to the Lord, "Please, help me. Why does this keep happening to me? Please, help me."

After that desperate night in my closet, when God spoke to me and sent me out to find Him, I believe He led me to the Healed and Set Free Bible study. God, in His amazing supernatural power, brought me to Himself. Jesus has used the tools in Healed and Set Free to save my soul from self-destruction. HSF has taught me who God is. What price He paid to save me. That He created me for a specific purpose. What that purpose is. And that He is powerful enough to heal me where I was broken; to forgive my every transgression; to give me a new start; to empower me to put off the old man, and be transformed and renewed in His Spirit.

Healed and Set Free Bible Study has given me the tools to practice forgiveness; to leave the past in the dust; to look to the future, toward the goal-the prize of Christ Jesus and living in eternity with Him. HSF has taught me how to love like Jesus does, as I have been loved by Him; to be the wife, mother, daughter and sister that He created me to be. Healed and Set Free has shown me the meaning of freedom.

He has delivered me from the shackles of the enemy. I am living free of regret. I was lost and broken, my heart busted and beaten, but now I am truly complete and whole. Today I am living the abundant life, serving my Lord, the King of Kings.

Tools to Become Healed and Set Free

To equip yourself in God's truth, look over the tools and verses that will be introduced in the coming weeks. Thinking about the past won't change it, but you can change your future by being set free from your past.

TOOL #1 - SEE: I must SEE the truth about what is in my heart so I am not defiled.

> **Definition**: To defile means to make filthy or dirty; to pollute.
>
> **Bible Verse**: "Looking carefully lest anyone fall short of the grace of God; lest any root of bitterness springing up cause trouble, and by this many become defiled" (Hebrews 12:15).

TOOL #2 - GIVE: I must GIVE my sin to God through repentance, knowing that Christ is waiting to take it. I must be sorry enough to change, and choose to go God's way over my own.

> **Definition**: To repent means to feel such sorrow for sin or fault as to be disposed to change one's life for the better; be penitent.
>
> **Bible Verse**: "For godly sorrow produces repentance leading to salvation, not to be regretted; but the sorrow of the world produces death" (2 Corinthians 7:10).

TOOL #3 - FORGIVE: I must FORGIVE as I am forgiven by Christ: Forgiving those who hurt, bruised, wronged, rejected, betrayed or harmed me, whether unintentionally or deliberately. I must ask God to forgive me for holding on to unforgiveness and know that He will.

> **Definition**: To forgive means to stop feeling angry or resentful toward someone for an offense, flaw or mistake.
>
> **Bible Verse**: "...Bearing with one another, and forgiving one another, if anyone has a complaint against another; even as Christ forgave you, so you also must do" (Colossians 3:13).

TOOL #4 - FORGET: I must FORGET by no longer dwelling on the hurt or the painful reminders, such as: phrases, smells, places, songs and comments. Instead, I am putting my mind on the higher calling that Christ has for me.

> **Definition**: To forget means to choose not to remember or notice, "forgive and forget".
>
> **Bible Verse**: "Brethren, I do not count myself to have apprehended; but one thing I do, forgetting those things which are behind and reaching forward to those things which are ahead" (Philippians 3:13).

Be Healed and Set Free: Christ will heal me from my past, showing me the truth, so I can become a cleansed vessel, healed and set free.

> **Definition**: To set free means to make free; set at liberty; release from bondage, imprisonment, or restraint.
>
> **Definition**: To heal means to make whole and healthy; to cure; to remedy or repair.
>
> **Bible Verse**: "And you shall know the truth, and the truth shall make you free" (John 8:32).

Two Become One:
God's Design for Marriage

This week we will be growing in our understanding of the four tools and how they apply in the context of marriage.

Tool #1 - SEE: I must SEE the truth about what is in my heart, so I am not defiled (see Hebrews 12:15).

Tool #2 - GIVE: I must GIVE my sin to God through repentance, knowing that Christ is waiting to take it. I must be sorry enough to change, and choose to go God's way over my own (see 2 Corinthians 7:10).

Tool #3 - FORGIVE: I must forgive as I am forgiven by Christ. Forgiving those who hurt, bruised, wronged, rejected, betrayed or harmed me, whether unintentionally or deliberately. I must ask God to forgive me for holding on to unforgiveness and know that He will (see Colossians 3:13).

Tool #4 - FORGET: I must FORGET by no longer dwelling on the hurt or the painful reminders such as: phrases, smells, places, songs and comments. Instead, I am putting my mind on the higher calling that Christ has for me (see Philippians 3:13).

Prayer: Ask God to help you be willing to SEE what's in your heart and GIVE Him the lingering strongholds. Continue to ask God to fill you with the knowledge of His will through all the wisdom and understand that the Spirit gives.

Week 8: Day 1

Prayer: Bow your heart before the Lord in prayer prior to completing today's Bible study. Ask Him to give you a new understanding of marriage.

Marriage is a divine union, instituted by God between a man and a woman. It's the most sacred of human relationships, the most important institution in society, the cornerstone of strong families, and the foundation of future generations.

The Bible speaks in detail about the role marriage plays in our lives. It was created by God, allowing men and women to experience the deep and unique nature of human relationships, and to mold us into the people that God desires us to become. It is a holy, beautiful gift from our Father in Heaven, who loved us so much that He gave us a spouse: a companion and partner to love, honor and cherish.

When it comes to marriage, we need to think and act biblically, not emotionally. We need a biblical worldview, because our marriage is under attack daily from the world and from the enemy. It's inevitable that our marriages will face pressure and hardship. What are you building your foundation on: The solid ground of God's Word? Or the shifting sands of this world? Is your marriage on the rocks or on the Rock? In this chapter, we will look at God's unique design for marriage, and how to participate in this relationship with His purpose and for His glory.

Now Do It!

"Let each one of you in particular so love his own wife as himself, and let the wife see that she respects her husband" (Ephesians 5:33). "Now Do It!" is a devotional by The Active Word[1] which expands on this verse. They write:

> Most marital issues in the church aren't due to a shortage of counseling or biblical instruction. They're not the result of husbands and wives not knowing what they're supposed to do. No, quite honestly, most problems are due to a lack of application—not lack of information.
>
> Think about it: the Bible has been around for a while now. We've had the New Testament for nearly 2,000 years, and it hasn't changed in all that time. The point is that most of us know what God's Word has to say about marriage. We know that the two are one and that marriage is a reflection of God's nature and of our relationship with Christ. Husbands know they're to love their wives as Christ loves the Church, and wives know their role. Christian couples already know all these things. So the question is, why are so many Christian marriages hurting?
>
> It's not because the Word is insufficient or unreliable. A big part of the problem is that we simply don't do what it says. That's the danger in even doing a devotional like this one. We can nod our head in agreement when we read truth but never follow through with it in our actions. We run the risk of being hearers of the Word only, and not doers (James 1:22).
>
> Let's not make that mistake, not with something as important as this. In this day and age, a godly marriage speaks louder about Jesus and His presence in our lives than just about anything else. Let's allow His Spirit to turn up the volume and be doers of what we know the Word says.

Tools to Become Set Free

In this chapter, we will continue to use **Tool #1 - SEE, Tool #2 - GIVE, Tool #3 - FORGIVE,** and **Tool #4 - FORGET**.

These tools will help you to become set free. It is crucial to memorize these powerful tools and review them regularly in order to apply them to your daily life.

#1 - SEE: I must SEE the truth about what is in my heart so I am not defiled.

#2 - GIVE: I must GIVE my sin to God through repentance, knowing that Christ is waiting to take it. I must be sorry enough to change, and choose to go God's way over my own.

#3 - FORGIVE: I must FORGIVE as I am forgiven by Christ: Forgiving those who hurt, bruised, wronged, rejected, betrayed or harmed me, whether unintentionally or deliberately. I must ask God to forgive me for holding on to unforgiveness and know that He will.

#4 - FORGET: I must FORGET by no longer dwelling on the hurt or the painful reminders such as: phrases, smells, places, songs and comments. Instead, I am putting my mind on the higher calling that Christ has for me.

Be Healed and Set Free: Christ will heal me from my past, showing me the truth, so I can become a cleansed vessel, healed and set free.

This Week's Focus

Prayer: Ask God to help you be willing to SEE what's in your heart and GIVE Him the lingering strongholds. Continue to ask God to fill you with the knowledge of His will through all the wisdom and understand that the Spirit gives.

By Memory: My challenge to you is to be able to recite the Bible verse from this chapter without looking. I know that by hiding these words of wisdom in your heart you are providing yourself with tools to be truly healed and set free. May we rise up to be women of the Word.

Tool #1 - SEE: I must SEE the truth about what is in my heart, so I am not defiled (see Hebrews 12:15).

Tool #2 - GIVE: I must GIVE my sin to God through repentance, knowing that Christ is waiting to take it. I must be sorry enough to change, and choose to go God's way over my own (see 2 Corinthians 7:10).

Tool #3 - FORGIVE: I must forgive as I am forgiven by Christ. Forgiving those who hurt, bruised, wronged, rejected, betrayed or harmed me, whether unintentionally or deliberately. I must ask God to forgive me for holding on to unforgiveness and know that He will (see Colossians 3:13).

Tool #4 - FORGET: I must FORGET by no longer dwelling on the hurt or the painful reminders such as: phrases, smells, places, songs and comments. Instead, I am putting my mind on the higher calling that Christ has for me (see Philippians 3:13).

"And you shall know the truth, and the truth shall make you free" (John 8:32).

Tammy's Reflections

Marital Expectations

One hot July day, I was visiting with my daughter Jessica, a new bride of three years. As we sat out in the summer sun, enjoying a piece of watermelon, I asked her: "If you had one piece of advice for a new bride, what would it be?"
Jessica said, "I have learned that you should never place expectations that are too great on your mate, it's not healthy. Too many expectations create an opportunity for the enemy to fill your mind with lies."

If you have one of those crazy days when you haven't spent time with Jesus, sometimes you can't shake the lies of the enemy, saying, "You're all alone... Your husband couldn't care less about spending time with you... All you think about is 'me, me, me!'" So many new brides expect their husband to be Prince Charming, the man of their dreams, able to read their mind and understand their emotions. Too high of expectations can really damage a relationship.

Then that still small voice says, "I love you. I want to spend time with you. I created you, and care about every detail of your life. I will protect you; I will watch out for you. I will give you the strength and joy it takes to live your life!"

Jessica went on, "When you spend time with Jesus first, and hear those words from Him, you melt in His arms. He alone satisfies the deep desire in your heart to be cherished and loved. My expectations are met in Him, and no matter how hard it gets, I can always count on Jesus to love and cherish me, even when I don't deserve it." Why? Because that's the promise He has given each and every one of us.

Having Our Expectations Met: In Jesus

It's unfair to expect our husbands to meet all our needs. Humans aren't meant to have all the answers, to heal every heart or to be perfect. After all, we are created beings. But God, the Creator, knows the very fiber of our being, and the deep feelings, insecurities, wounds and pain in our hearts. Only He can quench our need for love, understanding, companionship and peace.

Talking to Jessica about expectations in marriage made me think about the wisdom of focusing our expectations on Jesus. Luke 7 gives the story of a Roman centurion who interceded for one of his sick servants. He sends a messenger to Jesus, but tells Him not to bother coming to his house: "For I am not worthy," he said. "But say the word, and my servant will be healed" (v.6,7).

"This man has focused everything on Jesus. That's the point!" writes Dr. Shimmy Kotu. "We never go wrong in looking to Jesus as our Shepherd, Sustainer, Strength, Salvation and Song... He is our Alpha, Almighty, Apostle, Amen, Author and Advocate; Brightness, Beloved, Beginning, Bridegroom, Bread of life and Branch; Chosen, Captain, Comforter, Cornerstone, Chief and Counselor! Convinced? We can never expect too much of the One who is our All in All."[2]

Higher Expectations on Ourselves

The person who expects perfection in marriage has set themselves up for a great disappointment. After all, who is perfect? Yet so often we fail to see that even *we* don't measure up to our own expectations!

Again in Luke 7, we see Jesus setting expectations straight. Jesus is the guest of honor at the house of Simon the Pharisee. They're just sitting down to eat when a woman comes in, pours expensive oil over Jesus' feet, then wipes His feet with her hair. Simon the Pharisee, although he doesn't say anything, is thinking, "If you knew what kind of woman she is, you wouldn't let her touch you!"

But Jesus sees his heart and says, "I entered your house; you gave Me no water for My feet, but she has washed My feet with her tears and wiped them with the hair of her head. You gave Me no kiss, but this woman has not ceased to kiss My feet since the time I came in. You did not anoint My head with oil, but this woman has anointed My feet with fragrant oil. Therefore I say to you, her sins, which are many, are forgiven, for she loved much" (v.44-47).

It's easy to read this story and judge Simon. It would have been better for him to view himself through the lens of his own expectations. But we, like Simon, get things backward so quickly! We expect "everything from other people... while asking little from Jesus."[2] As a result, we go through life frustrated and critical toward our husbands and the people around us. We think, "Why aren't they satisfying my needs? Why? Why? Why?" Because it's easier to pass the blame than to take responsibility for ourselves.

If we want to have our expectations met in the Lord, we must learn to take responsibility for our thoughts, words, attitudes and actions. Too many people never really look inside and get honest with themselves. They don't get down to the root of the problem. We must deal with the bad root. It's like having a big, ugly weed in the middle of your front yard. You can pull the weed, but if you simply clip it off at the surface, you aren't really getting down to the root. A couple of days go by, and when you look in your yard, that same ugly weed is back.

For lasting change—and to be healed and set free—you must go deeper and not simply look at what you do, but ask yourself, "What is the root of the problem?"

Ask Yourself These Questions

- Why do I act this way?
- Why am I so defensive?
- Why am I out of control in this area?
- Why do I have too high of expectations in my relationship with my spouse?

We need to carefully examine where we constantly struggle. Is our spouse really at fault? Is our boss at fault? Is our friend at fault? Is it our upbringing? Or could it be that we have something buried deep within that is causing us to be infected? Many people have a root from the hurts in the past, but they hold onto it rather than let it go. Some people have roots of insecurity that cause them to feel defensive. Some have a root of bitterness, causing them to feel angry and critical.

We're sure it's our spouse. We're sure it's our boss. So often we can't seem to get along with a particular person, and we're sure it must be their fault. But hold on a moment! Could *you* be the problem? Could it be that you have a root of pride that is causing you to withhold forgiveness, or blinding you to someone's opinion? Get to the source.

Vicki and Jason

Vicki and Jason were always having problems in their marriage, especially in the area of communication and understanding each other. With almost every conversation, if Jason didn't agree with Vicki she would get extremely defensive. She'd feel upset, hurt and angry, and they would end up in an argument. "Why can't you just let me have my own opinion? You have your opinion, so let me have mine," Jason said. "Why do you get so upset when I don't agree with you?"

Vicki didn't have a good answer, but she obstinately opposed Jason's opinion when he disagreed with her. This went on year after year, with the growing tension damaging their marriage. Finally, Vicki decided to be honest with herself: She looked deep down and realized the reason she became defensive so easily was that she was very insecure. She had been through a lot of hurt and rejection in her life, and every time Jason didn't agree with her, Vicki felt that he was rejecting her, making her feel foolish. Rather than agreeing to disagree on some matters, Vicki took it personally. She tried to control and manipulate Jason so she wouldn't have to feel rejected.

Turn Over a New Leaf

Maybe you're stuck in a marriage where you're having a hard time communicating with your spouse. Turn over a new leaf today! Our prayer should be, "God please show me the truth about myself. I don't want to be in this same place six months from now. Show me why I respond and act the way I do. Help me, Father, to change. Help me to put my expectations on You, Lord. Help me to get to the root of the problem."

As we read this chapter, let's keep our expectations in perspective, and learn how to see our spouses as God sees them, rejoicing in the gift He has given us!

1. Do you place too high of expectations on your husband? If so, how does it affect your marriage? Explain.

2. Are your past hurts causing you to have these high expectations? Explain.

3. What can you do to take responsibility for your own actions, and put your expectations in Christ?

Tammy's Reflections

Are Grudges Holding Your Marriage Back?

If you're anything like me, it's easy to hold a grudge. Grudges can become a part of life at a very young age. After all, do you remember learning the alphabet or how to count in elementary school? Of course you do! Do you remember learning "hurt + grudges = a negative, unforgiving heart"? I think you see my point. I wore glasses as a child, and most days I received the brunt of jokes and name calling, playground teasing that was harmless child play. We've all done it, making fun of someone for a laugh. That's where the sinful habit of grudge holding can start. Harboring grudges can be harmful not only in friendships, but also in marriage.

"One of the most common grudges outside of a marriage is being angry with your parents for past hurts, for a lousy upbringing or for breaking up their marriage and family," Lori Lowe, creator of the "Marriage Gems" website, writes. "Another common grudge is against a friend who wronged us, and who we feel has never made amends. It eats away at us, and we complain to our spouse whenever we get the chance."[3]

Have you ever found yourself harboring a grudge? I didn't think holding a grudge toward someone outside my marriage could be harmful inside my marriage. Yet, as Lowe writes, "When we focus on these past wrongs, they affect all our relationships, including our marriage. They sap our energy, and our thoughts become negative, our time is wasted." It's time to move on. It's time to put it to rest by giving it to Jesus.

While grudges against those outside our marriage are certainly harmful, even more destructive are grudges within our marriage. They create a cold, unresponsive attitude that lurks at the door of our heart and mind. "Often, they are unexpressed, but closely held. They cloud our interactions and cause defensiveness or an inability to fully celebrate life with our partner. Maybe the grudges are based on old hurts your spouse has long forgotten about," continues Lowe.

I remember reading a story Heather Long shared about a women who said, "I keep grudges for so long, I retreat in my cocoon, never talking about the issue and assuming that my hubby will somehow figure out why I have not been communicating with him for the last two weeks." She went on to express, "I think I have a real problem. The recent incident is the worst so far, I have retreated to my cocoon for 3 months."[4]

Keeping a grudge and refusing to forgive won't help you or your relationship. I don't know why we don't see the danger of holding grudges until we have inflicted pain on the very person we care about the most! Even if your grudge isn't against your spouse, remember that unforgiveness eats at our mind and heart, gnawing away at us bit by bit. Isn't that energy spent brewing over an old wound energy that you would rather spend positively in your life, to bless your spouse and family? Rather than harboring grudges, realize that it's time to begin the process of forgiving and letting them go, as Heather Long explains in "How to Avoid a Grudge."[4]

> Grudges and marriages do not make happy partners. Not everyone carries a grudge, but many of us may, whether we are aware of it or not. When you carry a grudge, you invite the grudge, and the negativity associated with it, to move into your marriage with you and your spouse.

When you invite a grudge into your relationship, you add the variety of spices: paybacks, petty remarks and revenge. The negativity on both sides is far from constructive and loving. Carrying a grudge is not in the vows you took to get married, and the disharmony it generates can be the reason your marriage dissolves.

At one time or another, you or your spouse will do something that can be perceived as injurious or hurtful to the other. Forgiveness may be difficult, but getting angry about the injury—carrying it around like a badge, waving it like a flag—does not help you or your spouse.

Men can offer payback for a perceived slight by neglecting household chores and repairs. They can let the yard go, taking a slightly perverse joy in their spouse's unhappiness over it. By the same token, a wife may withhold sexual relations because he's been so neglectful of the chores. Every couple is different in the way they express a grudge. If you are guessing this can become a vicious cycle, you're right. In fact, the viciousness is often so distinct that a couple can find their marriage disrupted, but never really pinpoint what actually started the cascade effect.

We should never take pleasure in paying back our spouse, which will not help resolve the issue or repair the ill feelings. Instead of a grudge, we need forgiveness. Instead of revenge, we need repair. Instead of anger, we need love. Instead of fury, we need understanding.

In "the heat of the moment" is a difficult place for any couple to be. That's why it's best to never make decisions in the heat of the moment; that's why it's better to take a deep breath before saying something in the heat of the moment. But even if you can't manage to cool down "the heat" of the moment, don't allow the actions or grudges to fester between you and start the cycle of paybacks. Loving, honoring, caring and respecting are never about revenge and payback. Ultimately, forgiving and letting go of a grudge is as much about you as it is about the spouse you are forgiving.

It's not always easy to forgive those wrongs, whether real or imagined. Yet, even more difficult than forgiving a wrong is forgetting one. Now bear with me, because the old saying goes, "Fool me once, shame on you; fool me twice, shame on me." We all tend to get a little gun shy. However, if love and passion are going to survive in your marriage, you have to learn how to wipe the slate clean: forgive each other and forget. While you do not necessarily need to forget the incident, you do need to forget the negative feelings, or you will find it very difficult to keep anger and resentment from building up.

Forgiveness with a Side of Grudge

When I read the title of Stephanie Anderson's "Forgiveness with a Side of Grudge,"[5] I thought, "That sounds interesting." But Stephanie gives some very good reasons why grudges may still be lingering toward your spouse.

> Have you told your spouse you forgive them, only you're still harboring a grudge? According to dictionary.com, a grudge is defined as "a feeling of ill will or resentment." Maybe your spouse hurt you or broke your heart, and has set off a cascade of negative thoughts and painful emotions.
>
> What causes a person to feel a grudge toward another person isn't random,

it's triggered by another person inflicting pain of some sort upon us—whether the pain was intended or not. When you hold a grudge, you're psychologically placing a barrier up to protect yourself from further harm by this person.

This becomes a double-edged sword. You want to protect yourself from further hurt. After all, you were probably shocked that your spouse was capable of acting this way. However, if a grudge is in place, you may struggle to let it go. It's a comfort because it's protection, and yet, it's a wedge between you and your spouse.

If you and your spouse have discussed reconciliation, a grudge will stand in the way. Also, if your spouse has begged your forgiveness and you've offered it, you may be resentful because you felt pushed to patch things up before you were emotionally ready.

Here are three tips to help you discover whether or not you've been too quick to forgive, which may be why you are holding a grudge:

1. If you have offered your spouse forgiveness but your spouse has not done the work to rebuild trust, then you are likely to hold a grudge because it's too soon.

2. If your emotions are still volatile, you may hold a grudge against your spouse if you've offered forgiveness and yet are still reeling from pain.

3. Before you can realistically think about forgiveness, you must work through difficult emotions.

We've all heard the saying, "To err is human, to forgive is divine," but you simply may not be ready to forgive. While you may believe the right thing to do is forgive, your emotions may not be there yet. But it doesn't mean you can't come to forgiveness.

SEEING and GIVING are the first steps before moving on to forgiveness. But it all starts with getting real with God, with eyes wide open to look carefully inside your heart. Again, look at what Hebrews 12:15 has to say: "Looking carefully lest anyone fall short of the grace of God; lest any root of bitterness springing up cause trouble, and by this many become defiled."

4. Do you have a tendency to hold a grudge against your spouse? What do you think makes it so difficult for you to let things go?

Week 8: Day 2

Prayer: Bow your heart before the Lord in prayer prior to completing today's Bible study. Ask Him to give you a new understanding of marriage.

God's Commandment for Marriage

God establishes an order for us to follow, especially in marriage: "Wives, submit to your own husbands, as to the Lord. For the husband is head of the wife, as also Christ is head of the church; and He is the Savior of the body. Therefore, just as the church is subject to Christ, so let the wives be to their own husbands in everything. Husbands, love your wives, just as Christ also loved the church and gave Himself for her" (Ephesians 5:22-25).

Ephesians establishes the order of authority for men and women:

- Jesus is the head of the Church.
- The husband is the head of the wife, as Christ is the head of the church.
- Wives need to submit to their husbands as an act of submission to the Lord.

1. Define the word "submission" from page 301.

_____

_____

_____

_____

What Can I Do for My Marriage?

A friend of mine told me this story about how God worked on her heart and blessed her marriage in the process. She says:

> We are on an assignment from God to submit to our husbands. Okay, you're sitting there thinking, "Forget that!" But the Bible makes it clear that we are to submit! "Therefore, just as the church is subject to Christ, so let the wives be to their own husbands in everything" (Ephesians 5:24). The only thing that held me back from submitting was fear! I was afraid the kids wouldn't be properly disciplined if my husband did it, or that he would ask me to do something I didn't particularly like to do.
>
> Submission is your choice; no one can make that decision but you! You must face God's plan for marriage, or beware the world infesting and destroying your marriage. I had to face this by force from the gracious Lord's hand—not as much fun as choosing to submit out of obedience! I was horribly sick for three years, and had no choice but to allow my husband to take the lead. I learned that my husband never demanded the headship, and would have never demanded it. It had to be a free gift from me to him.
>
> At our 2000 New Year's party, my best friend said to me, "I've noticed such a difference in your marriage. You have stepped back and your husband has blossomed! By coming underneath his authority, you have helped him grow in the Lord! Your marriage is so much closer and intimate."

The relationship between men and women isn't just about submission. God has commended us as women to respect our husbands and to be helpers to them. Scripture calls us to respect and help our husbands win! "Your desire shall be for your husband" (Genesis 3:16). "It is not good that man should be alone; I will make him a helper comparable to him" (Genesis 2:18). "Comparable to him" doesn't mean doormat, slave or insignificant other. The Hebrew "helper" means someone who enables a person who is otherwise incapable. Take a lesson from this friend of mine when she says, "I'm asking myself these days, 'What I can do for my marriage?' Not, 'What can I get out of my marriage?'" Her marriage is blessed because of it. She desires to be a servant like Jesus, and this includes the "S" word: submission.

Letting Go and Choosing to Serve

If we are try to control our marriage in the flesh and use our own tactics of strategy, manipulation and intelligence, we are looking for disaster. Our hearts become a desert because we don't get what we want. We lose the joy and contentment of marriage, because our focus is on what we want and not on trusting the Lord with our marriage.

Today, you have a choice to serve your husband. Not because I told you to, but because the Lord encourages you to do so. You can make a choice to see the assignment from God as a blessing to your Savior and your husband. You will be amazed at the blessings that flow from heaven because of your heart of obedience! So many marriages are not experiencing fulfillment. In fact, most marriages are failing, not thriving. Why? Because they aren't following God's perfect plan in the Bible.

2. Who is the head of the Church?

3. Who has authority over our husbands?

4. As wives, who has authority over us?

5. What were your feelings about submission before reading this chapter?

6. Describe your feelings about submission now.

7. Do you see the importance of submission in the home and the importance of having God's order and design for submission in marriage? Yes or No?

8. Does submission mean that you lose yourself?

9. Does the thought of submission make you upset or angry? Why?

10. What changes do you desire for God to work in you so that you can submit willingly and even joyfully to your husband?

Tammy's Reflections

God Wasn't Finished With Me Yet

One area of my life that was affected by my past was my marriage, especially in regard to submission. I can remember reading the Bible's description about our roles as wives, "Wives, submit to your owns husband, as to the Lord" (Ephesians 5:22). I cringed at the thought of giving anyone total control over my life. Never would I be another person's doormat. I balked at this submission bit for years. It wasn't fair! I was scared, but then I realized that my husband hadn't asked to be the head or leader of our home. That responsibility was placed on him by the Almighty God; that is God's plan for the husband.

One day husbands will stand accountable for what they did in the leadership of their home. This realization was a turning point for me: I'm not a doormat; that's not God's plan. Biblically, submission simply means yielding my own will to that of my husband, as unto the Lord. When I am willing to lay down my own will and submit to God by letting my husband lead, I embrace God's will for my life. Author Elizabeth George shares some wonderful insight about submission:

The Fact of Submission
By Elizabeth George

When it comes to marriage, God arranged for the sake of order that the husband lead and the wife follow. For marriages to run smoothly, God has said, "The head of every man is Christ, the head of woman is man, and the head of Christ is God" (1 Corinthians 11:3).

Now don't be alarmed. The husband's headship doesn't mean we wives can't offer wise input (Proverbs 31:26), enter into a discussion, or ask questions for clarification during the decision making process. But the husband's headship does mean that he is responsible for the final decision. Author Elisabeth Elliot describes her father's headship in her childhood home. She writes, "'Head of the house' did not mean that our father barked out orders, threw his weight around, and demanded submission from his wife. It simply meant that he was the one finally responsible."

In the end, the husband is accountable to God for his leadership decisions, and we are accountable to God for how we follow that leadership. Our husbands answer to God for leading, and we answer to Him for following. Now I ask you, which responsibility would you rather have?

Submission is a wife's choice. She decides whether or not to subject herself to her husband. No one can do it for her, and no one can make her do it. Her husband can't make her submit and follow, her church can't make her, her pastor can't make her, and neither can a Christian counselor. She must choose to defer to her husband and follow his leadership. Do you know the main reason why we wives hesitate to follow our husband's leadership? God says it is *fear*. We are afraid of what will happen if our husbands do things their way instead of our way... or another way.

Once again it became clear to me that my submission has nothing to do with my husband and everything to do with God! God has instituted submission, commanded submission, and given me the faith in Him to be able to submit—and He is honored when I do! My obedience to my husband testifies to all who are watching that God's Word and His ways are right. This call to submit is indeed a high calling!

Helpful Hints to Encourage Submission

- **Dedicate your heart to honoring your husband**: Change requires a decision, and that's definitely the case with submission.

- **Remember to respect**: Submission flows from the basic heart-attitude of respect. God states, "Let the wife see that she respects her husband" (Ephesians 5:33). God isn't telling us to *feel* respect, but to show respect, to act with respect. A good way to measure our respect for our husband is to answer the question, "Am I treating my husband as I would treat Christ Himself?"

- **Respond to your husband's words and actions positively**: Old ways die hard. We can snort, buck, kick and fight with our husbands about everything: Which lane he should drive in... his method of disciplining the children versus mine, how he should handle his ministry... On and on our struggles go. For me the breakthrough came with developing a positive response. I trained, yes, *trained* myself to respond positively to anything and everything my husband said or did. The training was a two-phase process:

- **Phase One—Say nothing**: Have you ever been in the presence of a woman who doesn't respect her husband? She nags at him, picks on him, and disagrees with him in public. She corrects him, struggling with him over every little thing. Or she cuts him off, interrupts, or worse, finishes his sentences for him. Clearly, saying nothing is a great improvement over that kind of behavior.

- **Phase Two—Respond with a single positive word**: After I had mastered saying nothing in Phase One, I graduated to Phase Two. I chose the word *sure!* (with an exclamation mark behind it and melody in my voice). I began to use this positive response and say *sure!* on the small things. My friend Dixie also chose *sure!* Let me tell you something that happened in her family as a result: Her husband loved to go to Sam's Club, a crowded and noisy discount warehouse. Many times he would announce after dinner, "Hey, let's all go to Sam's Club!"

Well, Dixie—with three children, one of them a baby at the time—could have presented a watertight case against dragging the entire family out to Sam's Club on a school night after dark, but she didn't. She never challenged Doug's leadership in front of her little family. Instead, she just smiled, responded, "Sure!" and got everyone into the car for another trip to Sam's Club.

Many years later, as one by one, Dixie's family members shared around the Thanksgiving dinner table about their favorite thing to do as a family, all three of her grown-up children said, "Going to Sam's Club together." A favorite family memory born out of her obedience and sweet word, "Sure."

A Small But Meaningful Gesture

Early one morning while I was drying my hair with a blower, Jim asked if I could help him find something. My first (and fleshly) thought was, "Can't you hear? I'm drying my hair!" A less selfish option, and a better one, was to yell above the noise of the blower, "Sure, I'll be right there as soon as I finish drying my hair." But God gave me the wisdom and grace to do the least selfish, and best, I said "Sure!" as I turned off the blower. Then I asked my husband, "Do you need me to do that right now, or is there time to finish drying my hair?" I stopped to communicate with Jim, indicating my willingness to serve. He had no problem with me finishing my hair, but the point was my readiness and desire to respond to him. My simple but positive response meant no power struggle, no hurt feelings, no raised voices, and a much better start to our day.

A Lovelier Sermon

Sometimes we're tempted to dismiss God's plan, saying, "My husband isn't walking with God, so I don't have to submit to him," or "My husband isn't a Christian, so I don't have to submit to him." The apostle Peter wrote the following words to help women in those situations who have unbelieving and/or disobedient husbands: "Wives, likewise, be submissive to your own husbands, that even if some do not obey the word, they, without a word, may be won by the conduct of their wives" (1 Peter 3:1). In other words, our submission to our husband (whether or not he is a Christian or being obedient to God) preaches a lovelier and more powerful sermon than our mouth ever could!

It's important to mention here the one exception to following your husband's advice, and that is if he asks you to violate some teaching from God's Word. If he's asking you to do something illegal or immoral, go to a trusted pastor and follow the counsel you receive there.

Once you've begun to respond positively to the small things, you'll quickly find it becoming easier and even natural to respond positively to larger and larger issues, like car purchases, job changes and household moves.

From *A Woman After God's Own Heart*, Harvest House Publishing, © 1997. p.79-80,84-88,111. Used by permission.

11. How are you going to show your husband that you are willing to give him the leadership role in your home?

Week 8: Day 3

Prayer: Bow your heart before the Lord in prayer prior to completing today's Bible study. Ask Him to show you ways that you can make your marriage a priority.

Prioritizing Our Relationships

As women, we have many different kinds of relationships in our lives, but sometimes we forget the most important human relationship we have—our husbands! In order for a marriage to thrive and be all that God intended it to be, we need to prioritize the relationships in our lives and make sure they are in balance. Now that we have established the importance of submission to our husbands, let's take a look at ways that we can make our relationship with our husbands the most important human relationship we have.

Practice These Priorities

"Each day presents many opportunities and challenges to practice our priorities."[6] One way to simplify our moment-by-moment decision making might be to assign the following priorities to our lives:

1. God (spiritual growth)
2. Our husband
3. Our children
4. Our home
5. Our ministry and other activities

Celebrate, Plan and Keep the Priorities

1. Complete the following thought with ways in which you can celebrate and cherish your husband every day.

    I will celebrate my husband by:

    _____
    _____
    _____
    _____
    _____
    _____

> "Each passage in the New Testament... about the husband-wife relationship either begins or ends with a command for mutuality."
> -Clifford and Joyce Penner

The Little Things Make a Difference

There are lots of ways you can show your husband he is the most important person in your life. Here are some examples:

- Let him know how wonderful he is.
- Take an interest in his work and know what he does.
- Let him know how much you appreciate him working.
- When he gets home, greet him with a kiss and hug, and hang up the phone!
- Make him master of your home.
- Don't unload your day's problems; once he's had a chance to rest, then engage in conversation.
- If he's had a rough day, bring him his favorite beverage, make him his favorite meal, and tell him to relax in his favorite chair until dinner.
- Respect his advice.

2. Is your husband your number one human relationship? What steps will you take to re-prioritize your life?

_____

_____

"My beloved is radiant and ruddy, outstanding among ten thousand. His head is purest gold; his hair is wavy and black as a raven. His eyes are like doves by the water streams, washed in milk, mounted like jewels. His cheeks are like beds of spice yielding perfume. His lips are like lilies dripping with myrrh. His arms are rods of gold set with topaz. His body is like polished ivory decorated with lapis lazuli. His legs are pillars of marble set on bases of pure gold. His appearance is like Lebanon, choice as its cedars. His mouth is sweetness itself; he is altogether lovely. This is my beloved, this is my friend..." (Song of Solomon 10:5-16).

How to Be the Wife Your Husband Needs

I enjoy gleaning wisdom from godly women that I love and admire. One evening my dear friend, Cathy Caldwell, was visiting from Boise to be a guest speaker at our women's conference. While sitting by the fireplace in my living room enjoying a trusted friendship, I remember asking her one simple question: "Cathy, how do you know how to best serve and help your husband?" Her answer completely changed my life: "I just pray, 'God, help me to be the wife my husband needs.'"

I have prayed that prayer every day since. I'm amazed how God teaches me what my husband needs, and how to respond and help him, because every husband is fearfully and wonderfully made, and each of their needs are different. After I prayed and tried to follow God's leading, my husband Rick made a comment that blessed my heart. He said, "There is something really different about you and our relationship. What's going on? Because I really love it!" I thought, "Wow, God is really teaching me how to be the wife my husband needs!"

3. Ask yourself: "What will help or hinder my spouse?" How can you make your husband feel like he is the number one human relationship in your life? Explain and write down your plan:

_____
_____
_____
_____
_____
_____

God's Gift of Trust for the Future

God gives us a gift of assurance for our future: "All things work together for good to those who love God [and] are called according to His purpose" (Romans 8:28). We can trust God with our future, because He is a God that can be trusted. Again and again in my life, He has given me exactly what I need in order to grow spiritually. He's healed me from my past and set me free. Let's keep Jesus first in our daily lives!

Satan uses trials and suffering to try to destroy us, but we must let the trials and suffering drive us to Christ, becoming Christians who survive in God's perfect love. May we have a heart to finish this race well, and be steadfast in the will of God.

4. Do you believe God can make your future better? Can you trust Him to help you in your marriage? Explain.

_____
_____
_____
_____
_____
_____

This Week's Memory Verse

"Therefore a man shall leave his father and mother and be joined to his wife, and they shall become one flesh" (Genesis 2:24).

Trusting God with My Past, Present and Future

Our God is the God who transforms. I have seen His transforming power over and over in my life, and in the lives of those I love and respect. I think of Joni Eareckson Tada, who became a quadriplegic as a teenager, but who speaks, writes, draws and sings so eloquently about God's goodness.

I think of my dear friend, Kelly Vincent, who lost her beloved husband in an accident when she was four months pregnant with their first child. I wondered what she would do as a single parent, how would she go on without her husband? But it's been a privilege to see how God has provided for my sweet friend through the years. He has taken her step by step—helping her to trust Him for all of her needs—transforming her from a widow that was going to take her own life to a new bride blessed with a wonderful godly husband.

I think of my husband, Rick, coming from a broken home, with a convict stepfather who was in and out of prison. Rick followed that example, constantly in and out of trouble with the law. But God took a man who had no future—who stole, lied, used drugs, partied, got in drunken fights, was sexually immoral—and forever changed him when he gave his life to Christ Jesus.

Rick learned the real meaning of life: the great fulfillment of serving his Savior. He left his old lifestyle of emptiness and reached toward the higher calling in Christ Jesus. He became a senior pastor at the age of 25, and started two other Calvary Chapels before the age of 30, as well as a Christian school. He is truly a man after God's own heart. His daily devotions and relationship with Christ are his first and most important desire. Everything else (being a husband, dad, leading our home, pastoring the church and school) comes after his time with Christ Jesus. When you seek God first, He gives you the strength and wisdom to face the rest.

I think of my own life: God took a girl who distrusted men and healed that distrust by giving her a godly, protective, dependable and loving husband. God took an angry, confused, broken woman and set her free to become, by God's grace, a loving wife and mom. God took a shy little girl who was in a shell of shame from sexual abuse and assumed retarded in the second grade, and healed her from her past. God took the past that could have destroyed my life, and turned it around to comfort others with the same comfort He gave me. He has offered a fresh beginning to other hurting people through the writing of the *Healed and Set Free Bible Study*.

Greg Laurie writes, "Next to your relationship with God, there is no greater investment on earth than in a happy and successful marriage. Finding God's counsel, warnings, and wisdom on marriage and the home is better than pure gold."[7] So what do we do to build a happy and successful marriage?

> "A good marriage consists of two good forgivers."
> -Ruth Graham

Not only does God speak to us in a still small voice, He speaks to us through His Word, through circumstances and through other believers and ministries. Harvest Ministries is one of those voices that God is using to point out the wisdom of how to have a happy and strong marriage, as exhibited in the following piece:

A Happy and Strong Marriage
From Harvest Ministries

Some people spend more time planning a wedding than preparing for marriage; more time thinking about what they'll wear for the ceremony than what they'll do to build a strong marriage. They spend more time building a house than a home.

Sometimes we hear the term, "a marriage made in heaven," implying that some marriages are destined to be good, and others destined to be bad. But having a good marriage doesn't happen by luck! Marriage is a lot like a mirror. It gives back a reflection of you. If you don't like the way you look, don't blame the mirror! In order for a marriage to be strong and fulfilling, it takes the effort of both partners.

A strong and happy marriage is the result of obedience to God, and laying aside the world's distorted concept of marriage. Marriage God's way, next to salvation itself, is the most fulfilling and wonderful thing I know. As Proverbs 18:22 says, "He who finds a wife finds a good thing, and obtains favor from the Lord."

Are you willing to place your spouse's needs and wants above your own? Are you willing to make whatever sacrifice is necessary to make your marriage what God wants it to be? Are you willing, without reservation, to do what the Bible tells you to do? If you are, you can begin by praying that God would fill you with His Holy Spirit so you can be the spouse He wants you to be. Then submit to your spouse in the fear of God. Your life and marriage will never be the same.

She is Trustworthy

"The heart of her husband safely trusts her; so he will have no lack of gain. She does him good and not evil all the days of her life" (Proverbs 31:11–12). Truth is such an important virtue in a successful marriage. This is one of the reasons adultery is so devastating: Trust is dramatically damaged because a pattern of lying has usually preceded it. Yet a Proverbs 31 woman has her husband's complete trust. The husband knows that she will always be supportive of him, no matter what; he knows his money, resources and possessions are safe in her care.

Here is something worth remembering in a Christian marriage: Never criticize your mate to others or in a public setting. If you want to correct or disagree with him, do it privately. Publicly, however, always support him. Let people know that you and your husband are one.

Christian Wives and Unbelieving Husbands

Sometimes Christian women who are married to non-believers will meet wonderful godly men at church, and in time, they think the Lord is leading them to leave their husbands and remarry. But scripture teaches: "If any brother has a wife who does not believe, and she is willing to live with him, let him not divorce her. And a woman who has a husband who does not believe, if he is willing to live with her, let her not divorce him. For how do you know, O wife, whether you will save your husband? Or how do you know, O husband, whether you will save your wife?" (1 Corinthians 7:12–13, 16).

In God's ideal order, both partners would be living and thinking about the other more than about themselves. Yet in less than ideal situations, Peter tells us how a believing wife can effectively reach a nonbelieving husband for Jesus Christ, or motivate a complacent husband to greater spirituality:

- Reach your husband without a word (1 Peter 3:1). He won't be won to the Lord by telling him what to do, but by showing him what to do. Your actions speak louder than words; you live a godly life, and God will do the saving.

- Avoid the temptation to manipulate. "Manipulate" means to manage or to influence by artful or devious skill; to change to suit one's purpose or advantage. Manipulation is never lasting change. If someone is manipulated into doing something, he can be manipulated out of it.

- Avoid the temptation to nag. A woman usually resorts to this when she feels her husband is not paying attention to her. King Solomon wrote, "The contentions of a wife are a continual dripping" (Proverbs 19:13), and "Better to live in a desert than with a contentious and angry wife" (Proverbs 21:19). Nagging drives a husband away. Remember to notice what he has done, not what he hasn't done. Watch what you do and say. "Reckless words pierce like a sword, but the tongue of the wise brings healing" (Proverbs 12:18 NIV).

- Cultivate the peace of God in your life. Peter tells women not to let their adornment be merely outward, but "let it be the hidden person of the heart, with the incorruptible beauty of a gentle and quiet spirit, which is very precious in the sight of God" (1 Peter 3:4). The J.B. Phillips translation reads, "the unfading loveliness of a calm and gentle spirit." Quiet doesn't mean lack of noise or activity, but lack of agitation or harshness. It doesn't mean a woman cannot differ with her husband. She has a God-given right and responsibility to set her husband straight if he is off course. Instead, it means she is to cultivate the peace of God in her life. Then when she speaks, her husband will listen.

The Root of the Problem

The problems married people face could be summed up in one simple word: self. The traits of sin and selfishness, coupled with a desire to concentrate on our own needs and wants, all started at the Fall. Sin creates a false hunger, not for communion and fellowship with God, but for individuality of a destructive nature. You might say, "Well, that's human nature. There's nothing we can do to change that." But there is. God can give us a new nature to be the husbands and wives, and the mothers and fathers that we need to be.

From Harvest Ministries, PO Box 4000, Riverside, CA 92514 © 2012. Used by permission.
http://www.harvest.org/knowgod/new-believer/foundations-for-living/marriage-family.html.

"For I know the thoughts that I think toward you, says the Lord, thoughts of peace and not of evil, to give you a future and a hope" (Jeremiah 29:11).

Week 8: Day 4

Prayer: Bow your heart before the Lord before completing today's study. Ask God to show you His intent for the intimacy between husbands and wives.

Sexual intimacy between a husband and wife is holy, pure, good and most importantly, designed by God. Men and women were created for one another and, like a puzzle, fit perfectly together in a beautiful design. Unfortunately, many things try to destroy this perfect union and undermine its importance in relationships.

The Marriage Bed is Honorable Between a Husband and Wife

The hurtful memories of sexual abuse, rape or sexual relationships outside of marriage can bring difficulty with sexual intimacy in a marriage, damaging a couple's relationship. Satan has harmed children through sexual abuse, and corrupted sex in the media, on TV and in movies and magazines. We need to transform our minds from the defiled past where sex may be a painful subject. We need to see the truth of God's undefiled design for sex in the marriage bed, where married couples enjoy sexual fulfillment as God designed it to be—holy and pure.

"Marriage is honorable among all, and the bed undefiled; but fornicators and adulterers God will judge" (Hebrews 13:4). In the Greek, "honorable" (*timios*) means valuable, of costly price, most precious, dear, desirable, honored, esteemed and beloved. "Undefiled" in the Greek (*amiantos*) means unsoiled, pure, unpolluted, unstained by sin. *Amiantos* is only used four times in the New Testament; notice the holy beauty of its uses in these verses:

- **Of Jesus**: "For such a High Priest was fitting for us, who is holy, harmless, undefiled, separate from sinners, and has become higher than the heavens" (Hebrews 7:26).

- **Of True Religion**: "Pure and undefiled religion before God and the Father is this: to visit orphans and widows in their trouble, and to keep oneself unspotted from the world" (James 1:27).

- **Of Our Heavenly Inheritance**: "To an inheritance incorruptible and undefiled and that does not fade away, reserved in heaven for you" (1 Peter 1:4).

- And last but not least, it's used of the holy and beautiful bed where married couples enjoy sexual fulfillment as God designed it: "Marriage should be honored by all, and the marriage bed kept pure..." (Hebrews 13:4 NIV).

1. Read Lamentations 3:40-41: "Let us search out and examine our ways, and turn back to the Lord; let us lift our hearts and hands to God in heaven."

    Is sexual intimacy in your marriage fulfilling for both of you?

    _____
    _____

2. How are you to look at your marriage bed?

    _____

What's Your Focus?

"Let the only measure of your expectations for yourself be the resurrection power of Jesus Christ. You can then live a truly powerful life, not because you are no longer weak, but because being weak, you count on His power to work in you," writes Anne Ortlund.[8] We can be healed and set free to be the people God has made us to be. Satan wants us to take our eyes off the blessings that God showers on us, and put our focus on the negative to rob us of our blessings. When you're faced with reminders of the past—smells, phrases, places or songs—recognize that it's coming from the enemy, planning his attack to get you back in the chains of your past.

3. Is sexual intimacy pure or dirty to you? Is your mind defiled or undefiled concerning sex in marriage?

4. When we realize we have held on to negative thoughts and emotions rather than release them to God, what are we to do? What is our responsibility?

5. Do you want to forget the past corruption of sex? Confess these things to Christ and He will help you move on.

6. What will you do when sinful things from your past come to your mind?

The Marriage Bed Is Honorable: Physically Love Him

Elizabeth George said, "I remember hearing God's view of physical love taught at a seminar I attended as a new Christian. I was so impressed and convicted, I went straight home and announced to my husband that I was available to him physically at any and all times for the rest of our life together! That may have been an overreaction, but I wanted to act on God's Word, and my husband got the message."[9]

7. Read 1 Corinthians 7:3-5: "Let the husband render to his wife the affection due her [likewise] the wife to her husband. The wife does not have authority over her own body, but the husband does... Likewise the husband does not have authority over his own body, but the wife does. Do not deprive one another except with consent for a time, that you may give yourselves to fasting and prayer; and come together again so that Satan does not tempt you because of your lack of self-control."

A fundamental principle for marriage is "rendering affection" to one's mate. Song of Solomon details physical love in marriage, and Proverbs 5:19 says our husband is to be "enraptured" with our sexual love. When you start thinking about sex as dirty within your marriage bed, what scripture can you memorize to keep you from believing this lie? Quickly go to prayer. Hold on to God's grace, and remember Philippians 3:13: "Brethren, I do not count myself to have apprehended; but one thing I do, forgetting those things which are behind and reaching forward to those things which are ahead."

Write down your thoughts.

_____
_____
_____

8. Read Proverbs 5:15-21 on page 304.

   How can your fountain or relationship be blessed?

   _____
   _____

9. Write down four things that make you rejoice over your spouse.

   1. _____
   2. _____
   3. _____
   4. _____

10. Write down ways you can show your husband how much you care about him.

    _____
    _____
    _____
    _____

Helpful Hints

Proverbs 31:22 says, "She makes coverings for her bed; she is clothed in fine linen and purple." Here are some helpful hints to make your sexual relationship more fulfilling and special, and make your husband feel wanted and loved.

Make Your Bedroom a Special Place

- Decorate your bedroom. Make it cozy and romantic.
- Keep your bedroom clean and uncluttered. As one woman said, "The worst thing we ever did was try to make our bedroom the office/bedroom. We had to move the computer downstairs! Now it's just our 'love nest.'"
- Show your husband that you are interested in sexual intimacy; make him feel wanted, loved and attractive.

Week 8: Day 5

Prayer: Bow your heart before the Lord in prayer. Ask Him to show you ways that you can improve your relationship with your husband.

Creating the Right Environment

As wives and managers of our homes, God has given us a great responsibility in creating an environment that is peaceful and inviting for our husbands. An environment that they want to come home to is nurturing for your relationship. It is also important to make sure that you and your husband have quality and quantity time together to nurture your relationship. In this section, we will discuss ways to create the right environment for your marriage and family to thrive.

Prepare for His Homecoming Daily

- Before your husband gets home, quickly pick up the house. Have your kids help and put away their toys. I enjoy lighting scented candles, turning on relaxing Christian music, and even having dinner on the stove, so my husband comes home to a peaceful refuge that says, "I'm glad you're home."

- Welcome him home with a hug, kiss and planned greeting. "A good man ponders what to say" (Proverbs 15:28). Ask God to give you the right words!

- Get your children ready to greet their father. Be sure the TV is off.

Elizabeth George writes, "It is a privilege to be able to prepare for our husbands' arrival and to lavish love on them. Pour out God's love, which is poured out in your heart (Romans 5:5), when your husband walks through the door of his home! Make sure he's not treated like the man who wrote 'The Homecoming'":

> When I get home after work, the only one who acts like she cares is my little dog. She is really glad to see me and lets me know it. I always come in the back door, because Doris is in the kitchen about then. She always looks up from whatever she is doing with a startled look in her eyes and says, "Oh, are you home already?"
>
> Somehow she makes me feel like I've done something wrong just by getting home. I used to try and say hello to the kids, but I don't do that anymore. It seems like I would just be getting in the way or step in front of the TV at just the wrong minute. So now, I just pick up little Suzy, my dog, stick her under my arm and go out in the yard. I act like I don't care, and maybe I shouldn't, but I do. It makes me feel like the only reason I'm here is to pay the bills and to keep the place up. If the bills are paid and nothing breaks, no one would ever know I was gone.[10]

"Let the wife make her husband glad to come home."
-Martin Luther

Make Home a Place to Cherish

- Seek God daily to keep your heart clean from having a junk drawer.
- Seek ways daily to do something special for your spouse.
- Keep a neat and orderly home.
- Meet your spouse's needs: consult him every day to see if there's anything he would like you to do for him.
- Respond positively.
- Work diligently to send every member of your family off in a good mood every day; personally meet and greet each of them as they return home.
- Make dinner for your family.
- Grow daily in your God-given roles as a wife, mom and Christian woman.

1. Are you taking the time to prepare for your husband? Yes or no? What kind of environment does your husband come home to?

2. What steps can you take to make your home a place that your husband wants to come home to?

War Maker or Peacemaker?

Skip Heitzig is another one of those people God is using to point out wisdom and truth. In his devotional titled "The Right Words,"[11] Skip expands on the importance in our choice of words.

> Sometimes we can be ironic in our use of words. For instance, the word "peacemaker" has been applied to both the huge B-36 bomber of the 1950s and the Colt .45 revolver used by lawmen and the Army in the late 1800s. Jesus uses the word for something a lot less intimidating. In the Sermon on the Mount, He says, "Blessed are the peacemakers, for they shall be called sons of God" (Matthew 5:9). 1 Samuel 25 gives us a great example of what it means to be a peacemaker.
>
> David was living in the wilderness, keeping his distance from Saul and protecting the people. He sends men to ask for provisions from a man named Nabal. Nabal is a rich man, whose name means "fool." That's a volatile combination! He's described as "harsh and evil in his doings;" even his own servants call him a "scoundrel."
>
> Nabal quickly lives up to his name. He not only refuses the request but insults David, comparing him to a runaway servant. David's response is to go ballistic. He and his men grab their swords and march out to kill Nabal. So the hard-headed Nabal is about to be destroyed by the hot-headed David.
>
> Here's where the peacemaker steps into the picture. The wife of the fool Nabal is a woman named Abigail, who is called "a woman of good

understanding and beautiful appearance." Opposites do attract! She's the "rose between two thorns," and she keeps the two men from coming to bloodshed. She quickly gathers supplies for David and rushes out to meet him. With soothing words, she takes responsibility for the insult against David, and she cools his hot anger. Mark Twain once said, "The difference between the right word and the almost-right word is the difference between lightning and the lightning bug." Abigail has the right words and the right demeanor, and it makes all the difference: David, faced with the sweetness and humility of Abigail, repents of his anger.

Here's my point about peacemakers: They seek solutions to problems rather than arguments. Peacemakers seek to calm the waters rather than stirring them up, and peacemakers work hard for reconciliation rather than retaliation. By seeking to make peace, Abigail not only keeps her husband from being killed, she also keeps David from doing something he would regret. Peacemakers are courageous, but they're also humble. They know that "a soft answer turns away wrath" (Proverbs 15:1).

Expressing Our Hurt Instead of Anger

One of the ways that we can create the right environment for our husbands is to be careful how we respond to them. Like Abigail, God can use us to be peacemakers in our marriages. Let's look at some ways that we can create a more peaceful, enjoyable and inviting environment for our husbands.

Most problems start with someone getting hurt. Most hurts simply come from misunderstandings because men and women think so differently. If you're married, I'm sure you can relate: A wife feels hurt when her husband doesn't include her in a decision, doesn't help around the house, or doesn't listen when she is sharing something important. A husband feels hurt when his wife doesn't respect him, isn't sensitive about the pressure he's under at work, criticizes him in front of someone, or doesn't support his decisions.

"Hurt is a legitimate response to disappointment and offense," writes Bill Hybels, "and it should never be denied or kept hidden… Hurt becomes a problem when people let it build up inside and turn into anger. This is why it is so important to plan peace talks as soon as possible, before hurt turns to anger."[12]

Most spouses are moved when their partner shares his or her hurt feelings, and expressing hurt becomes the bridge to understanding and compassion. On the other hand, "venting hostility blows up bridges, because people are repelled by angry assaults. Another mistake that causes hurt to turn to anger is accumulating grievances. One hurt is manageable, two hurts are a little harder to deal with, and more than that is almost impossible to keep from turning into anger."[13] Grievances pile up quickly, eventually becoming so overwhelming that anger is inevitable.

So deal with offenses as they arise. Don't let them pile up until they turn into out-of-control anger or deep-seated bitterness. Have "heart to heart" talks as often as needed. Remember, under-your-breath remarks are counterproductive.

Have you ever handled conflict with the "freeze out" method? During our early years of marriage, when Rick did something that hurt my feelings or angered me, I would simply "freeze him out." I wouldn't look him in the eye, engage in conversation or smile. I'd just walk around detached as if he were a stranger. When Rick would ask me what was wrong, I would look away and say, "Nothing." But of course, he knew something was wrong. He would try to lighten up the mood by being kind, or ask me if I wanted to go do something fun, but I wouldn't respond. After many attempts, and my lack of response, he would give me a taste of my own medicine and give me the "freeze out."

Instead of the "freeze out," I needed to have a "heart to heart" with my husband to share my hurt and get to the bottom of it, so we could move past the situation and avoid it in the future. My method simply allowed the wound to fester, leading to more anger, bitterness and a vicious cycle that was difficult to break. Now that I have learned the tools to be set free from my anger, I love being married to Rick. He's the only man I have ever loved or plan on loving. Investing in your marriage and in each other should be the most important role you have as a married person—of course, apart from your relationship with Christ Jesus.

Yes, "heart to heart" conversations take an enormous amount of energy, but every "heart to heart" brings you a little closer to understanding how your spouse thinks and what their needs are. For example, I appreciate how diligent Rick is in maintaining our vehicle: filling the tank with gas, regular oil changes and getting the car tuned up. He never ignores our car.

In the same way, marriages need constant maintenance to have a smooth running, meaningful and fine-tuned relationship. We need to fill the marriage tank every day, notice when the marriage needs attention, and tune up by reading a Christian book on marriage from time to time. Try investing in your marriage by planning a romantic getaway. Look for new ways to engage in meaningful conversations. Never ignore your marriage relationship. Each day is another opportunity to fall in love all over again. Marriage is a gift from God! Tune up your marriage, forgive each other, pray for each other and invest in each other every day!

Don't Give Up!
- Be willing to humble yourself.
- Have "heart to heart" talks as often as needed.
- Don't take blame you don't deserve, but fully accept blame that's rightly yours.
- Be willing to say, "I'm sorry." When these words are said sincerely and with a humble heart, they open a line of communication to reconcile with your spouse. Show you want to make it right! Life is too short to let anger rule!

How to Say "I'm Sorry"
- "Forgive me for letting my pride get in the way. I'm sorry. Can we start over?"
- "I'm sorry for blowing up in front of the kids. I don't want to keep doing that."
- "I'm sorry I was selfish. I was wrong."
- "I'm sorry I have an expectation of you. That's not right of me."
- "I'm sorry, forgive me for thinking you could read my mind. I didn't communicate clearly."
- "I should never have said what I said. Please forgive me."

Praise Him

Ladies, never pass up an opportunity to bless your husband in public, and bless him to his face. Again, Elizabeth George offers her wisdom: "If you catch yourself speaking critically about him, quickly quit speaking and do two things:

- "Search your heart. 'Hatred stirs up strife, but love covers all sins' (Proverbs 10:12).
- "Seek a solution. If some area in your husband's life needs attention, choose a better path: devote yourself to prayer; if you need to speak up, do so after much preparation and with gracious, edifying, sweet speech (Ephesians 4:29). You may need to speak to your pastor, but remember: time with the pastor is not for venting about your husband, but getting help so that you can properly deal with the issue. Blessing your husband in public and in private is one way to sow seeds of love for him in your heart."[14]

3. How do you speak to your husband?

_____

_____

4. Will you put the lessons you've learned from this section about praising your husband into practice?

_____

_____

5. How will you do this?

_____

_____

The Right Perspective

Our perspective is how we see things. We tend to see what we want to see, and that's why changing our perspective calls for a willingness to see things differently. No matter where you find yourself today, know that God has put you in this place for such a time as this, as author Elizabeth George cheers us women on to have "the right perspective."[15]

> As I prayerfully prioritize the activities of my day, God not only gives me a vision for the day, but for my life. This prioritizing also gives me a passion for what I am trying to achieve with my life's efforts. That passion has been fueled by the following comments I first heard at a women's retreat. Since the day I heard these statements, they have motivated me to follow after God's plan for my life with all of my heart, soul, mind and strength! First let me set the stage: A reporter interviewed four women, asking each of them what she thought about "the golden years," that period in life "after middle age, traditionally characterized by wisdom, contentment and useful leisure." These are their thoughts and fears.
>
> **Age 31:** "Golden years? I have so much to do before then that I doubt I'll ever have them. I have to help my husband succeed. I want to raise our children... And, of course, I want time for me, to find myself, and to be my own person."

Age 44: "Only 20 years to go! If I can just get the kids through college and on their own. If we can just help keep my husband's blood pressure under control and get through menopause sanely. I'm just hoping we get there."

Age 55: "Doubtful. Sometimes I think our golden years will never come. My parents are still alive and need constant attention. Our daughter was divorced last year and lives with us again. She had a baby, and of course my husband and I feel responsible for both her and our grandson."

Age 63: "I'm supposed to be on the brink, but I'm not. I'll be frank. I thought we were saving enough to live comfortably, but we haven't. Inflation has eaten up our savings and now my husband talks about deferring his retirement. If he does, I will too. We're both unhappy about the way things have turned out."

Sobering comments, aren't they? As we stand looking down the corridor of time, life can appear hopeless, pointless and futile! But what does God think? Let's look at a godly perspective from a woman to whom I sent a copy of what you just read. Here's her inspiring response: "We should treat each day as if it and it alone was our golden day. Then what a beautiful string of golden days we will have that will become golden years to give back to the Lord!" Imagine being a woman who treats each day as if it were her golden day! When I thought about this, I said, "That's it!"

Treating each day as if it and it alone were our golden day is the "how" of practicing priorities. It's also the "why," the motivation and the perspective we need for practicing them! If you desire a good life, focus on having one good quality day today! After all, as Joseph Hall famously quoted, "Every day is a little life, and our whole life is but a day repeated."

But what if your day was a failure? A day of merely trying to survive? A day of taking shortcuts? A day of neglecting things you wanted to focus on? We all have those days. But thanks be to God who enables us to forget the day that's done, reach forward the next morning, and press on toward the goal (Philippians 3:13-14). In His power and grace, we keep following after God's heart, no matter what! After all, every morning He gives you a fresh new day, an unspoiled opportunity to live according to His priorities.

Furthermore, by exercising the privilege of confession, and because of Jesus' forgiveness, you have a clean start with the dawn. "God's mercies are new every morning" (Lamentations 3:22). So remember, your goal is simple: have one good day of living your priorities and God's plan for your life. When the day is done, you'll be exhausted as you drop into bed, but you'll also know an unmatched peace in your heart: peace from resting in the Lord and doing things His way, peace from knowing you're living a life of promise with no regrets.

This Week's Memory Verse

"Therefore a man shall leave his father and mother and be joined to his wife, and they shall become one flesh" (Genesis 2:24).

Home Management

Again, looking to the wisdom that Elizabeth George shares in *A Woman After God's own Heart*,[16] we find some great insights into home management. She says:

> To "guide a house" means to be the head of or to rule a family. The one who manages a house is the householder. This management has built-in accountability, describing the work of a steward or servant. The woman who manages her house is not the head of the home. Her husband is, if she is married, and God is if she isn't. Instead, she is the house manager.
>
> 1 Timothy 5:14 says, "I desire that the younger women guide the house." The women of Timothy's church were idle, wandering from house to house, and also gossips and busybodies, saying things which they ought not (1 Timothy 5:13). Their undisciplined behavior led those outside the church to think and speak poorly of Christianity (v. 14). Obviously, having a home to manage would contribute positively to these women's lives by eliminating the opportunity for negative behavior.
>
> It's a blessing for women to serve God in this capacity! And what a blessing we are to our families when we properly manage the household and keep the right perspective. Martin Luther wrote, "The greatest blessing is to have a wife to whom you may entrust your affairs." That's what being a home manager is all about! Titus 2:4-5 has given women an assignment to love their husband and children, to be discreet, chaste homemakers, good and obedient to their own husbands.

How to Manage a Home

"Home management is God's best for us," writes Elizabeth George.[17] Every company has a manager who oversees their customer service, quality control and employees. If not, the company would fall apart. Choosing to manage our homes is choosing God's way. He is simply calling us, as women, to do it. Home management is His plan, and it is His good, acceptable and perfect will for us (Romans 12:2). If we don't manage our homes, they too will fall apart.

6. Decide to take home management seriously. Read Proverbs 31:27: "She watches over the ways of her household."

    Pray and ask God what you can do to be the best house manager for God and your family. Then plan your day to accomplish it. Write down your thoughts.

    _____

    _____

    _____

7. What lessons could you learn from an older woman? If you work outside the home, who could give you pointers on new skills for better "home management"? Ask God to show you the right woman, and to help you follow through on what you learn. Write down some of the questions you might ask.

    _____

    _____

8. We can't share what we don't possess. We can't help our children learn, read, study, discuss, memorize or recite the Bible if we're not doing it ourselves. What are you doing or what will you do to fill your own heart with the law of the Lord? Develop a plan. What will you read? What will you teach your children?

Teaching Our Children

When my kids, Caleb and Jessica, were young, they would clean their room and help with household chores. They each had their own clothes basket, and from the time they were nine, they could add the laundry soap, turn the dials on the washing machine, wash their clothes, fold them and put them away in their drawers. This was important preparation for real life. It's never too late to begin to build your house and to create a wonderful home. Only the enemy, Satan, would want us to think otherwise. We can begin at any time, even today! I was blessed to the place of tears as I read my friend Shelley Spady's thoughts on motherhood, presented below in "When Is It My Turn?"[18]

> Life used to be quiet. Noise and chaos could be turned on and off. The word "I" was used often. Life was good. Then something strange happened and my life turned upside down. A miraculous event took place that left my previous self a thing of the past, along with bikinis and belts. The strange event was called "having children," and life was no longer quiet.
>
> There were dishes to wash, laundry to fold, diapers to change and events that required my attention when normal people were sleeping. Peanut butter was smeared on the couch, crayon on the walls, a million toys everywhere, and it was my responsibility to take care of it all. Many times late at night, as I threw my battered body on the couch after a long day of battle, I was left to ponder one question: When will it be my turn? When will I get 5 minutes to myself? How about a massage? How about a maid? How about a phone call without children screaming in the background? How about a shower? When will the "I" be back in my vocabulary?
>
> Then something would happen: As I pondered life's most daunting question, I was reminded of the truth. Like many things in life, it was the difficult journeys that were filled with the most joy and happiness. But how could giving every ounce of my being to others be joyous? It just was, and I knew it. And it wasn't just joy. It made my life complete.
>
> The truth is, it had been my turn all along: My turn to love, my turn to bandage scraped knees and dry little tears. My turn to answer life's most difficult questions. My turn to watch an angel sleep. My turn to hear the words "I love you" from the most beautiful voices in the world. It was my turn to put another person's needs before my own. My turn to be a mother.
>
> So go ahead. Throw Cheerios on the floor. Scream and yell and laugh. Hide and seek and play to your heart's content. Track mud on the floor. Rearrange the furniture. Throw toys in the toilet. Even let the snake out of its cage; it will turn up one of these days. Yes, I will get tired and irritated and want to jump off a cliff now and then, but I will always remember one thing: I am the luckiest woman in the world and I have loved every minute.

Celebrating Life

"The thief does not come except to steal, and to kill, and to destroy. I have come that they may have life, and that they may have it more abundantly" (John 10:10). Christ came to make eternal, abundant life available to all. We who have accepted Him have eternal life, but few Christians enjoy the abundant life. Satan can't steal eternal life, but he can rob you of the joy of living abundantly. Be aware of Satan's schemes, and SEE, GIVE, FORGIVE, FORGET and BE SET FREE to enjoy abundant life.

One day we'll be in Heaven. There will be no tears, no pain and no failures. We need to celebrate the life we've been given now, as we live in anticipation of Heaven. The air you breathe is a gift from God. Celebrate! The husband and children you have are gifts from God. Celebrate them! The love you give and receive is a gift from God because God is love. Celebrate your love! Your very salvation is a gift from God and ensures your future. Celebrate your future in Heaven!

First: Commit to focus on God in celebration. "Lord, what can I do today to live out and celebrate the fact that you are the Ultimate Priority in my life?"

Second: Commit to help and focus on your spouse. I try to focus on Rick and his responsibilities by asking him two questions: "What can I do for you today?" and "What can I do to help you make better use of your time today?"

When Elizabeth George's husband became a full-time seminary student, a full-time staff member at church, and traveled extensively with a missions pastor, she read every book she could find about Ruth Graham, wife of evangelist Billy Graham. Ruth's husband was absent from home almost ten months a year. Elizabeth learned from Ruth Graham's experience: "We have to learn to make the least of all that goes and the most of all that comes." Elizabeth said, "This encouragement made me a better helper to my husband as he serves as a senior pastor preparing for speaking, preaching, early morning and late night counseling appointments; elder, leadership and school staff meetings; and late night hospital visits week after week. It has also decreased my urge to pout and give the cold shoulder to my husband."[19]

Third: Commit to focus on your children in celebration. "Lord, what can I do today for Caleb and Jessica to let them know that, after Rick, they are more important than all other people in my life?" Many times the answer was to show patience, kindness and not lose my temper. I scheduled specific times to play with them. After school I might surprise them by going out for ice cream or making their favorite snack.

Fourth: Commit to focus on your home in celebration. "Lord, what can I do in my home today?" The answer is to watch over my home as the house manager and make my home a refuge for my family and guests.

Fifth: Commit to focus on your ministry in celebration. "Lord, what can I do today to minister to Your people?" Call friends, organize women's retreats, write, or prepare food for events to show support for the Body of Christ.

9. What would you like to do to celebrate your life?

Chapter Review

1. What have you learned about the word "submission"?

2. Have your attitudes or feelings about submission changed after reading this chapter?

3. What changes will you make to prioritize the most important human relationship you have: your husband?

4. What can you do to improve the intimacy between you and your husband?

5. What things can you do to make the environment in your home a more inviting place for your family, especially your husband?

7 Secrets to a Great Marriage

1st Secret:
If it's God's will for you to marry, re-live all of the little things and reasons that made you fall in love with the other person, and then start counting all of the new ones.[20]

2nd Secret:
Start your day by reading the Bible and praying. This allows you to bring the power of the Spirit into your marriage, and helps take the "I" out of marriage (ie: choosing to be selfless).

3rd Secret:
Being "there" for your spouse is what being married is really about. It takes time to get to know another person. If you're not available, it can't happen.[21]

4th Secret:
Be appreciative. "Thank you": Two words spouses don't hear often enough—from one another: "Thank you for being my love" or "thank you for supporting me." Gratitude is not an option. (1 Thessalonians 5:18, "Give thanks in all circumstances.")[21]

5th Secret:
Your attitude does matter. Changing behavior is important, but so is changing attitudes. Bad attitudes often drive bad feelings and actions.[22]

6th Secret:
Resist holding grudges. As Ruth Graham reminds us, "A happy marriage is the union of two good forgivers." We choose not to bring up the past. No marriage is perfect, because no husband is perfect and no wife is perfect.

7th Secret:
Is it possible to build a marriage that lasts. We focus on this verse, "Love the Lord your God with all your heart and with all your soul and with all your strength and with all your mind'; and, 'Love your neighbor as yourself'" (Luke 10:27).

Stories of Real People and a Real Savior

My Marriage Was Over! How God Restored Our "Love Account"
By Teresa, Idaho

"He heals the brokenhearted and binds up their wounds"- (Psalm 147:3).

Thank you for the opportunity to share my testimony, and thank you, Tammy Brown, and all the others who shared their life stories with us. I would also like to thank Vicki for being a great teacher, leader and friend through this process.

My husband and I have been married for fourteen years. Somewhere along the way we stopped investing in our "love account" and did a lot more investing in our "self-serving account." We had begun drinking. It started with special occasions, then weekends, then before we knew it, it was several times a week. I was under the illusion that I was a much "happier" person if I drank. That was far from the truth! I usually found myself pointing an accusatory finger at my husband, followed by nagging. My husband would turn a deaf ear to me, giving me the cold shoulder. During this time we found ourselves in very unsavory situations, even dangerous. Our family life began to suffer, as well as our spiritual life. I very rarely went to church. Although I was saved, I felt very distant from God. By this point in my life I had already felt the cold sting of being molested as a child, and the fear of physical and verbal retaliation from a much older brother. But my fear, shame and guilt would not end there; life was about to deal me the biggest blow of my life—betrayal.

Betrayal was one of my biggest fears, and I shared that very openly in my marriage. I have learned that Satan works our fears against us, that is, if we give him the power to do so. My husband strayed for a moment, and in that moment our lives were forever changed. I found out about his betrayal from the person with whom he had betrayed me. I felt so hopeless. I screamed a colorful array of phrases at him over the phone. I found myself circling his car with a very large mallet, trying to decide which part was going to be taken out first. Eventually, I relented and took my anger out on our picnic table, which, needless to say, did not survive. I spent most of that night plotting revenge, even swearing he would come home to an empty home left in shambles. The next day I drained our savings account and even went as far as going to a lawyer.

But as I stepped into the lawyer's office, I knew I could not end things on those terms. When we said our vows it was "for better or for worse, in sickness or in health." I had every reason—and God's given blessing—to walk out of my marriage that day. But I didn't. When my husband came home, we had a very long heartbreaking talk. I even went as far as giving my ring back to him and told him he needed to prove his love to me.

That was the weekend we began rebuilding. We began a couples' devotional, and for the first time in thirteen years, we actually joined hands and prayed. I would love to tell you that our recommitment to God, family, and to one another made everything easy, and that we sailed on calm seas into the sunset. But it was the worst storm I had ever gone through in my life. I found myself in bed for very long stints of time. I began cutting. I felt so numb, and the pain hurt so bad. I had lost all control over my life, and cutting seemed to mask some of my internal pain.

During our struggles my mom passed away. By all accounts and definition I was an orphan. I knew I needed help. My bitterness, shame and hate continued to grow like a wild fire inside of me. Then I began the Healed and Set Free Bible study. What a blessing it has been. It taught me to see my "roots of bitterness" that began to spring up within me. It made me see that my choices, no matter how much I felt justified in that moment, were not OK if they were not the will of God.

"See to it that no one falls short of the grace of God and that no bitter root grows up to cause trouble and defile many" (Hebrews 12:15). Forgiveness is for me as much as it is for the person who has wronged me. "For if you forgive other people when they sin against you, your heavenly Father will also forgive you. But if you do not forgive others their sins, your Father will not forgive your sins (Matthew 6:14-15). At many points during this healing process, I would find myself pointing out all my husband's failures only to have three fingers pointed back at me. I needed as much forgiveness and grace as I thought my husband did. I gave my pain, bitterness, shame and hate to the Lord, and in return He has given me peace, joy and love. Pretty good trade I think!

Finally I have begun to heal and be set free from all my burdens. It does not happen overnight. I still sometimes pray with clinched teeth for those who have hurt me so deeply, but it's getting easier. God has done great things in me, in my husband, and in our family. Since the first day we joined our hands in prayer together, there have been very few days we have missed a day of prayer. We have seen both our kids saved and baptized through our journey, and it's only been a year! I can only imagine what other blessings He has in store for our lives. My husband was and is my best friend; I love him with my whole heart. I am thankful for God, for His abounding grace and for second chances.

Tools to Become Healed and Set Free

To equip yourself in God's truth, look over the tools and verses that will be introduced in the coming weeks. Thinking about the past won't change it, but you can change your future by being set free from your past.

TOOL #1 - SEE: I must SEE the truth about what is in my heart so I am not defiled.

> **Definition**: To defile means to make filthy or dirty; to pollute.

> **Bible Verse**: "Looking carefully lest anyone fall short of the grace of God; lest any root of bitterness springing up cause trouble, and by this many become defiled" (Hebrews 12:15).

TOOL #2 - GIVE: I must GIVE my sin to God through repentance, knowing that Christ is waiting to take it. I must be sorry enough to change, and choose to go God's way over my own.

> **Definition**: To repent means to feel such sorrow for sin or fault as to be disposed to change one's life for the better; be penitent.

> **Bible Verse**: "For godly sorrow produces repentance leading to salvation, not to be regretted; but the sorrow of the world produces death" (2 Corinthians 7:10).

TOOL #3 - FORGIVE: I must FORGIVE as I am forgiven by Christ: Forgiving those who hurt, bruised, wronged, rejected, betrayed or harmed me, whether unintentionally or deliberately. I must ask God to forgive me for holding on to unforgiveness and know that He will.

> **Definition**: To forgive means to stop feeling angry or resentful toward someone for an offense, flaw or mistake.

> **Bible Verse**: "...Bearing with one another, and forgiving one another, if anyone has a complaint against another; even as Christ forgave you, so you also must do" (Colossians 3:13).

TOOL #4 - FORGET: I must FORGET by no longer dwelling on the hurt or the painful reminders, such as: phrases, smells, places, songs and comments. Instead, I am putting my mind on the higher calling that Christ has for me.

> **Definition**: To forget means to choose not to remember or notice, "forgive and forget".

> **Bible Verse**: "Brethren, I do not count myself to have apprehended; but one thing I do, forgetting those things which are behind and reaching forward to those things which are ahead" (Philippians 3:13).

Be Healed and Set Free: Christ will heal me from my past, showing me the truth, so I can become a cleansed vessel, healed and set free.

> **Definition**: To set free means to make free; set at liberty; release from bondage, imprisonment, or restraint.

> **Definition**: To heal means to make whole and healthy; to cure; to remedy or repair.

> **Bible Verse**: "And you shall know the truth, and the truth shall make you free" (John 8:32).

Chapter 9

Healed and Set Free

This Week's Focus

As our last week, we will go over the four tools we've learned and discover the summation of our journey, which is to "Be Healed and Set Free."

Be Healed and Set Free: Christ will heal me from past hurts, showing me the truth, so I can become a cleansed vessel who is healed and set free.

Definition: To heal means to make whole and healthy; to cure; to remedy or repair.

Definition: To free means to make free, set at liberty; release from bondage, imprisonment or restraint.

Bible Verse: "And you shall know the truth, and the truth shall make you free" (John 8:32).

Prayer: Ask God to strengthen you through His Spirit so that Christ may dwell in your heart, through faith, that you may be filled with all the fullness of God.

Week 9: Day 1

Prayer: Bow your heart before the Lord in prayer prior to completing today's Bible study. Thank God for the truth that has set you free.

Each of us is capable, by the power of the Holy Spirit, to lay down our own will, but not all are willing. It's our free choice to either embrace or reject the truth from the scriptures we learn. But one day we will stand accountable for what we know. When we reject the will of God, we seem okay on the outside, but on the inside our hearts are filled with:

- Bitterness
- Resentment
- Pride
- Unforgiveness
- Hopelessness
- Unhappiness
- Self-centered desires
- Defensiveness
- Jealousy
- Anger

When we embrace the will of God, we will be able to deal with and acknowledge our true feelings, get real with God, get rid of the strongholds, and follow the truth. We can have victory over the flesh day by day and choice by choice! Jesus said, "If you abide in My word, you are My disciples indeed" (John 8:31).

What God Hath Promised

Annie Johnson Flint

God hath not promised skies always blue

Flower-strewn pathways all our lives through;

God hath not promised sun without rain,

Joy without sorrow, peace without pain,

But God has promised strength for the day,

Rest for the labor, light for the way

Grace for the trials, help from above,

Unfailing sympathy, undying love

"God is preparing you today for something greater tomorrow!"
- Greg Laurie

Tools to Become Set Free

In this chapter, we will continue to use **Tool #1 - SEE**, **Tool #2 - GIVE**, **Tool #3 - FORGIVE** and **Tool # 4 - FORGET**.

These tools will help you to become set free. It is crucial to memorize these powerful tools and review them regularly in order to apply them to your daily life.

#1 - SEE: I must SEE the truth about what is in my heart so I am not defiled.

#2 - GIVE: I must GIVE my sin to God through repentance, knowing that Christ is waiting to take it. I must be sorry enough to change, and choose to go God's way over my own.

#3 - FORGIVE: I must FORGIVE as I am forgiven by Christ: Forgiving those who hurt, bruised, wronged, rejected, betrayed or harmed me, whether unintentionally or deliberately. I must ask God to forgive me for holding on to unforgiveness and know that He will.

#4 - FORGET: I must FORGET by no longer dwelling on the hurt or the painful reminders such as: phrases, smells, places, songs and comments. Instead, I am putting my mind on the higher calling that Christ has for me.

Be Healed and Set Free: Christ will heal me from my past, showing me the truth, so I can become a cleansed vessel, healed and set free.

This Week's Focus

Prayer: Ask God to strengthen you through His Spirit so that Christ may dwell in your heart, through faith, that you may be filled with all the fullness of God.

By Memory: My challenge to you is to be able to recite the tool, definition and Bible verse from this chapter without looking. I know that by hiding these words of wisdom in your heart you are providing yourself with tools to truly be healed and set free. May we rise up to be women of the Word.

Be Healed and Set Free: Christ will heal me from past hurts, showing me the truth, so I can become a cleansed vessel who is healed and set free.

Definition: To heal means to make whole and healthy; to cure; to remedy or repair.

Definition: To free means to make free, set at liberty; release from bondage, imprisonment or restraint.

Bible Verse: "And you shall know the truth, and the truth shall make you free" (John 8:32).

Preparing You Today for Something Greater Tomorrow

"For we are His workmanship, created in Christ Jesus for good works, which God prepared beforehand, that we should walk in them" (Ephesians 2:10). There are daily preparations we make, whether it's our hair or meals for our family; life takes preparation. "Preparing" is defined as making something ready for use or consideration. It's important to know you are being prepared for a purpose and can trust God for the outcome, as Greg Laurie[1] explains:

> A visitor to a logging area in the Pacific Northwest, was interested in seeing how the logs used to make furniture are chosen. As the logs came down the stream, a logger would suddenly reach out and hook one, pull it up, then set it down. He would sometimes wait a few minutes before grabbing another. There didn't seem to be any rhyme or reason to his choices.
>
> After a while, the visitor said, "I don't understand what you're doing." The logger replied, "These logs may look alike to you, but some are quite different. The ones that I let pass came from trees that grew in a valley. They were always protected from the storms. The grain is rather coarse. The logs I pulled aside are from high up on the mountain, where they were beaten by strong winds from the time they were small; that toughens the trees and gives them a fine grain. We save these for choice work. They're too good to be used for ordinary lumber."
>
> It was through trying and testing that the logs were prepared for choice work. The same could be said of us as Christians. If you were to ask Moses how he became who he was, he would remind you of his trials with Pharaoh and his times of testing in the wilderness. If you asked Joseph, he would refer back to his years as a slave and his imprisonment on a false accusation. Talk to Peter and he would probably point back to his denial of Christ, and how he learned many difficult yet important lessons.
>
> Maybe you find yourself facing something similar in your life. Maybe God is preparing you for a choice work. All Christians have eternal life, but very few Christians experience abundant life. God wants us to have life here and now that glorifies Him, even in the midst of our trials, disappointments and failures.

1. Read Hebrews 12:12: "Therefore strengthen the hands which hang down, and the feeble knees, and make straight paths for your feet, so that what is lame may not be dislocated, but rather be healed."

   Define the word "strengthen" from page 301.

   _____

2. What has strengthened, renewed and invigorated your life during this time of healing? Quiet your heart before the true Healer, pouring out thanks to Him for what He has healed.

   _____

Walking in the Light

The world we live in thrives on vengeance while mocking forgiveness. This is Satan's trap, creating bondage which has the potential to destroy our lives and relationships! But when you walk in the light, you live to please only one person: God. Walking in the light makes life so much easier and happier. Examine your heart daily and get real with God. Continue to be on your guard and don't harbor bitterness. Be set free to be "kind to one another, tenderhearted, forgiving one another, even as God in Christ forgave you" (Ephesians 4:32).

3. Jesus wants to bridge the gap between the broken, unforgiving heart and His freedom. Have you let Him guide you to wholeness through His Word?

_____

_____

4. Ask yourself, "Who am I really seeking to please? Am I seeking to please God, or am I more concerned with being a friend to the world, pleasing other people or satisfying my own desires?" Explain your thoughts.

_____

_____

_____

_____

5. If you don't have a personal relationship with Jesus Christ, or if you're unsure, take a moment to read the following:

   - "For when we were still without strength, in due time Christ died for the ungodly. For scarcely for a righteous man will one die; yet perhaps for a good man someone would even dare to die. But God demonstrates His own love toward us, in that while we were still sinners, Christ died for us. Much more then, having now been justified by His blood, we shall be saved from wrath through Him. For if when we were enemies we were reconciled to God through the death of His Son, much more, having been reconciled, we shall be saved by His life" (Romans 5:6-10).

   - "For God so loved the world that He gave His only begotten Son, that whoever believes in Him should not perish but have everlasting life" (John 3:16).

   God loves us so much that He sent His Son to die for us on the cross. He said our sins would be washed away and His light would shine through us! All we have to do is believe in Him, and He will take up residence in our hearts. The things of this world pale in comparison to the brilliant light of God's glory.

   There's nothing we can do to earn God's mercy, but also nothing we could do that would tear us away from His love. He gives mercy and love freely to all who believe. "For God… has shone His light in our hearts to give the light of the knowledge of the glory of God in the face of Jesus Christ" (2 Corinthians 4:6).

   If you've never asked Jesus to come into your life, why don't you do it right now? It will be the best decision you ever make. Pray this prayer to ask Him into your life, and He will forgive you:

"Lord Jesus, I know I'm a sinner and need Your forgiveness. I need the love, peace and hope You offer, so I turn from my own ways now. Come into my heart and fill me with Your Holy Spirit. Help me to follow You all the days of my life. Thank You that I am now going to Heaven. In Jesus' name, amen."

Write down what you are feeling right now.

_____

_____

_____

When we sin or go our own way, we are drawn away from the truth. It's important to recognize our sinful thoughts and emotions when they begin to get stirred up.

"Keep sound wisdom and discretion; so they will be life to your soul and grace to your neck. Then you will walk safely in your way, and your foot will not stumble. When you lie down, you will not be afraid; yes, you will lie down and your sleep will be sweet. Do not be afraid of sudden terror, nor of trouble from the wicked when it comes; for the Lord will be your confidence, and will keep your foot from being caught. Do not withhold good from those to whom it is due, when it is in the power of your hand to do so" (Proverbs 3:21-27).

Let's Go Over the Tools to Stay Healed and Set Free!

Tool #1 - SEE: I must SEE the _____ about what is in my _____, so I am not _____ (see Hebrews 12:15).

Tool #2 - GIVE: I must GIVE the _____ to God through _____, knowing that Christ is waiting to take it. I must be sorry enough to _____, and choose to go God's way over my own (see 2 Corinthians 7:10).

Tool #3 - FORGIVE: I must _____ as I am _____ by Christ: Forgiving those who hurt, bruised, wronged, rejected, betrayed or harmed me, whether unintentionally or _____. I must ask God to forgive me for holding on to unforgiveness and know that He will (see Colossians 3:13).

Tool #4 - FORGET: I must forget by no longer _____ on the hurt or the painful reminders such as: phrases, smells, places, songs and comments. Instead I am putting ____ _____ on the higher calling that Christ has for me (see Philippians 3:13).

BE SET FREE: I will choose God's will over my own. Choice by choice, I will experience freedom from having a junk drawer in my heart where records of wrong are kept. I will become an open vessel that's *healed and set free!*

This Week's Memory Verse

"And you shall know the truth,
and the truth shall make you free"
(John 8:32).

Week 9: Day 2

Prayer: Bow your heart before the Lord in prayer prior to completing today's Bible study. Thank God for the truth that has set you free.

Author Hal Lindsey said, "Man can live about forty days without food, three days without water, eight minutes without air, but only for one second without hope."[2] No matter what our lives bring, hope is what keeps us going. Greg Laurie's "A Purpose in the Storm"[3] shows how vital that God-given hope is to our lives. He points to 1 Corinthians 2:9, "Eye has not seen, nor ear heard, nor have entered into the heart of man the things which God has prepared for those who love Him." He writes:

> It has been said that the hammer shatters glass, but forges steel. God has His purposes in the storms of our lives. He is in control, He has a plan, and He knows all things in the past, present and future. He alone is uniquely qualified to know when to permit evil and suffering, and when not to allow them. Therefore, if He allows, or even brings something into your life, then He has a plan in mind for it.
>
> We love to follow the Lord when things are going our way. But when we come across a rough patch, we put on the brakes. That's why I like Psalm 23, one of the greatest passages in the Bible: "The Lord is my shepherd; I shall not want. He makes me to lie down in green pastures; He leads me beside the still waters... Yea, though I walk through the valley of the shadow of death, I will fear no evil; for You are with me; Your rod and Your staff, they comfort me." We love those green pastures and still waters, but we aren't very excited about a valley, especially when the shadow of death hovers over it. But God is with us in those times as well.
>
> For the believer, life on earth is as bad as it will ever get. If you are a Christian, the worst time of your life is as bad as it will ever be. That's the hope we have. And through the hardships of our lives, God can accomplish great things.

Keep Pressing Forward

1. Read Philippians 3:14: "I press toward the goal for the prize of the upward calling of God in Christ Jesus." After all the tears have been shed, and the brokenness of a contrite heart felt, what great hope is there to look forward to?

2. Read Romans 15:4: "For whatever things were written before were written for our learning, that we through the patience and comfort of the Scriptures might have hope." What are you reaching for today?

3. In the future, where can you find hope and encouragement when you are reminded of painful experiences?

_____

_____

4. Why is it important to ask God to expose the root cause of our thoughts and emotions?

_____

_____

5. Read Job 12:22: "He uncovers deep things out of darkness, and brings the shadow of death to light."

   Fill in the blanks below to begin memorizing Job 12:22.

   "He _____ _____ _____ out of darkness, and brings the shadow of death _____ _____" (Job 12:22).

6. Read Romans 15:13: "Now may the God of hope fill you with all joy and peace in believing, that you may abound in hope by the power of the Holy Spirit."

   According to Paul's prayer in Romans, what does God want to fill you with?

   _____

   _____

Reaching Others with the Hope We Have

In *A Woman After God's Own Heart*, Elizabeth George writes, "Everyone needs edification and encouragement, and we are free to offer that when we have hearts filled by God,"[4] and I would add, hearts that are healed and set free from lingering hurts. Here are some hints for encouraging God's people from Elizabeth:

- **A Heart that Encourages**: With every encounter, make it your aim to leave people better off for having been in your presence; try to give something to the other person. What a great and simple way to positively influence the lives of other people!

- **Take Time to Be Filled**: If you take time to sit at Jesus' feet and be filled with God's Spirit as you study the written Word, if you focus on overcoming internal obstacles to doing God's work, you will never lack for ministry. God's fullness in you will naturally overflow into the lives of others.

- **Memorize Scriptures of Encouragement**: If you "let your speech always be filled with grace and seasoned with salt" (Colossians 4:6), your life and lips will offer refreshing encouragement to all who cross your path. Like our Messiah, you will be able to "speak a word in season to him who is weary" (Isaiah 50:4). But we can't give away what we do not possess. So it's good to memorize some pertinent words of encouragement from the Bible to share with people in need.

- **Make Phone Calls to Encourage**: An easy way to encourage and to make a heart glad is to reach out and touch someone by phone. I'm not talking about making lengthy calls. A simple, quick call can do much to brighten the heart of the recipient!

- **Write Notes of Encouragement**: Writing notes, by mail or email, to those who need encouragement is another way to share a good word that makes the heart glad (Proverbs 12:25). It's as simple as three sentences: Sentence one conveys "I miss you," "I appreciate you," or "I'm thinking of you." Sentence two lets readers know they are special to me and why. Sentence three says I'm praying for them and includes the verse I'm praying for them.

- **Ministry Opportunities**: Ministry happens in greater ways when we take time to develop our skills and overcome our weaknesses. After all, how much can a teacher teach, a counselor counsel, or an administrator administrate? Only as much as he or she has grown! As each of us grows, each of us finds power and knowledge for overcoming personal weaknesses and for more effective ministry in Jesus Christ. Evangelist Corrie Ten Boom had a problem with shyness. Corrie enrolled in a Dale Carnegie course so she could learn to talk to people. If she could talk to people, then she could witness to them about Jesus Christ! Developing herself led to greater ministry.

Working on Our Weaknesses

In my early 20s, when my husband, Rick, was on staff as the youth pastor at Calvary Chapel San Jose, the senior pastor's wife, Jean McClure, asked me to administrate and emcee a sexual purity seminar. I was so nervous, but also excited about the chance to serve God and take a step in overcoming my shyness. Standing before 500 teen girls and women at the seminar, God's grace poured over me, enabling me to serve Him in my weakness.

7. What would you consider to be a major weakness in your life, one that hinders you in the area of ministry to others? (For example, I suffered from shyness.) What causes you to suffer and/or fail to minister to others? Name it, and list steps you can take this week to strengthen this weakness, and move toward overcoming it altogether. Create a plan of action.

_____

_____

_____

_____

_____

8. In what areas of your life have you found new hope springing forth from your past experience?

_____

_____

_____

Again and again Jesus tells us to give. Give to everyone (Luke 6:30), hoping for nothing in return (v.35). Give in the generous way that God, who is kind to the unthankful and evil, gives (v.35). Care for others by giving (v.38). You and I can learn to give in this way, to overflow with care for all others. Do you SEE why you and I must be healed and set free from lingering hurts and selfish tendencies? That way we can give to others! Again, Elizabeth George offers a few ideas:

Learn to Reach Out
By Elizabeth George

- **Develop a Bountiful Eye**: When I'm in public, I intentionally look for wounded sheep—and, believe me, they are there! I've found women and teen girls in the church lobby crying, in the ladies bathroom, on benches sobbing. We can ask questions like, "Can I do anything to help you? Can I get you something? Would you like to talk or pray?" People all around us need a tender word, or ministry from us.

- **Offer Your Presence**: Your presence, and sometimes a single touch, is worth a thousand words. When it comes to reaching out, remember this principle of ministry: your very presence is a source of comfort. You may not have the exact words to say or the perfect scripture to share, but in many, if not most situations, your touch can bring comfort far greater than words.

- **Be a Giver**: Just as you and I learned with our husbands and children, we can give a smile, a greeting, a warm question, a touch, or a hug to offer comfort to those around us—always try to remember the person's name.

- **Be Bold**: Give to the people God places in your path. If, however, you find yourself avoiding a certain person, ask God to show you why. Sin in our heart, a heart meant to overflow with care for others, keeps us from being confident in our relationships. So find out what is going on in your heart that's hindering your ministry. Then go a step further and decide what you will say the next time you see that person. Actively search for him or her and give the greeting you planned. With a heart clean before God, you should have nothing to hide, nothing to withhold. Learn to reach out to the people you meet every day.

- **Go to Give**: Missionary and martyr Jim Elliot once said, "Wherever you are, be all there. Live to the hilt in every situation you believe to be the will of God." I keep these words in mind whenever I attend any church or ministry event, and I go expecting God to use me. Here's an overview of my approach and I encourage you to make it yours:

    1. **Be all there**: Before I go to an event, I pray that I will go to give, to reach out, to look out, to be direct and to withhold nothing. Then, as I go, I put my thought-life on guard. While I'm at Bible study, I don't want to be thinking about what I'm going to fix for dinner that night. During my pastor's message, I don't want to be planning my week. I don't want to be concerned about what happened before I got there or what will happen after the event. I want to be all there!

    2. **Divide and Conquer**: Agree with your closest girlfriends, mother, sister or daughter not to visit the entire time. Instead share the commitment to "divide and conquer." Remember that you came to give! Your closest

friends have greater access to your life, plenty of one-on-one time with you in private, so why should they also have all your public time? They can talk to you later. One Christian woman and her friend made a pact that, when they find themselves gravitating toward each other in a crowd, one of them will announce, "Come on! Let's go touch some sheep!"

From *A Young Woman After God's Own Heart*. Harvest House Publishers, © 2003. p.176-179. Used by permission.

9. Can you comfort hurting people with the comfort you've received from the Lord?

10. Write down four important truths you've learned from *Healed and Set Free*:

    1. _____
    2. _____
    3. _____
    4. _____

11. Read 1 Corinthians 13:1-7 on page 304.

    Love holds no record of wrong, according to 1 Corinthians 13. What do we become if we have no love in our eyes for our husband, children, God or others?

12. Have you moved past the wrongs that were done to you? In what way are you pressing toward Jesus Christ?

This Week's Tool and Memory Verse

BE SET FREE: Christ will _____ ____ from past hurts, showing me the _____, so I can become a _____ _____ who is healed and set free.

"And you shall know the truth,
and the truth shall make you free"
(John 8:32).

Week 9: Day 3

Prayer: Bow your heart before the Lord in prayer prior to completing today's Bible study. Thank God for the truth that has set you free.

Learning to Love Through God's Word

Let's take a moment to look at the life of Hannah. As you read the story about Hannah in 1 Samuel 1:2-10,1:19-21 on page 305, you see a woman who had tears and heartache. Hannah's name means "grace and favor," but before she could embody God's grace and favor, she had to be prepared. Her character had to be refined, her will broken, and her devotion tested to the roots of her being. She had to come to the place of surrendering all to the Lord.

Following God doesn't always mean life is easy. Life was certainly not easy for Hannah. Knowing God in a new way, she realized that He really did order her life. With unshakable faith, she knew God would take care of Samuel, her son, sensing that he had an important destiny in Israel. With her heart freed of harassment, Hannah rejoiced over the Lord's goodness toward her. Overflowing with grateful praise, she described how God took her on a journey from disgrace to honor.

Even when nothing outwardly seems to change, keep pressing on to know God, love Him, trust Him, see His purpose and believe His promises. Let us remember, "Now faith is the substance of things hoped for, the evidence of things not seen" (Hebrews 11:1). As Hannah wrestled in prayer for her miracle, she found that perseverance, spiritual strength and faith began to grow in her spirit.

1. Do you suffer from some sort of debilitating struggle?

2. How does Hannah's story encourage you?

3. How can God use your trial for ultimate good?

From Mourning to Dancing

Once you have accepted God's forgiveness in your life, joy replaces shame and guilt; forgiveness replaces resentment and bitterness.

4. Let's read about King David in Psalms 16:11 and 30:11-12:

    - "You will show me the path of life; in Your presence is fullness of joy; at Your right hand are pleasures forevermore" (Psalm 16:11).

    - "You have turned for me my mourning into dancing; You have put off my sackcloth and clothed me with gladness, to the end that my glory may sing praise to You and not be silent. O Lord my God, I will give thanks to You forever" (Psalm 30:11-12).

    David accepted God's forgiveness. How did he respond in the Psalms above?

5. What burdens from the past have turned your mourning into dancing?

6. Fill in the blanks for this week's memory verse.

    "And you shall _____ the truth, and the truth _____ make you free" (John 8:32).

7. Read Romans 1:21-22: "Because, although they knew God, they did not glorify Him as God, nor were thankful, but became futile in their thoughts, and their foolish hearts were darkened."

    Knowing that you are set free, what are you thankful for?

> Lord, I pray, help me to move past futile thoughts to keep my heart from being foolish and darkened by hurts. Help me to SEE what I can be thankful for each and every day. In Jesus' name, amen.

8. Satan doesn't want us to see the blessings in our life. When you are thankful for the trials and hard times of the past, then you have truly been set free. Can you see five things you are thankful for? Write them down.

   1. _____
   2. _____
   3. _____
   4. _____
   5. _____

   Offer a prayer of thankfulness to God for allowing painful circumstances to lead you to His love, mercy and forgiveness. God has made the way straight so the heart can be healed and set free.

9. Read Matthew 24:12: "And because lawlessness will abound, the love of many will grow cold."

   Jesus is coming back soon. Is your heart cold, lukewarm or hot for Jesus?

   _____
   _____
   _____
   _____

> Let's tell the truth in love, then concentrate on keeping our hearts right before God. We cannot do anything to keep another person's heart right, only our own.

Tammy's Reflections

Wounding Words

One of Satan's greatest methods of attack is tempting God's people to hurt or wrong one another. Whether intentional or not, the hurt is done and bridges are burned. People are cut out of each others' lives, but the difficulty surrounding the relationship continues, especially if one decides to hold a grudge.

Satan has come to kill, steal and destroy, especially Christian relationships. Christians who gossip, criticize and find fault will always maintain the chain reaction Satan loves: having tongues that work overtime tearing down causes division. Greg Laurie's "Attack Through Division"[5] illustrates this point so well. He says:

> Show me a church where people want to reach out and impact the culture around them, where people want to live godly lives, and I will show you a church that can expect satanic opposition. In the book of Acts, we see the early church being attacked through persecution (Acts 4). We see the enemy trying to infiltrate the church through compromise (Acts 5). Then we see the devil using one of his most effective tactics against the church: division (Acts 6).
>
> Probably more havoc has been wreaked on the church through division than anything else, and when you get down to it, many divisions in a church are actually over minor things. You can always find something wrong; no church is perfect. But as St. Augustine wrote: "In essentials, unity; in nonessentials, liberty; in all things charity." Because one of the devil's most effective ploys is causing division among believers.

Praying Blessings Over Those Who Curse You

We shouldn't be surprised by divisive attacks. Even Jesus, the only perfect One, was misunderstood, rejected, disliked, hated and abandoned—we will be also. Our response should be to walk in unity as the Body of Christ, including leadership, and others you are serving with: "Being like-minded, having the same love, being of one accord, of one mind" and being "perfectly joined together in the same mind and in the same judgment" (Philippians 2:2, 1 Corinthians 1:10).

Just recently, I had to use the four tools to set me free from a new hurt. I had to SEE, GIVE, FORGIVE, FORGET and BE SET FREE because a fellow Christian was gossiping and criticizing me behind my back. Of course I was hurt and disappointed to hear about it, but I immediately applied the four tools and was set free from the situation. Then God led me to Matthew 5:44: "But I say to you, love your enemies, bless those who curse you, do good to those who hate you, and pray for those who spitefully use you and persecute you."

Every day for two weeks when I thought about it, I would replace the hurtful words they said with what God's Word says about me. I prayed for God to shower blessings on their life, home and hands. At first this was just the opposite of what I wanted to do, but before I knew it, I was so filled with God's love for this person that the hurt was gone! It's wonderful to BE SET FREE and have a sincere heart of love for the one who hurt me, which is only possible through God's grace and mercy.

Don't Be a Victim: Be a Woman with a Mission

Try this for two weeks: Pray that God would shower blessings on the lives of those who have hurt you, and in return your heart will be blessed. You can't think about yourself and others at the same time, and as you settle your personal needs with God in private prayer, you will then rise up and focus all your attention outward—on to others. You can't hate the person you are praying for. Jesus instructed us to pray for our enemies (Matthew 5:44), and as we do, God changes our hearts, putting an end to our selfishness and dissolving our negativity, which heals and sets us free.

10. Read 1 Peter 1:4-9 on page 305.

    Why were the believers filled with inexpressible joy, even during trials?

11. List four ways that you are rejoicing with inexpressible joy, through faith in Jesus, concerning your trials from the past?

    1.
    2.
    3.
    4.

12. Read Luke 11:39-40: "Then the Lord said to him, 'Now you Pharisees make the outside of the cup and dish clean, but your inward part is full of greed and wickedness. Foolish ones! Did not He who made the outside make the inside also?'"

    In your own words, what does it mean to make the outside clean, but leave the inside dirty?

13. Read 2 Timothy 2:21: "Therefore if anyone cleanses himself from the latter, he will be a vessel for honor, sanctified and useful for the Master, prepared for every good work."

    As you look toward the higher calling Christ has for you, what will you become?

A Lifestyle of Forgiveness

"Lifestyle" is defined as a way of life or style of living that reflects the attitudes and values of a person or group. Everyone has a lifestyle. There are many phrases regarding lifestyles, for example, "a millionaire's lifestyle" or "a healthy lifestyle." True beauty is to humbly walk in a lifestyle of forgiveness. Doug Easterday expands on this thought in his article "Restoration Through Forgiveness."[6]

> What happens when you recall a certain situation? What goes on internally? It might be something you only remember once a year, but when you do remember, your blood starts to boil, and there's bitterness in your heart. And bitterness will kill you spiritually, emotionally and physically.
>
> We can't just forgive one time and say, "That's over with!" It's something that has to be maintained. I can't guarantee that after you've forgiven you won't be hurt again. In fact, I can almost guarantee that you will be hurt again! Forgiveness isn't saying, "I'll forgive, but just this once!" That's not forgiveness. Forgiveness is a lifestyle of taking our rightful place in God and saying to the person who continues to hurt us, "I'm sorry you feel the way you do about me, but I'm not going to respond back to you in the same way." Taking this stand puts my emotional health and destiny in the Lord's hands, instead of letting the other person rule my emotional life. This is hard to do, but it is possible. And it's the only way we're going to really rise above the constant conflicts we have to deal with in human relationships. Forgiveness says, "No! In the name of Jesus, I am going to rise above that and not let your problem become my problem."

This Week's Tool and Memory Verse

BE SET FREE: Christ will _____ ____ from past hurts, showing me the _____, so I can become a _____ _____ who is healed and set free.

"And you shall know the truth,
and the truth shall make you free"
(John 8:32).

Week 9: Day 4

Prayer: Bow your heart before the Lord in prayer prior to completing today's Bible study. Ask Him to show you what new direction or new outlook He wants you to have as He works all things together for good.

From Tears to Joy

As a person moves from tears to joy, their eyes are off their past. They seek the face of the Lord, His direction and His plan for their life through prayer and the Word. God wants us to turn our hurts into healing, believing He will make all things work together for good, including pain and heartache from the past.

1. Read Acts 26:16: "But rise and stand on your feet; for I have appeared to you for this purpose, to make you a minister and a witness both of the things which you have seen and of the things which I will yet reveal to you. I will deliver you from the Jewish people, as well as from the Gentiles, to whom I now send you, to open their eyes, in order to turn them from darkness to light, and from the power of Satan to God, that they may receive forgiveness of sins and an inheritance among those who are sanctified by faith in Me."

   What did the Lord tell Paul He had planned for his life?

2. How was Paul using his past to work out the plans God had for him?

3. Read Ephesians 1:18: "The eyes of your understanding being enlightened; that you may know what is the hope of His calling, what are the riches of the glory of His inheritance in the saints."

   Compare your future with Paul's. How have your eyes been opened to your past? What darkness in your heart has been replaced with light?

4. How can you use your past to glorify the Lord as Paul did, and not give Satan power over you?

5. How can you help others move past their hurts? Remember, don't waste the pain, tell them to use it to drive them into a deeper walk with God.

Today I'm Set Free to Be...

If you're anything like me, you will always have a filing cabinet in your mind of life's moments that involve different people and different circumstances. Some of these have stayed with me, and tried to keep me from believing that I am who God says I am. Now, the more we learn about Jesus and His thoughts toward us, memories that once defeated and defined us are replaced with the truth of God.

Let's be women who rise up to be all God has created us to be! Together let's say, "Jesus does indeed bring beauty for ashes! I am who God says I am. I can be who He says I can be, and I can do what He asks me to do!"

A Lesson From Peter

Stop with me for a moment to envision Jesus asking Peter to walk on water. I envision Peter's mouth dropping open as he says, "I can't!" But because he trusted Jesus, he went for it, and Jesus accomplished the impossible through his life. God wants to do the same through you. Jesus said one simple word to Peter, "Come." God has healed and set you free to do impossible things by faith.

God is asking you from this point forward, as a daughter of the King, to be set free to live the life He has called you to, "Looking to Jesus, the author and finisher of our faith" (Hebrews 12:1-2).

Start This Week

"I can do all things through Christ who strengthens me" (Philippians 4:13). Believe that this verse is true! In John 8:32 Jesus said, "And you shall know the truth, and the truth shall make you free."

6. What will you be healed and set free to be? Pray and start living it out! Ask for more of God's attributes in your life such as: love, kindness, hope, courage, joy, peace, justice, forgiveness, wholeness, compassion, encouragement, a heart of service and an uncompromising faith. Write down your thoughts.

Obedience or Disobedience?

Before I was healed and set free, I thought my past altered the plans God had for my future. I thought I would always be a critical, angry and rebellious woman. I thought that was who I was; if Rick, my kids and others didn't like it, well too bad! But, as Doug Easterday writes, "The real issue is obedience to God."[7] He continues:

> What's the opposite of obedience? Disobedience. So if you don't forgive, what are you doing? Disobeying. And what is disobedience? Sin. It's pretty plain, isn't it? If we choose not to forgive, we choose to sin. Psalm 66:18 says, "If I regard iniquity in my heart, the Lord will not hear." Do you want the Lord to hear you? Then I believe you need to forgive.
>
> I'm convinced many Christians stop growing in the Lord, and go through the same problems over and over again, because they're holding on to unforgiveness. Unforgiveness will bring your spiritual life to a halt. God wants to bring you to a place in your life where the past no longer has any bearing on your present or future in Him. He even promises to "restore to you the years that the swarming locust has eaten" (Joel 2:25).

Letting go of the past is crucial to thriving in our healing, but equally important is making the choice to rejoice everyday. This list of ways to "seize the day" in *God Is in the Small Stuff*[8] gives some great insight!

- Live life on purpose, not by accident.
- There is a time and a place for love: anytime, anyplace.
- What you think determines what you do.
- Discover your spiritual gifts, and get involved in ministry so God can use you.
- Always go the extra mile, whether for a spouse, child or friend.
- Always keep your promises, no matter how long it takes.
- Display what you believe by how you behave.
- Be positive whenever you look back on your life.
- If you seek God's wisdom over opportunity, opportunity will usually follow.
- Change is a process, not an event.
- Follow the prompting of your heart rather than the desires of your flesh.
- Enjoy each day as if it were your last.
- Spend time with God, His Word and other people: you are investing in eternity.

Seize the Day

"For I know the thoughts that I think toward you, says the Lord, thoughts of peace and not of evil, to give you a future and a hope. Then you will call upon Me and go and pray to Me, and I will listen to you. And you will seek Me and find Me, when you search for Me with all your heart. I will be found by you, says the Lord, and I will bring you back from your captivity..." (Jeremiah 29:11-14).

Again, these thoughts from Bruce Bickel and Stan Jantz[9] in *God Is in the Small Stuff* inspire a new outlook:

> We easily find God in nature: the majesty of a rainbow, the intricacy of a colony of ants, the deafening roar of Niagara Falls. God is there, and we marvel at His handiwork. We identify Him in the celebrations of our lives: the birth of a child, the new job, the car crash that left the vehicle

totaled but our kids unscathed. God is there, and we thank Him. We even acknowledge Him in the midst of tragedy: the report from the pathology lab, the severance notice. God is there, and we depend upon His strength. Seeing God in these "big things" is easy. More difficult—yet just as rewarding—is seeing God in our everyday, mundane activities. We need "divine perspective." When we realize that He is in the ordinary, our daily grind suddenly has meaning and purpose.

You can't change yesterday, and only God knows what will happen tomorrow. Today is the only day you have. How do you seize the day? First, build upon the knowledge that God is working in your life. Second, have faith that God has secured your future; no matter what happens, He has given you hope. You will live in God's power today when you know that God works through your circumstances; it will energize you. Go out and make a difference: Leave an impression on everything and everyone you touch because of what God has done for you!

The Life-Altering Love of Christ

In "May I Have Your Attention Please,"[10] The Active Word talks about Jesus' love. It reminds me how our hearts should be toward others when we are healed and set free: displaying His love. They point to John 13:34-35: "A new commandment I give to you, that you love one another; as I have loved you, that you also love one another. By this all will know that you are My disciples, if you have love for one another." They then write:

> What gets a person's attention? Is it a beautiful face, a mountain of material possessions, an impressive physique, an extensive education, or a winsome wit? All these things have the power to capture attention, but over time the fixation fades. So what gets a person's attention and keeps it?
>
> As usual Jesus has the answer: His love. When Christ's love is actively expressed through a believer, it becomes the most powerful force that Planet Earth has ever witnessed. The love of Jesus is the one point that has no counterpoint. It ends all arguments, accomplishes the unimaginable, and opens hearts that have been cynically sealed up for a lifetime.
>
> Knowing this, Jesus told the disciples on the night before His crucifixion that if they were to have an impact on this world, they had to love one another. What wisdom! For as the world watches the Church, where the love of God is exchanged and expressed, it sees something that gets its attention... and keeps it. When God's love is flowing freely all lines of separation and segregation are erased: "There is neither Jew nor Greek, there is neither slave nor free, there is neither male nor female; for you are all one in Christ Jesus" (Galatians 3:28). The world is drawn to this because it cannot find it within itself. It longs to experience the peace, harmony, and oneness that is ours, found exclusively in Christ. When our "love level" for one another is at its highest, our witness to the world is at its strongest. May the Lord make us mindful of this. May He fill our hearts with His love for our brothers and sisters. Ask yourself these questions:

- What does this passage reveal to me about God?
- What does this passage reveal to me about myself?
- Based on this, what changes do I need to make?
- What is my prayer for today?

7. What plans does the Lord have for your life?

8. Read 2 Corinthians 5:17-19: "Therefore, if anyone is in Christ, he is a new creation; old things have passed away; behold, all things have become new. Now all things are of God, who has reconciled us to Himself through Jesus Christ, and has given us the ministry of reconciliation, that is, that God was in Christ reconciling the world to Himself, not imputing their trespasses to them, and has committed to us the word of reconciliation."

   What three things will you do when you believe God has a future for you?

   1.
   2.
   3.

How to Know If You've Forgiven

Lewis Smedes writes, "None of us wants to admit that we hate someone. It makes us feel mean and malicious. Hate is too ugly for us [so] we deny, we disguise, and we suppress the real hate that ferments in our souls. [But] when we deny our hate, we detour around the crisis of forgiveness. We do not dare to risk admitting the hate we feel because we do not dare to risk forgiving the person we hate."[11] So how do you know whether you've truly forgiven someone? Again, Doug Easterday[12] offers his wisdom:

> The moment God's love can freely flow through you to that person, where you want to bless them rather than curse them, as the Lord commands, that is when you have truly forgiven. That doesn't mean you have to trust them or be their best friend. It only means that you're not holding a grudge in your heart, and that you have peace toward them.
>
> I want to encourage you to ask the Lord to reveal any unforgiveness that still might be in your heart. I never thought I had a problem with this because I was "spiritual." Spiritual people don't have problems with unforgiveness, right? But God began to bring things to the surface and convict my heart about unresolved issues in my past. The Lord will do the same for you if you'll just allow Him to show you specific individuals whom you may need to forgive.
>
> I have learned that there is no substitute for forgiveness. Forgiveness frees God to move on your behalf; it frees you from the bondage, bitterness and resentment in your life. Best of all, forgiveness will free you to continue growing in the Lord and to become the woman the Lord intends you to be.

A Fresh Beginning

9. Through all the pain, suffering and heartache of examining your past, what is one thing you have gained?

10. To summarize your feelings, finish the following statement:

    In the future when I am confronted with painful feelings, I will remember to get real with God by using the four tools to be set free:
    (Try to fill in the blanks below by memory.)

    Tool #1. _____
    Tool #2. _____
    Tool #3. _____
    Tool #4. _____

11. What if your child, friend, spouse or other family member begins to grow a root of bitterness from a hurt, and they become weighed down with a junk drawer in their heart? What tools can you share with them to help them clean out the junk drawer?

12. Read 2 Corinthians 1:3-4: "Blessed be the God and Father of our Lord Jesus Christ, the Father of mercies and God of all comfort, who comforts us in all our tribulation, that we may be able to comfort those who are in any trouble, with the comfort with which we ourselves are comforted by God."

    Fill in the blanks below to start memorizing 2 Corinthians 1:3-4:

    "Blessed be the God and Father of our Lord Jesus Christ, the Father of _____ and God of ____ _____, who _____ us in all our tribulation, that we may be able to _____ those who are in any trouble, with the _____ with which we ourselves are _____ by God."

Freedom in Grace

13. Grace grants us freedom from sin and the flesh. You have been called to live in freedom—not to satisfy your sinful nature, but to serve one another. Read Galatians 5:13: "For you, brethren, have been called to liberty; only do not use liberty as an opportunity for the flesh, but through love serve one another."

    What are we called to live in?

14. Read Ephesians 2:4-10 on page 305. Grace enables us to have a new life in Christ. What do these verses say about what this new life will include?

15. Read John 8:32: "And you shall know the truth and the truth shall make you free." Where do you find the truth?

Freedom

Having the freedom to love God with our entire mind is to truly experience His love for us. We can't change the way we think on our own, but when we draw near to God and spend time getting to know Him in His Word, He uses the truth to transform how we think. When we feel weak or overwhelmed by life, scriptures give us the strength to go on.

I love how Elizabeth George puts it: "God's holy Word as an instrument He uses to guide, comfort, correct, rebuke and teach us. The passages we commit to memory are like a surgeon's sterilized tools, carefully arranged on instrument trays and ready for His expert use. When there's a problem in our lives, God can pick up exactly the verse we need and cut right to our heart."[13] He has done it for me, and I know He will do it for you.

We can also love God with our entire mind by the choices we make. We can choose to dwell on the negative, on our weaknesses and pain, or we can let those things turn us to God. Regardless of how life looks or feels, we can make the deliberate decision to yield to God's wisdom and His ways. We can choose to:

- Believe the truths of the Bible rather than trust our emotions.
- Work on what is real rather than worry about what is unreal.
- Reach forward rather than remain a prisoner of the past.
- Act on the truth of scripture rather than on what appears to be true in the world.

By making these choices, we are choosing to love God with our entire mind. The result is what I call the right perspective—the peace and well-being the Spirit gives us when we think and act on the truth of the Bible.

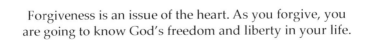

Forgiveness is an issue of the heart. As you forgive, you are going to know God's freedom and liberty in your life.

Chapter 1: "Getting Real with God" Review

1. Which tool comes first: SEE or FORGET when your heart is hurting or you've made a mistake? Circle the correct answer.

2. Why do we need to SEE what is in our hearts?

3. Write down Hebrews 12:15 from memory. (Go to page 5)

Looking carefully lest _____

_____ and by this many become defiled.

Chapter 2: "Knowing God's Heart" Review

1. John 10:27 says, "My sheep hear My voice, and I know them, and they follow Me." How will you follow God when you are faced with a trial or heartache? Will you hold a grudge or follow His Word?

2. Write down Lamentations 3:22-23 from memory. (Go to page 302)

Chapter 3: "Letting Go of Anger" Review

1. Which tool comes second, GIVE or FORGET once you SEE what is in your heart? Circle the correct answer.

2. Why do we need to GIVE the sin in our hearts over in repentance?

3. Write down 2 Corinthians 7:10 from memory. (Go to page 5)

Chapter 4: "Forgiving the Unacceptable" Review

1. Which tool comes third, FORGIVE or FORGET? Circle the correct answer.

2. Write down the names of those whom you have forgiven:

   _____

   _____

   _____

3. Write down Colossians 3:13 from memory. (Go to page 5)

   _____

   _____

   _____

Chapter 5: "Conquering Depression" Review

When we are depressed, we suffer from "ingrown eyeballs." Our eyes are turned inward and we focus on our own problems and on ourselves. The more we focus inward, the worse we feel and the harder it is to take the necessary steps to SEE the truth and allow the Lord's love and grace to flow through our lives.

1. Write down Proverbs 12:25-26 from memory. (Go to page 148)

   _____

   _____

   _____

Chapter 6: "Body Image" Review

You must reject the false values of society and accept your own worth, based on who you are in Christ and not on what your body looks like. You'll find that you must exercise the fruit of the Spirit of self-control in your life. And no, you don't have to get heavy to get well. It's a matter of the choices you make at mealtimes. Food is just fuel for your body. Food is not your enemy and food is not your companion!

1. Write down Galatians 5:1 from memory. (Go to page 181)

   _____

   _____

   _____

Chapter 7: "Remember to Forget" Review

When you are faced with reminders of the past, realize that it's the enemy trying to get you focused on the past. Like Paul, we must keep forgetting those things which are behind us. Paul didn't rest on his past accomplishments, failures or the failures and mistakes of others, and neither should we. Don't let the past hold you back!

Get real with God about what is in your heart. Then SEE, GIVE, FORGIVE and FORGET. God has given us permission to forget the past and move forward.

1. Which tool comes fourth, BE SET FREE or FORGET? Circle the correct answer.

2. Write down the changes you see in your heart as you move forward.

_____

_____

3. Write down Philippians 3:13 from memory. (Go to page 5)

_____

_____

Chapter 8: "Two Become One: God's Design for Marriage" Review

Deal with issues as they arise. Don't let them build into raging anger or bitterness. Have "heart to hearts" as often as you need, remembering that off-hand remarks are counterproductive. The first step in a hurting marriage is forgiveness.

1. What changes will you make to prioritize your relationship with your husband?

_____

_____

2. Write down Genesis 2:24 from memory. (Go to page 247)

_____

_____

Chapter 9: "Healed and Set Free" Review

Christ will heal us from our past hurts and show us the truth so we become cleansed vessels that are HEALED AND SET FREE.

Each of us is capable, by the power of the Holy Spirit, to lay down our own will; but not all are willing. It's our choice to either embrace or reject the truth from the scriptures we learn. Embracing the will of God means acknowledging our true feelings, getting real with God, getting rid of the strongholds, and following the truth to have victory over the flesh, day by day and choice by choice!

1. Write down John 8:32 from memory. (Go to page 5)

_____

_____

_____

Tammy's Reflections

Lord, Help Me Finish Well

"...He who has begun a good work in you will complete it until the day of Jesus Christ" (Philippians 1:6).

I am not perfect by any means, and I am still confronted by challenges. But God has given me hope for the future. His desire for me is to fight the good fight and finish well!

Remember

Don't put this study on the shelf and forget about it. Constantly be renewing your thinking in order to: SEE, GIVE, FORGIVE, FORGET and BE SET FREE! And pass on the lessons you've learned: Comfort others the way you have been comforted in His Word!

We Want to Hear From You

Many people have said the stories in the Healed and Set Free Bible study have left a lasting impression and an encouraging impact.

We invite you to share your story. How did God use the Healed and Set Free Bible study in your life? How were you set free from the wounds of your past? What insights, stories or Bible verses encourage you to let go and move forward? Every story is important in God's plan. Share your story online at www.hsfministries.org/healed-and-set-free-testimonies.php (500 words maximum please).

God doesn't change the past,
but He can change the meaning of the past.

Stories of Real People and a Real Savior

My Marriage Was Mended
By Dyan, Idaho

I would like to share my testimony about what Healed and Set Free has done in my life!

First I would like to thank Tammy Brown for letting God use her to make an impact on my life through this study! I know Tammy, and I will always have a special place in my heart for her because of this amazing gift. Also my Healed and Set Free teacher Leah! Thank you Leah for the late night studies, the love and compassion you showed each and every one of us ladies, and sharing your testimony with us!? I had lead a life of bitterness and it had started to affect my marriage and my motherhood.

It all started from my parents divorced, my dad became an every-other-weekend dad, a family member molested me for most of my childhood years, when I was 13 my aunt's boyfriend murdered my 22 month-old cousin and she died in my arms at the hospital, and I became pregnant at the age of 15 and gave birth to my beautiful daughter named McKenna.

I had always shoved my feelings along with everything else in my "Junk Drawer." ?

I married my husband is June of 2002 had another daughter Kyrsten in August of 2002 and then had my third daughter Keyana in 2003. They were only 11 months apart.

By the time I had my last daughter I was going through Post Partum depression along with me was my "Junk Drawer." I had been on a rampage for months, I remember one time my husband calling home from work asking, "Do I need to come home, are you going to hurt the kids?" One morning I got my 5-year-old daughter up for school and she wouldn't get dressed and it set me off. I smacked her across the face! I fell to my knees crying and she says to me not ever knowing who God is or anything about praying, "Mommy we need to pray!" So we did!

That same day my husband said, "We need God in our home, in our marriage, and in our lives!" We started to go to church and my husband and I both became BORN AGAIN! That's when I got into the bible study "Healed and Set Free!" It gave me the tools to see, forgive, and just let go!

I remember coming home from study and that night we talked about forgiveness and it's about you and God not the person who has sinned against you, and I truly forgave my parents, my brother, my aunt's boyfriend and most of all myself. I came home and took a bath and the water was so soft and I could breathe and cry for joy it was unlike anything I had ever felt. Many nights my husband did the study with me, so through Gods love and this study my marriage was mended! Praise be to God!

There is nothing God can't do! I was filled with so much hate, anger, and always felt yucky but I am healed and set free from all of it! Thank you for letting me share!

> HEALING... it's what God does.
> Invigorating others about His healing power in our lives...
> it's what He longs for us to do.

Stories of Real People and a Real Savior

My Abortion, Healed and Set Free From My Secret Heartache
By Julie, Idaho

I had a good childhood growing up and it wasn't until I became an adult that I started to suffer so much loss. It started when I chose to terminate two separate pregnancies while in my 20's. I was scared and filled with such pain and shame that I kept it a deep, hidden secret for many years. I was married for several years, divorced and married again years later. During that marriage I had several miscarriages. More loss.... I actually thought that God was punishing me for my earlier abortions. That marriage too ended in divorce. We had a son from this marriage which was a wonderful blessing. But, now I was alone, raising my son mostly on my own. I felt like my whole life I was always searching. Searching for love and happiness.

I was always going from one relationship to another, never satisfied until I found the one relationship that does satisfy, Jesus Christ. He began to transform my life in so many ways! My life started to have meaning and purpose and I finally began to understand love. However, even though I was a Christian, I still carried the guilt and shame, pain and failures. I thought what I had done was too horrible for God to forgive.

It wasn't until I started to pour myself into God's Word and His presence that I started discovering God's mercy and love. He began to restore what the locusts had eaten. Joel 2:25. In 2010, I met a loving, Godly man and we married a year later.

It wasn't until I heard about the "Healed and Set Free" ministry where I would find true healing. It was in this bible study where the Lord showed me and helped me to overcome the unforgiveness and bitterness in my heart towards my ex-husband and the deep shame and pain over my past pregnancies. The Lord showed me what was still in my heart, the emotions still lingering deep within. He helped me to give all those emotions, - the pain, guilt and shame over to Him. He showed me the true essence of what forgiveness is all about. I hadn't realized that unforgiveness was a sin. It was through the tools explained in this wonderful, God inspired bible study that I was able to not only forgive my ex-husband but also I was able to receive God's forgiveness for myself from my abortions, and secret heart ache. Forgiving ourselves is many times the most difficult. I knew God loved me no matter what I had done. I discovered that there is no sin that God won't forgive. I was able to completely surrender and give it all to Him.

I felt such a freedom and weight lifted off and I knew then I wanted other women to experience the same JOY of finding freedom IN CHRIST. Nothing is too difficult for Him and there is nothing we have done that He won't or can't forgive. What a marvelous truth that is. You will know the truth and the truth will set you free! John 8:32.

I now facilitate the "Healed and Set Free" bible study and have the privilege to walk alongside other women on their journey to find freedom in Christ. My life is forever changed. God works all things together for good to those who love God and are called according to his purpose. (Romans 8:28)

God doesn't change the past but He can change the meaning of the past.

Questions and Answers About Everlasting Life

Question: In whom must I believe to have eternal life?

Answer: "That whoever believes in Him (Christ Jesus) should not perish but have everlasting life" (John 3:16).

Question: Why did Christ have to die? Why did God give Jesus, His only Son?

Answer: "So Christ was offered once to bear the sins of many. To those who eagerly wait for Him He will appear a second time, apart from sin, for salvation" (Hebrews 9:28). "For God so loved the world that He gave His only begotten Son, that whoever believes in Him should not perish but have everlasting life" (John 3:16).

Question: What is the way to Heaven? What is the truth?

Answer: "Jesus said to him, 'I am the way, the truth, and the life. No one comes to the Father except through Me'" (John 14:6).

Question: What does God promise you will lose if you follow anything other than Jesus Christ, who was sacrificed for your sins?

Answer: "For whoever desires to save his life will lose it, but whoever loses his life for My sake will find it. For what profit is it to a man if he gains the whole world, and loses his own soul? Or what will a man give in exchange for his soul?" (Matthew 16:25-26).

Questions and Answers About How to Pray

Question: What do I pray for?

Answer: Anything! You can pray when you're thankful, sorry for sinning, afraid, uncertain, discouraged or asking God to help you share Christ with others. The most important thing is to have a personal relationship with Him, sharing the issues of your heart and life like you would with your spouse or close friend.

Question: Should I close my eyes to pray? Should I pray on my knees? Should I pray alone or in a group? Can I pray while driving down the road?

Answer: All God is concerned with is your heart. You can talk to Him anywhere, anytime. The key is to talk to God on a daily basis to keep your relationship with Him close. Start by picking a special time each day. He loves you and is always with you, waiting joyfully to hear from you. Remember, "The Lord is near to all who call upon Him, to all who call upon Him in truth" (Psalm 145:18).

Question: Can I tell God anything?

Answer: Yes. You can tell Him anything, because He already knows everything. Be transparent before Him. There is nothing you could say to Him that would make Him stop loving you. You can tell Him when you are sad, thank Him when everything is going well, ask Him to provide for your needs, or tell Him when you have bitterness in your heart toward someone. You can tell Him anything, as 1 Peter 5:7 says, "Casting all your care upon Him, for He cares for you."

How To Receive Christ and Have Everlasting Life

1. Admit that you are a sinner who needs forgiveness and a Savior.
2. Be willing to turn from your sins.
3. Believe that Jesus Christ died for you on the cross and rose from the grave.
4. Through the Holy Spirit, receive Jesus as your Lord and Savior.

Life Changing Prayer: What to Pray

"Dear Lord Jesus, I know I'm a sinner. I need Your forgiveness. I want to turn from my sins. I believe You died for my sins, and I invite You to come into my heart and life. I want to trust and follow You as my Lord and Savior. In Jesus' name, amen."

This is the beginning of a new life in Christ! To deepen this relationship you should:
- Read your Bible every day to know Christ better.
- Talk to God in prayer every day.
- Tell others about Christ.
- Worship, fellowship and serve in a church where Christ is preached.

Definitions

Bitterness: Anger and disappointment at being treated unfairly; resentment: "he expressed bitterness over his dismissal without notice."

Contrite: Feeling or expressing remorse or penitence; affected by guilt: "a broken and contrite heart."

Carousing: drinking large amounts of alcohol with others in a noisy, lively way.

Defile: To make foul, dirty or unclean; pollute; to violate the chastity of.

Discipline: Give instruction to, educate, train. The controlled behavior resulting from discipline: "he was able to maintain discipline among his men."

Iniquity: Immoral, unrighteous, or harmful action or conduct.

Judging: [when] a person [is] able or qualified to give an opinion on something; form an opinion or conclusion about.

Lame: a condition in which [a person or animal] is unable to walk normally because of an injury.

Relent: Abandon or mitigate a harsh intention or cruel treatment: "she was going to refuse his request, but relented."

Remedy: a medicine or treatment for a disease or injury; a means of counteracting or eliminating something undesirable.

Remorseless: Without regret or guilt: "a remorseless killer;" (of something unpleasant) never ending or improving; relentless.

Repent: to feel such sorrow for sin or fault as to be disposed to change one's life for the better; be penitent.

Restitution: the restoration of something lost or stolen to its proper owner.

Righteousness: The quality of being morally right or justifiable.

Sin: An immoral act considered to be a transgression against divine law: "a sin in the eyes of God."

Strengthen: Give moral support, courage or confidence to; encourage, hearten; give defensive or physical strength to; fortify or reinforce.

Submission: The action or act of submitting or yielding to authority, another person, etc.; the state or condition of being submissive or obedient; deferential conduct, attitude or bearing; humility.

Definitions from oxforddictionaries.com. © 2012, Oxford University Press.

Scripture References

Chapter 1
Matthew 18:21-35:
>[21]Then Peter came to Him and said, "Lord, how often shall my brother sin against me, and I forgive him? Up to seven times?"
>[22]Jesus said to him, "I do not say to you, up to seven times, but up to seventy times seven. [23]Therefore the kingdom of heaven is like a certain king who wanted to settle accounts with his servants. [24]And when he had begun to settle accounts, one was brought to him who owed him ten thousand talents. [25]But as he was not able to pay, his master commanded that he be sold, with his wife and children and all that he had, and that payment be made. [26]The servant therefore fell down before him, saying, 'Master, have patience with me, and I will pay you all.' [27]Then the master of that servant was moved with compassion, released him, and forgave him the debt.
>[28]"But that servant went out and found one of his fellow servants who owed him a hundred denarii; and he laid hands on him and took him by the throat, saying, 'Pay me what you owe!' [29]So his fellow servant fell down at his feet and begged him, saying, 'Have patience with me, and I will pay you all.' [30]And he would not, but went and threw him into prison till he should pay the debt. [31]So when his fellow servants saw what had been done, they were very grieved, and came and told their master all that had been done. [32]Then his master, after he had called him, said to him, 'You wicked servant! I forgave you all that debt because you begged me. [33]Should you not also have had compassion on your fellow servant, just as I had pity on you?' [34]And his master was angry, and delivered him to the torturers until he should pay all that was due to him.
>[35]"So My heavenly Father also will do to you if each of you, from his heart, does not forgive his brother his trespasses."

Chapter 2
Matthew 9:9-13:
>[9]As Jesus passed on from there, He saw a man named Matthew sitting at the tax office. And He said to him, "Follow Me." So he arose and followed Him.
>[10]Now it happened, as Jesus sat at the table in the house, that behold, many tax collectors and sinners came and sat down with Him and His disciples. [11]And when the Pharisees saw it, they said to His disciples, "Why does your Teacher eat with tax collectors and sinners?"
>[12]When Jesus heard that, He said to them, "Those who are well have no need of a physician, but those who are sick. [13]But go and learn what this means: 'I desire mercy and not sacrifice.' For I did not come to call the righteous, but sinners, to repentance."

"The *mind* of God never changes." Numbers 23:19 (NIV):
>God is not human, that he should lie, not a human being, that he should change his mind. Does he speak and then not act? Does he promise and not fulfill?

"His *compassion* never fails." Lamentations 3:22-23 (NIV):
>Because of the Lord's great love we are not consumed, for his compassions never fail. They are new every morning; great is your faithfulness.

"His *love* never fails." Psalm 18:50 (NIV):
>He gives his king great victories; he shows unfailing love to his anointed, to David and to his descendants forever.

Scripture References

Chapter 2 (Continued)

"The *promise* of God never changes." 2 Peter 3:9 (NIV):
> The Lord is not slow in keeping his promise, as some understand slowness. Instead he is patient with you, not wanting anyone to perish, but everyone to come to repentance.

Hebrews 12:5-11:
> [5]And you have forgotten the exhortation which speaks to you as to sons:
> "My son, do not despise the chastening of the Lord,
> Nor be discouraged when you are rebuked by Him;
> [6]For whom the Lord loves He chastens,
> And scourges every son whom He receives."
> [7]If you endure chastening, God deals with you as with sons; for what son is there whom a father does not chasten? [8]But if you are without chastening, of which all have become partakers, then you are illegitimate and not sons. [9]Furthermore, we have had human fathers who corrected us, and we paid them respect. Shall we not much more readily be in subjection to the Father of spirits and live? [10]For they indeed for a few days chastened us as seemed best to them, but He for our profit, that we may be partakers of His holiness. [11]Now no chastening seems to be joyful for the present, but painful; nevertheless, afterward it yields the peaceable fruit of righteousness to those who have been trained by it.

Chapter 3

Proverbs 15:1:
> A soft answer turns away wrath, but a harsh word stirs up anger.

Proverbs 16:32:
> He who is slow to anger is better than the mighty, and he who rules his spirit than he who takes a city.

Proverbs 29:11:
> A fool vents all his feelings, but a wise man holds them back.

Proverbs 29:22:
> An angry man stirs up strife, and a furious man abounds in transgression.

Chapter 4

Matthew 19:26:
> But Jesus looked at them and said to them, 'With men this is impossible, but with God all things are possible.'

Matthew 18:21-35 (see above in chapter 1)

Philippians 4:8:
> Finally, brethren, whatever things are true, whatever things are noble, whatever things are just, whatever things are pure, whatever things are lovely, whatever things are of good report, if there is any virtue and if there is anything praiseworthy—meditate on these things.

Chapter 5

Philippians 4:8 (see above in chapter 4)

Scripture References

Chapter 6
2 Peter 1:3-9:
> ³As His divine power has given to us all things that pertain to life and godliness, through the knowledge of Him who called us by glory and virtue, ⁴by which have been given to us exceedingly great and precious promises, that through these you may be partakers of the divine nature, having escaped the corruption that is in the world through lust.
> ⁵But also for this very reason, giving all diligence, add to your faith virtue, to virtue knowledge, ⁶to knowledge self-control, to self-control perseverance, to perseverance godliness, ⁷to godliness brotherly kindness, and to brotherly kindness love. ⁸For if these things are yours and abound, you will be neither barren nor unfruitful in the knowledge of our Lord Jesus Christ. ⁹For he who lacks these things is shortsighted, even to blindness, and has forgotten that he was cleansed from his old sins.

1 Peter 4:2:
> That he no longer should live the rest of his time in the flesh for the lusts of men, but for the will of God.

Mark 10:46-52:
> ⁴⁶Now they came to Jericho. As He went out of Jericho with His disciples and a great multitude, blind Bartimaeus, the son of Timaeus, sat by the road begging. ⁴⁷And when he heard that it was Jesus of Nazareth, he began to cry out and say, "Jesus, Son of David, have mercy on me!" ⁴⁸Then many warned him to be quiet; but he cried out all the more, "Son of David, have mercy on me!" ⁴⁹So Jesus stood still and commanded him to be called. Then they called the blind man, saying to him, "Be of good cheer. Rise, He is calling you." ⁵⁰And throwing aside his garment, he rose and came to Jesus. ⁵¹So Jesus answered and said to him, "What do you want Me to do for you?" The blind man said to Him, "Rabboni, that I may receive my sight." ⁵²Then Jesus said to him, "Go your way; your faith has made you well." And immediately he received his sight and followed Jesus on the road.

Chapter 8
Proverbs 5:15-21:
> ¹⁵Drink water from your own cistern, and running water from your own well. ¹⁶Should your fountains be dispersed abroad, streams of water in the streets? ¹⁷Let them be only your own, and not for strangers with you. ¹⁸Let your fountain be blessed, and rejoice with the wife of your youth. ¹⁹As a loving deer and a graceful doe, let her breasts satisfy you at all times; and always be enraptured with her love. ²⁰For why should you, my son, be enraptured by an immoral woman, and be embraced in the arms of a seductress? ²¹For the ways of man are before the eyes of the Lord, and He ponders all his paths.

Chapter 9
1 Corinthians 13:1-7:
> ¹Though I speak with the tongues of men and of angels, but have not love, I have become sounding brass or a clanging cymbal. ²And though I have the gift of prophecy, and understand all mysteries and all knowledge, and though I have all faith, so that I could remove mountains, but have not love, I am nothing. ³And though I bestow all my goods to feed the poor, and though I give my body to be burned, but have not love, it profits me nothing.

Scripture References

Chapter 9 (Continued)

⁴Love suffers long and is kind; love does not envy; love does not parade itself, is not puffed up; ⁵does not behave rudely, does not seek its own, is not provoked, thinks no evil; ⁶does not rejoice in iniquity, but rejoices in the truth; ⁷bears all things, believes all things, hopes all things, endures all things.

1 Samuel 1:2-10, 19-21: (Life of Hannah)

²And he had two wives: the name of one was Hannah, and the name of the other Peninnah. Peninnah had children, but Hannah had no children. ³This man went up from his city yearly to worship and sacrifice to the Lord of hosts in Shiloh. Also the two sons of Eli, Hophni and Phinehas, the priests of the Lord, were there. ⁴And whenever the time came for Elkanah to make an offering, he would give portions to Peninnah his wife and to all her sons and daughters. ⁵But to Hannah he would give a double portion, for he loved Hannah, although the Lord had closed her womb. ⁶And her rival also provoked her severely, to make her miserable, because the Lord had closed her womb. ⁷So it was, year by year, when she went up to the house of the Lord, that she provoked her; therefore she wept and did not eat.

⁸Then Elkanah her husband said to her, "Hannah, why do you weep? Why do you not eat? And why is your heart grieved? Am I not better to you than ten sons?" ⁹So Hannah arose after they had finished eating and drinking in Shiloh. Now Eli the priest was sitting on the seat by the doorpost of the tabernacle of the Lord. ¹⁰And she was in bitterness of soul, and prayed to the Lord and wept in anguish.

¹⁹Then they rose early in the morning and worshiped before the Lord, and returned and came to their house at Ramah. And Elkanah knew Hannah his wife, and the Lord remembered her. ²⁰So it came to pass in the process of time that Hannah conceived and bore a son, and called his name Samuel, saying, "Because I have asked for him from the Lord." ²¹Now the man Elkanah and all his house went up to offer to the Lord the yearly sacrifice and his vow.

1 Peter 1:4-9:

⁴To an inheritance incorruptible and undefiled and that does not fade away, reserved in heaven for you, ⁵who are kept by the power of God through faith for salvation ready to be revealed in the last time. ⁶In this you greatly rejoice, though now for a little while, if need be, you have been grieved by various trials, ⁷that the genuineness of your faith, being much more precious than gold that perishes, though it is tested by fire, may be found to praise, honor, and glory at the revelation of Jesus Christ, ⁸whom having not seen you love. Though now you do not see Him, yet believing, you rejoice with joy inexpressible and full of glory, ⁹receiving the end of your faith—the salvation of your souls.

Ephesians 2:4-10:

⁴But God, who is rich in mercy, because of His great love with which He loved us, ⁵even when we were dead in trespasses, made us alive together with Christ (by grace you have been saved), ⁶and raised us up together, and made us sit together in the heavenly places in Christ Jesus, ⁷that in the ages to come He might show the exceeding riches of His grace in His kindness toward us in Christ Jesus. ⁸For by grace you have been saved through faith, and that not of yourselves; it is the gift of God, ⁹not of works, lest anyone should boast. ¹⁰For we are His workmanship, created in Christ Jesus for good works, which God prepared beforehand that we should walk in them.

Endnotes

Foreword
1. Caroline Cox, *Coxs Book of Modern Saints and Martyrs.* Continuum Books, New York, 2006.

Chapter 1
1. *Start! to Follow.* Harvest Ministries, 2011. www.harvest.org/pdf/1598.pdf
2. The Active Word, "Sweeping Statement." July 10, 2011. http://www.activeword.org/dailydevotion.cfm?keyword=10-Jul-11
3. Shelley Spady, "The Quilt." Used by permission.
4. Rick Brown, "The Power of Forgiveness." Sermon from November 27, 2011.

Chapter 2
1. Greg Laurie, "God's Cure for Heart Trouble." Knowing God, 2007. http://video.google.ca/videoplay?docid=8961639617231371863Q
2. Elizabeth George, *A Woman After God's Own Heart*. Harvest House Publishers, Eugene, OR, 1997. p.36.
3. Greg Laurie, "Our Great Physician." Harvest Daily Devotions, August 2, 2006. Harvest Ministries with Greg Laurie, PO Box 4000, Riverside, CA 92514. http://www.harvest.org/devotional/archive/devotion/2006-08-02.html
4. Greg Laurie, "You are Loved by God." Greg's Blog, October 19, 2009. http://blog.greglaurie.com/?p=2568
5. Bruce Bickel and Stan Jantz, *God Is in the Small Stuff*. Promise Press, Uhrichsville, OH, 1998. p.24-25.
6. Elizabeth George, *A Woman After God's Own Heart*. p.30-31.
7. Greg Laurie, "Trying to Explain the Inexplicable." WorldNetWeekly, June 22, 2012. http://www.wnd.com/2012/06/trying-to-explain-the-inexplicable/
8. Greg Laurie, "Preaching Through Pain" Sermon Notes, Harvest Ministries, 2009. Harvest Ministries with Greg Laurie, PO Box 4000, Riverside, CA 92514.
9. Bruce Bickel and Stan Jantz, *God Is in the Small Stuff*. p.23-24.

Chapter 3
1. Linda Cochrane, *Forgiven and Set Free*. Baker Books, Grand Rapids, MI, 1996. p.53.
2. Doug Easterday, "Restoration Through Forgiveness." Last Days Ministries, 2007. http://www.lastdaysministries.com/Publisher/Article.aspx?ID=1000008603
3. Verdell Davis, *Let Me Grieve But Not Forever*. Thomas Nelson, Inc., Nashville, TN, 2004. p.16,17-18.
4. Shelley Spady, "An Anchor in the Storm." Used by permission.
5. All scriptures NIV translation, unless otherwise noted.
6. Elizabeth George, *A Woman After God's Own Heart*. p.47.
7. Greg Laurie, "Finding Forgiveness." Harvest Daily Devotions, August 24, 2005. http://www.harvest.org/devotional/archive/devotion/2005-08-24.html

Chapter 4
1. James Blanchard Cisneros, *You Have Chosen to Remember*. Self published, 2004. p.151.
2. Mary Katherine Kohl, "Self-Preservation." © 1997. http://www.christianwritings.com/
3. Mary Hayes Grieco, *Unconditional Forgiveness*. Atria Books, a Division of Simon & Schuster, Inc., New York, 2011. pp.1,5.
4. The Active Word, "In His Hands," December 21, 2011. http://www.activeword.org/dailydevotion.cfm?keyword=21-Dec-11

[5] Doug Easterday, "Restoration Through Forgiveness."
[6] Max Lucado, *No Wonder They Call Him the Savior*. Thomas Nelson, Inc., Nashville, TN, 2004. p.5-6.

Chapter 5

[1] Archibald D. Hart, *Dark Clouds, Silver Linings*. Focus on the Family Publishing, Colorado Springs, CO, 1993. p.18.
[2] Dennis DeHaan in *Comfort: Strength for the Soul*. Discovery House Publishers, Grand Rapids, MI, 2006. p.9.
[3] Elizabeth George, *A Woman After God's Own Heart*. p.129.
[4] The Active Word, "The Power of Praise." April 28, 2010. http://www.activeword.org/dailydevotion.cfm?keyword=28-Apr-10
[5] Linda Ellis, "The Dash." © 1996.
[6] Kathy Babbitt, *Habits of the Heart*. Wolgemuth & Hyatt, Brentwood, TN, 1990. p.48.

Chapter 6

[1] Mia Evans, "Natalie Grant: Her Heart Revealed." The 700 Club, April 24, 2008. http://cbn.com/700club/Guests/bios/Natalie_Grant042408.aspx
[2] Janice Lloyd, "Eating disorders are common in older women, study shows." USA Today, June 21, 2012. http://www.usatoday.com/news/health/story/2012-06-21/eating-disorders-over-50/55720718/1
[3] Associated Press, "Schiavo case highlights eating disorders." USA Today, February 26, 2005. http://www.usatoday.com/news/health/2005-02-25-schiavo-eating-disorder_x.htm
[4] Information about anorexia nervosa taken from EatingDisordersOnline.com
[5] Information about bulimia taken from EatingDisordersOnline.com
[6] Greg Laurie, "Drawn Away by Desire." Harvest Daily Devotions. January 16, 2006. http://www.harvest.org/devotional/archive/devotion/2006-01-16.html
[7] Greg Laurie, "Excess Baggage." Harvest Daily Devotions. January 1, 2004. http://www.harvest.org/devotional/archive/devotion/2004-01-01.html
[8] James MacDonald, "Relationship Building." Our Journey. April 3, 2011. http://www.jamesmacdonald.com/teaching/devotionals/2011-04-03/
[9] Greg Laurie, "A Fresh Start." Harvest Daily Devotions. December 30, 2008. http://www.harvest.org/devotional/archive/devotion/2008-12-30.html
[10] This paraphrase and the bullets that follow found in the NIrV Adventure Bible for Young Readers

Chapter 7

[1] Greg Laurie, "How to Clear Your Conscience." Harvest Daily Devotions. May 3, 2011. http://www.harvest.org/devotional/archive/devotion/2011-05-03.html
[2] Greg Laurie, "Forget the Past." Harvest Daily Devotions. November 8, 2007. http://www.harvest.org/devotional/archive/devotion/2007-11-08.html
[3] Greg Laurie, "The Race We Must Run." Light Source. http://www.lightsource.com/ministry/greg-laurie-tv/articles/the-race-we-must-run-12521.html
[4] Greg Laurie, "How Not to Win the Spiritual Race." Harvest Daily Devotions. June 8, 2005. http://www.harvest.org/devotional/archive/devotion/2005-06-08.html
[5] Elizabeth George, *Loving God with All Your Mind*. Harvest House Publishers, Eugene, OR, 1998. p.40.
[6] Greg Laurie, "Can God bring good out of bad?" Greg's Blog. October 7, 2009. http://blog.greglaurie.com/?p=2527

Chapter 8

[1] The Active Word, "Now Do It!" May 31, 2010. http://www.activeword.org/dailydevotion.cfm?keyword=31-May-10

[2] Dr. Shimmy C. Kotu, "Where to Put Your Expectations." May 23, 2012. http://www.shimmykotu.com/where-to-put-your-expectations/

[3] Lori Lowe, "Are Grudges Holding Your Marriage Back?" Marriage Gems. March 27, 2010. http://marriagegems.com/tag/forgiviness/

[4] Heather Long, "How to Avoid a Grudge." Families.com. http://marriage.famiies.com/blog/how-to-avoid-a-grudge

[5] Stephanie Anderson, "Forgiveness, with a Side of Grudge." Marriage Sherpa. April 23, 2012. http://www.marriagesherpa.com/blog/marriage/forgiveness_grudge/

[6] Elizabeth George, *A Woman After God's Own Heart*. p.87,88.

[7] Greg Laurie, *Married. Happily*. NavPress Publishing, 2011.

[8] Anne Ortlund, *My Sacrifice, His Fire: Weekday Readings For Women*. Authors Choice Press, Canada, 2001. p.95.

[9] Elizabeth George, *A Woman After Gods Own Heart*. p. 109-110.

[10] Ibid., p.105.

[11] Skip Heitzig, "The Right Words," The Connection Daily Devotional. June 24, 2011. http://www.crosswalk.com/devotionals/theconnection/

[12] Bill Hybels, *Marriage*. Zondervan Publishers, Grand Rapids, MI, 1996. p.78.

[13] Ibid. p.79.

[14] Elizabeth George, *A Woman After God's Own Heart*. p.112.

[15] Ibid., p.273.

[16] Ibid., p.176.

[17] Ibid., p.108.

[18] Shelley Spady, "When Is It My Turn?" Used by permission.

[19] Elizabeth George, *A Woman After God's Own Heart*. p.72-73.

[20] Rachel Palm, "To the Singles from Married Couples"

[21] Karen O'Connor, "Staying Married for Life"

[22] Mitch Temple, "Ten Secrets to a Successful Marriage"

Chapter 9

[1] Greg Laurie, "God Is Preparing You Today for Something Greater Tomorrow!" Harvest Daily Devotions. May 5, 2012. http://www.harvest.org/devotional/archive/devotion/2012-05-05.html

[2] Hal Lindsay, *The Terminal Generation*. Baker Publishing, 1981. p.i.

[3] Greg Laurie, "A Purpose In the Storm." Harvest Daily Devotions. June 29, 2012. http://www.harvest.org/devotional/archive/devotion/2012-06-29.html

[4] Elizabeth George, *A Woman After God's Own Heart*. p.196,198-199.

[5] Greg Laurie, "Attack Through Division." Harvest Daily Devotions. June 4, 2012. http://www.harvest.org/devotional/archive/devotion/2012-06-04.html

[6] Doug Easterday, "Restoration Through Forgiveness."

[7] Ibid.

[8] Bruce Bickel, Stan Jantz, *God Is in the Small Stuff*. p.241-243,247-249.

[9] Ibid., p.240,245.

[10] The Active Word, "May I Have Your Attention Please." July 21, 2012. http://www.activeword.org/dailydevotion.cfm?keyword=21-Jul-12

[11] Lewis B. Smedes, *Forgive and Forget*. HarperCollins, New York, 1984. p.22.

[12] Doug Easterday, "Restoration Through Forgiveness."

[13] Elizabeth George, *Loving God With All Your Mind*. p.276.

TAMMY BROWN

From Past Hurts

Leader's Guide

God doesn't change the past,
but He can change the meaning of the past

Healed and Set Free

Leader's Guide
Table of Contents

A Letter from Tammy	313
Before Getting Started	314
Transforming Truth: About the Tools	315
The Tools to Become Set Free	316
Lead by Example	317
Getting Started	319
First Class Checklist	320
For Leaders, From Leaders	321
Chapter 1: Getting Real with God	322
Chapter 2: Knowing God's Heart	324
Chapter 3: Letting Go of Anger	326
Chapter 4: Forgiving the Unacceptable	328
Chapter 5: Conquering Depression	330
Chapter 6: Body Image	332
Chapter 7: Remembering to Forget	334
Chapter 8: Two Become One: God's Design for Marriage	336
Chapter 9: Healed and Set Free	338
Acknowledgments	340
Q&A With Tammy	341
About The Author	343

Recommended supplemental leadership material:
<u>Principles of Leadership for Women</u> by Gail Mays

A Letter from Tammy

Dear Fellow Laborer in Christ Jesus,

If you ever wondered how God could use you to make a difference, just take a look at those He used in the Bible. God used *people* to make a difference. People! Ordinary people, like you and me.

God has a plan and a purpose for every believer. You've been set aside for a very special ministry if you're getting ready to lead a *Healed and Set Free* study. You have many blessings ahead as God's truth unfolds in the hearts of your group members.

I may or may not know you personally, but I know that if you're stepping out in faith with a God-given desire to see others set free from the chains of emotional scars, then you have most likely been deeply hurt in some way as well. You know all about past hurts, but you also know how incredible it feels to be set free from them.

It's exciting to open your arms to others so they can experience the same peace and freedom. As you reach out with God's love, you are making yourself available to others who are hurting, angry and scared. Some aren't sure that they will be accepted or loved by you, or if they can trust anyone with the deep, dark hurt that has chipped away at their peace.

If there is one clear lesson I can leave with you, one thing to remember from this letter, it is this: you will be walking on Satan's turf. Many of those in your group have been taken captive by the painful, heavy chains of their past, weighing them down for 10, 20 or 50 years. You are not going to a tea party where you can wear your high heels and a pretty white dress. You are going to war for those in your group. Get on your battle boots and the full armor of God. It's time to battle in the Spirit. Don't be afraid! God is bigger than all our hurts and fears!

The first thing to do is PRAY!

1. Pray to loose the bonds of wickedness.
2. Pray to undo the heavy burdens of the past.
3. Pray for the oppressed to be freed.

"He who is in you (Christ) is greater than he who is in the world" (1 John 4:4). Prayer will unleash the power of God in the lives of your group members. Prayer will remind you that you are not responsible to set anyone free in your own strength. Jesus is the only One who "heals the brokenhearted and binds up their wounds" (Psalm 147:3). It's "'not by might, nor by power, but by My Spirit,' says the Lord of hosts" (Zechariah 4:6).

Unhealed Wounds

There is one big mistake in ministering to victims of any type of abuse or hurting hearts and it's important to avoid repeating this traumatizing error. Telling them, "That's in the past. Forget it! Shape up and get on with your life! Time will heal your wounds."

Love is the essence of God. Love is also the handrail that helps move us along from one step to another. Be consistent to love people all the way to Jesus, be compassionate, be understanding and be a good listener. Knowing God encourages us to trust Him. We can be assured that God doesn't call the equipped, He equips the called- the best part is it's not us! It's Christ power in us!

In closing, my prayers and heart are with you as you open your arms to hurting people through God's love and truth.

Before Getting Started

- Pray and ask Jesus if He wants you to facilitate this study.

- Decide on a date, time and location for the study you will be facilitating.

- Spend time in prayer and devotions daily. God's Word will strengthen you to facilitate the *Healed and Set Free Bible Study* with joy in your heart. If you believe Jesus has directed you to facilitate, then when you are attacked by the enemy you will be equipped to stand in God's strength.

- Put the study in the church bulletin about four weeks prior to start date. Example announcement text: "For those who suffer from past wounds, depression or a broken heart, this Bible study will teach you God's power to heal a broken heart and give you tools that will set you free. To join a *Healed and Set Free Bible Study*, (add how your church will handle registration)."

- Ask your pastor if he will announce the *Healed and Set Free Bible Study*, with details on how to register, at church services four weeks prior to the start date. Announcement Example: "Our church will be hosting a *Healed and Set Free* women's Bible study (with the date, time and location). Please register, etc. The cost of the book is $13.00."

- Pray, pray, pray, pray before going to the introductory meeting.

General Guidelines

This study guide will help you lead your group through the *Healed and Set Free Bible Study*. Keep it available and read it each week to remind yourself of your role as a leader so you will be prepared to lead others on this journey.

It's critical that you, as the leader of the discussion group, be a cleansed vessel filled with God's love and wisdom, a living example of God's healing power. *Healed and Set Free* must be applied to your own life before you can be prepared to lead others. You can't give something you have never had yourself.

Transforming Truth: Four Healing Tools

As a group leader, you will need to become very familiar with the four tools: SEE, GIVE, FORGIVE and FORGET. You will need to be encouraging and keep the focus on getting real with God.

Satan Wants to Keep Us from Freedom

Those in your group must SEE what things from their past are affecting them, so they can BE SET FREE from the emotional prison that's keeping them from freedom. Encourage them to examine their heart and their way of thinking. Remind them that only the truth will set us free.

It's time to get real with God: Encourage those in your group to be completely honest with God and themselves in order to SEE the sin that has defiled their heart from past hurts and wrongs. As Hebrews 12:15 says, "Looking carefully lest anyone fall short of the grace of God; lest any root of bitterness springing up cause trouble, and by this many become defiled."

What's First: SEE or FORGET?

Notice the first tool is SEE, not FORGET. Many times we want to jump to FORGET because the past is so painful. We just want to push it away from our minds, hearts and lives, and pretend it never happened. But it doesn't work in that order. You can't bake a cake without first mixing the ingredients. If you do, you will have an empty, burned pan. If you try to FORGET your pain before you SEE what is really in your heart, you will come up empty and burned without being truly healed and set free.

There are four tools we will learn throughout this study: SEE, GIVE, FORGIVE and FORGET. As we deal with our past and present hurts, we can either embrace the truth and let go of the burdens we carry, or we can carry our burdens and reject the freedom that God's truth brings. It's an individual's choice. Getting real with God is the first step. It is a process, a sometimes painful journey, but it is a journey that brings freedom.

Weekly Review

Focus yourself and the group on becoming open and cleansed vessels, broken before Christ and dying to our own way of thinking, which is contrary to God's. Sometimes your weekly meetings will be emotional and difficult, but remind yourself and your group that the goal is to press on to freedom: walking in God's will for our lives!

Tools to Become Healed and Set Free

To equip yourself in God's truth, look over the tools and verses that will be introduced in the coming weeks. Thinking about the past won't change it, but you can change your future by being set free from your past.

TOOL #1 - SEE: I must SEE the truth about what is in my heart so I am not defiled.

Definition: To defile means to make filthy or dirty; to pollute.

Bible Verse: "Looking carefully lest anyone fall short of the grace of God; lest any root of bitterness springing up cause trouble, and by this many become defiled" (Hebrews 12:15).

TOOL #2 - GIVE: I must GIVE my sin to God through repentance, knowing that Christ is waiting to take it. I must be sorry enough to change, and choose to go God's way over my own.

Definition: To repent means to feel such sorrow for sin or fault as to be disposed to change one's life for the better; be penitent.

Bible Verse: "For godly sorrow produces repentance leading to salvation, not to be regretted; but the sorrow of the world produces death" (2 Corinthians 7:10).

TOOL #3 - FORGIVE: I must FORGIVE as I am forgiven by Christ: Forgiving those who hurt, bruised, wronged, rejected, betrayed or harmed me, whether unintentionally or deliberately. I must ask God to forgive me for holding on to unforgiveness and know that He will.

Definition: To forgive means to stop feeling angry or resentful toward someone for an offense, flaw or mistake.

Bible Verse: "...Bearing with one another, and forgiving one another, if anyone has a complaint against another; even as Christ forgave you, so you also must do" (Colossians 3:13).

TOOL #4 - FORGET: I must FORGET by no longer dwelling on the hurt or the painful reminders, such as: phrases, smells, places, songs and comments. Instead, I am putting my mind on the higher calling that Christ has for me.

Definition: To forget means to choose not to remember or notice, "forgive and forget".

Bible Verse: "Brethren, I do not count myself to have apprehended; but one thing I do, forgetting those things which are behind and reaching forward to those things which are ahead" (Philippians 3:13).

Be Healed and Set Free: Christ will heal me from my past, showing me the truth, so I can become a cleansed vessel, healed and set free.

Definition: To set free means to make free; set at liberty; release from bondage, imprisonment, or restraint.

Definition: To heal means to make whole and healthy; to cure; to remedy or repair.

Bible Verse: "And you shall know the truth, and the truth shall make you free" (John 8:32).

Lead By Example

- Be real. If you are real and transparent yourself, sharing your own failures, struggles and victories, it will be easier for those in your group to do the same.

- Be sensitive to the leading of the Holy Spirit. If you need to stop and pray during a study to let someone give an overwhelming hurt over to God, do so right away.

- Always make sure that the sharing is lined up with God's truth and that it points to Jesus.

- Remember, as the discussion leader, you are simply a channel that God is using to stimulate and guide the conversation. The Holy Spirit is always the teacher. Do not do all the talking, but instead involve every member of the group.

- As you ask questions, don't be afraid of silence. People need time to think before responding.

- Allow the Holy Spirit to direct your responses; He will give you discernment to encourage, give a hug, stop and pray, or contact someone in the group on the phone or in person to offer a special encouragement.

- Try to avoid answering your own questions. If the group gets used to you answering the questions, they will learn to keep silent. Make sure that those in the group understand the questions; if needed, rephrase a question until it's clearly understood.

- Encourage more than one answer to each question.

- Do not force anyone to share personal experiences, but do encourage each person to talk if they want to. Everyone should be free to say, "I don't feel comfortable talking about that right now." It's important to be a good listener, swift to hear and slow to speak.

- Everyone needs someone they can talk to who will give them undivided attention. Your eyes should always be focused on the person sharing. Always try to acknowledge them as much as you can. Just listen, let them cry, and listen again, always praying silently to God for His response. Try to really understand what each person is sharing. You may want to ask, "Is this what you're saying?" or "Do you mean...?"

- Bring a box of tissues to each meeting.

- Be an encourager. Set an example for your group by encouraging the members constantly, perhaps by sending encouraging notes, giving encouraging hugs or giving encouraging words at church or over the phone.

- Communication will not only be with your words, but also with your body language. Even when someone shares something shocking, acknowledge the person, all the while asking God to give you the love and wisdom you need to respond wisely.

- It's important not to criticize, make fun of or put down any person in your group, but always tell the truth in love.

- Learn how to correct a group member's answer in a tactful and loving way. Never let a wrong answer go uncorrected; it may lead others astray. You may want to ask, "What led you to that conclusion?"

- It's your responsibility to keep things on track and avoid going off on tangents.

- One of the most difficult roles for a leader is keeping one person from dominating the group. You need to allow each person to share her heart, but you must prevent any one person from doing all the talking (including you). You must not rush the person who's talking. Give the Holy Spirit time to minister, but remember that you are responsible for keeping the discussion moving.

- If someone is dominating the discussion, try to gently interrupt the person speaking. Thank her for sharing and repeat the question for the next member. It's now time for the next person to share. If this doesn't work, ask the person to please let other group members share their views.

- Remember to keep the main focus: This Bible study is designed to examine our own hearts, not gossip about everyone else. Continue to be on your guard concerning backbiting.

- Set an example for others by being the first to be trustworthy.

- Our example is Christ: His mercy and His forgiveness. Paramount to any Bible study is prayer. Be sure to pray for the group before and after each study and do much private prayer during the discussion itself. Remember, prayer is the only thing that unleashes the power of God to work in each of our lives.

Stories of Real People and a Real Savior

A New Direction

Jonnie, Idaho

Healed and Set Free is a blessing to a hurting world! The lessons taught in this study have changed people's lives. It's not just a one time study, it can be used over and over to remind God's people of His love, grace, mercy and forgiveness!

Healed and Set Free is about prayer, Bible reading, studying, sharing and relationships. What a joy and privilege it is to have a resource that helps to keep us from building stone walls in our hearts. "As iron sharpens iron, so a man sharpens the countenance of his friend" (Proverbs 27:17).

Prior to Your First Meeting

One week before the study begins, call the women signed up for your group to remind them of the time, date and location of the *Healed and Set Free Study*, making sure each woman has a book. Answer any questions she may have, and give clear directions to the location of the study.

A few days before the study begins, call those who will be in your group—it will encourage them to hear from you. Let them know that you are looking forward to seeing them. Remind them that you have been praying for them and that God has many blessings to unfold in their life. This will put you in touch with each person and prevent Satan from tempting them not to come.

Group Leader: Redeem the Time

You will be called to lead, exhort, warn, comfort, pray and be patient with those in your group. As part of the preparation process, take time to memorize 1 Thessalonians 5:14, Galatians 6:9 and Colossians 3:2, so the Holy Spirit can take the Word of God and weave it into the very fiber of your being:

"Now we exhort you, brethren, warn those who are unruly, comfort the fainthearted, uphold the weak, be patient with all" (1 Thessalonians 5:14).

"Let us not grow weary while doing good, for in due season we shall reap if we do not lose heart" (Galatians 6:9).

"Set your mind on things above, not on things on the earth" (Colossians 3:2).

Each Week

- Prior to meeting with your group, complete the assigned chapter in *Healed and Set Free*. Meditate and reflect upon each passage of scripture as you formulate your answers. Mark the questions you want to discuss in the group meeting, as there is never enough time to go over every question.

- Pray for the leading of the Holy Spirit to touch on the needs of the group and each individual.

- Have that each person write down any questions she has during the week while reading the assigned chapter. Discuss questions over the phone during your weekly calls or at the next group meeting.

- Always open and close group discussion with prayer. Pray that God will help each group member open up her heart to Him concerning the lingering hurts.

- Go around the circle and let each person share a thought concerning the opening question, if they desire. Review the tools: SEE, GIVE, FORGIVE and FORGET.

Remind Group Members Along the Way:

- You shouldn't compare yourself to others, just do the best you can.

- Just because someone doesn't love you the way you want them to doesn't mean they don't love you with all they have.

- No matter how good a friend is, they're going to hurt you every once in a while, and you must forgive them.

- It isn't always enough to be forgiven by others. Sometimes you have to forgive yourself.

- You can't make someone love you. All you can do is be someone who can be loved. The rest is up to them.

- Pain is pain, and no matter how seemingly big or small each person's situation is, God cares about them all.

First Class Checklist

- Arrange the chairs or couches in a circle.

- Bring a candle or something to make the room cozy, and perhaps refreshments. Put a few copies of *Healed and Set Free* on a side table; someone always forgets theirs or needs to purchase one for the first meeting.

- Go over the requirements for the study: prayer, honesty, and most of all the importance of completing each week's assignment.

- Bring a notebook for taking notes about each participant as they introduce themselves. (There is also a blank page next to each chapter in the Leader's Guide.)

- Open in prayer. Then start the study by sharing a little about yourself and how you have been healed and set free. Explain how the study will be facilitated each week. For example, "We will begin with an opening question each week, then we will go around in a circle to answer questions."

- Ask each participant to introduce and share a little about herself—if she is comfortable. This is a good time to take notes so you can pray for each person before the next study. This helps you remember the names of those in your group, and gives you compassion for them as you pray.

- Open the *Healed and Set Free Bible Study* and read the "Suggestions for Group Study" (page 2) and the "Group Accountability to Confidants" (page 3). Ask participants to sign and date. Cover the confidence requirements thoroughly, helping everyone understand the importance of these principles. Even their husbands and friends shouldn't know the names of those in the group.

- Let the participants know that the study will always begin and end on time; two hours is the study length. This is very important and makes the group members feel secure. They may have a sitter with their children or have another commitment.

- "Are outside guests welcome?" Politely, no. Because of the nature of the *Healed and Set Free* study, and the confidentiality needed to honor each member's feelings, no group member may invite anyone to come with them. Once a group has begun meeting, no additional participants may join that particular group. They will need to sign up for the next available *Healed and Set Free* Bible study.

- Ask members to share what they want to get out of *Healed and Set Free*. Take their responses to heart: Remember: this is going to be an emotional time for some. They may never have talked about their lingering hurts. Be sensitive to each person's needs.

- Give an assignment. Assign Chapter 1: "Getting Real with God," to be completed over the next week.

- Close the group in prayer. End by taking prayer requests from each participant and pray for them during the week.

From Leaders, For Leaders

"I took Healed and Set Free to Australia and New Zealand. Many hurting women 'down under'. Thank you Tammy for your faithfulness. We must leave no hostages in the enemy's clutches! God is raising up an army of fearless once-wounded, now- healed warriors to take the message to women of all ages.......JESUS HEALS!"

Debbi Bryson, is an author and pastor's wife at Calvary Fellowship, Vista, California. She is the Founder of the Bible Bus Stop, and author of Wisdom for Women. Debbi is a highly sought after speaker for various retreats, and conferences, mother of one, former missionary to Russia and wife of Pastor George Bryson.

I came across your study a few years ago, I began to use the book in individual counseling situations, only to discover that our church was full of hurting people still struggling in private places.

We are about to start our third group and I count it the greatest privilege the Lord has ever allowed me to be a part of. I love to watch the way the Lord works in and through His people, but in our groups, He proved Himself to be absolutely real, powerful, and yet intimately tender and involved with each of the ladies in the group. No one can reach and heal the soul but our God, and He has used this study as a valuable tool in His medical bag.

Thank you for your labor of love for Him and the family of God. Thank you and your husband for your willingness to surrender your testimony into His care. Thank you for staying the course despite the obvious warfare that comes with this ministry. It obviously will be attacked because it does eternal damage against the enemy. You are very appreciated by the flock in upstate New York.

Shannon Gallatin has been serving the Lord in a variety of ministries for more than 20 years. While serving as a missionary in Europe, she met and later married Scott Gallatin, who is now the senior pastor of Calvary Chapel of the Finger Lakes in upstate New York.

Chapter 1

Getting Real with God

Prior to Meeting with Your Group

Complete the assigned chapter in *Healed and Set Free*. Meditate on each passage of scripture or reflection as you formulate your answers. There is never enough time to go over every question, so mark the questions you want the group to answer and discuss in the next meeting.

Pray for the leading of the Holy Spirit to meet the needs of the group and each individual.

Arrange meeting chairs in a circle to give a more intimate setting and allow group members to see one another.

As Group Leader

Always open the discussion with prayer. After prayer, the group leader should respond to the opening question first. This will help members feel more relaxed and at ease when asked to participate.

After the leader has shared, group members will be asked to share (if they are comfortable) one after another. Always remind the group that they are not expected to share if they don't want to. The rule is, everyone works within their comfort level.

Opening Discussion Question for Chapter One

If you could change one thing about yourself or develop one quality that you don't have, what would it be?

The opening question is not for detailed conversation. Ask members to keep their comments brief. If a member is in obvious pain at any time during the session, the leader should interrupt the discussion and have prayer for the person in pain. After prayer, group discussion may resume. That's what *Healed and Set Free* is all about: seeking the true Healer when a person is shown the truth or is in pain. AMEN!

Closing

End the study with prayer. This can be done by the leader or by a group member.

Notes

Chapter 2

Knowing God's Heart

Prior to Meeting with Your Group

Complete the assigned chapter in *Healed and Set Free*. Meditate on each passage of scripture or reflection as you formulate your answers. There is never enough time to go over every question, so mark the questions you want the group to answer and discuss in the next meeting.

Pray for the leading of the Holy Spirit to meet the needs of the group and each individual.

Arrange meeting chairs in a circle to give a more intimate setting and allow group members to see one another.

As Group Leader

Always open the discussion with prayer. After prayer, the group leader should respond to the opening question first. This will help members feel more relaxed and at ease when asked to participate.

After the leader has shared, group members will be asked to share (if they are comfortable) one after another. Always remind the group that they are not expected to share if they don't want to. The rule is, everyone works within their comfort level.

Opening Discussion Question for Chapter Two

What do you believe God wants you to do this week? When and how do you intend to do it? After the opening question, read this week's memory verse to the group: "He heals the brokenhearted and binds up their wounds" (Psalm 147:3).

The opening question is not for detailed conversation. Ask members to keep their comments brief. If a member is in obvious pain at any time during the session, the leader should interrupt the discussion and have prayer for the person in pain. After prayer, group discussion may resume. That's what *Healed and Set Free* is all about: seeking the true Healer when a person is shown the truth or is in pain. AMEN!

Closing

End the study with prayer. This can be done by the leader or by a group member.

Notes

Chapter 3

Letting Go of Anger

Prior to Meeting with Your Group

Complete the assigned chapter in *Healed and Set Free*. Meditate on each passage of scripture or reflection as you formulate your answers. There is never enough time to go over every question, so mark the questions you want the group to answer and discuss in the next meeting.

Pray for the leading of the Holy Spirit to meet the needs of the group and each individual.

Arrange meeting chairs in a circle to give a more intimate setting and allow group members to see one another.

As Group Leader

Always open the discussion with prayer. After prayer, the group leader should respond to the opening question first. This will help members feel more relaxed and at ease when asked to participate.

After the leader has shared, group members will be asked to share (if they are comfortable) one after another. Always remind the group that they are not expected to share if they don't want to. The rule is, everyone works within their comfort level.

Opening Discussion Question for Chapter Three

What happens when we confess our sin? After the opening question, review the first tool (SEE) with the group. Read this week's memory verse to the group: "If we confess our sins, He is faithful and just to forgive us our sins and to cleanse us from all unrighteousness" (1 John 1:9).

The opening question is not for detailed conversation. Ask members to keep their comments brief. If a member is in obvious pain at any time during the session, the leader should interrupt the discussion and have prayer for the person in pain. After prayer, group discussion may resume. That's what *Healed and Set Free* is all about: seeking the true Healer when a person is shown the truth or is in pain. AMEN!

Closing

End the study with prayer. This can be done by the leader or by a group member.

Notes

Chapter 4

Forgiving the Unacceptable

Prior to Meeting with Your Group

Complete the assigned chapter in *Healed and Set Free*. Meditate on each passage of scripture or reflection as you formulate your answers. There is never enough time to go over every question, so mark the questions you want the group to answer and discuss in the next meeting.

Pray for the leading of the Holy Spirit to meet the needs of the group and each individual.

Arrange meeting chairs in a circle to give a more intimate setting and allow group members to see one another.

As Group Leader

Always open the discussion with prayer. After prayer, the group leader should respond to the opening question first. This will help members feel more relaxed and at ease when asked to participate.

After the leader has shared, group members will be asked to share (if they are comfortable) one after another. Always remind the group that they are not expected to share if they don't want to. The rule is, everyone works within their comfort level.

Opening Discussion Question for Chapter Four

Name several reasons you shouldn't set up conditions to forgive others that have hurt or wronged you. After the opening question, review the third tool (FORGIVE) and read this week's memory verse: "Bearing with one another, and forgiving one another, if anyone has a complaint against another; even as Christ forgave you, so you also must do" (Colossians 3:13).

The opening question is not for detailed conversation. Ask members to keep their comments brief. If a member is in obvious pain at any time during the session, the leader should interrupt the discussion and have prayer for the person in pain. After prayer, group discussion may resume. That's what *Healed and Set Free* is all about: seeking the true Healer when a person is shown the truth or is in pain. AMEN!

Closing Question

What is one thing I can see about the sins committed against me and the sin of unforgiveness?

Closing Prayer

Spend time together pouring your hearts out before Christ Jesus, confessing the hidden sins of hatred, unforgiveness and grudge holding. Loose the chains and be set free to have a clean heart.

Notes

Conquering Depression

Prior to Meeting with Your Group

Complete the assigned chapter in *Healed and Set Free*. Meditate on each passage of scripture or reflection as you formulate your answers. There is never enough time to go over every question, so mark the questions you want the group to answer and discuss in the next meeting.

Pray for the leading of the Holy Spirit to meet the needs of the group and each individual.

Arrange meeting chairs in a circle to give a more intimate setting and allow group members to see one another.

As Group Leader

Always open the discussion with prayer. After prayer, the group leader should respond to the opening question first. This will help members feel more relaxed and at ease when asked to participate.

After the leader has shared, group members will be asked to share (if they are comfortable) one after another. Always remind the group that they are not expected to share if they don't want to. The rule is, everyone works within their comfort level.

Opening Discussion Question for Chapter Five

What changes do you believe that you should make in your habits or actions this week? How will you tackle these? After the opening question, review the tools (SEE, GIVE and FORGIVE). Continue to encourage your group to get to the root cause of hidden sins that have defiled their hearts. Read this week's memory verse: "Anxiety in the heart of man causes depression, but a good word makes it glad. The righteous should choose his friends carefully, for the way of the wicked leads them astray" (Proverbs 12:25-26).

The opening question is not for detailed conversation. Ask members to keep their comments brief. If a member is in obvious pain at any time during the session, the leader should interrupt the discussion and have prayer for the person in pain. After prayer, group discussion may resume. That's what *Healed and Set Free* is all about: seeking the true Healer when a person is shown the truth or is in pain. AMEN!

Close in Prayer

End the study with prayer. This can be done by the leader or by a group member.

Notes

Chapter 6

Body Image

Prior to Meeting with Your Group

Complete the assigned chapter in *Healed and Set Free*. Meditate on each passage of scripture or reflection as you formulate your answers. There is never enough time to go over every question, so mark the questions you want the group to answer and discuss in the next meeting.

Pray for the leading of the Holy Spirit to meet the needs of the group and each individual.

Arrange meeting chairs in a circle to give a more intimate setting and allow group members to see one another.

As Group Leader

Always open the discussion with prayer. After prayer, the group leader should respond to the opening question first. This will help members feel more relaxed and at ease when asked to participate.

After the leader has shared, group members will be asked to share (if they are comfortable) one after another. Always remind the group that they are not expected to share if they don't want to. The rule is, everyone works within their comfort level.

Opening Discussion Question for Chapter Six

Read the memory verse: "Stand fast therefore in the liberty by which Christ has made us free, and do not be entangled again with a yoke of bondage" (Galatians 5:1). How is the Holy Spirit prompting you as a result of this Bible study? What will you do about it and when? After the opening question, review the tools (SEE, GIVE and FORGIVE). Continue to encourage your group to get to the root cause of the hidden sins that have defiled their hearts.

The opening question is not for detailed conversation. Ask members to keep their comments brief. If a member is in obvious pain at any time during the session, the leader should interrupt the discussion and have prayer for the person in pain. After prayer, group discussion may resume. That's what *Healed and Set Free* is all about: seeking the true Healer when a person is shown the truth or is in pain. AMEN!

Closing Question

What's one thing you have learned about the area of food in your life?

Closing Prayer

Lead participants through this prayer. Ask them to commit to God by signing and dating below.

Dear Lord,

Thank You for loving me unconditionally. Thank You for being intimately involved with every aspect of my life. Thank You for wanting to heal me. As I continue this journey of self-control, please give me insight and understanding concerning my eating disorder or wrong thinking about food and my body. Bring Your Word to my mind to give me the strength, courage and power to change. Be with me in a special way, as I desire to be healed and set free from this idol in my life.

Signed: _____

Date: _____

Notes

Chapter 7

Remembering to Forget

Prior to Meeting with Your Group

Complete the assigned chapter in *Healed and Set Free*. Meditate on each passage of scripture or reflection as you formulate your answers. There is never enough time to go over every question, so mark the questions you want the group to answer and discuss in the next meeting.

Pray for the leading of the Holy Spirit to meet the needs of the group and each individual.

Arrange meeting chairs in a circle to give a more intimate setting and allow group members to see one another.

As Group Leader

Always open the discussion with prayer. After prayer, the group leader should respond to the opening question first. This will help members feel more relaxed and at ease when asked to participate.

After the leader has shared, group members will be asked to share (if they are comfortable) one after another. Always remind the group that they are not expected to share if they don't want to. The rule is, everyone works within their comfort level.

Opening Discussion Question for Chapter Seven

In what ways can you recognize that Satan is trying to throw the past in your face by reminding you of places, smells or phrases? Read this week's memory verse: "Forgetting those things which are behind and reaching forward to those things which are ahead, I press toward the goal for the prize of the upward call of God in Christ Jesus" (Philippians 3:13-14).

The opening question is not for detailed conversation. Ask members to keep their comments brief. If a member is in obvious pain at any time during the session, the leader should interrupt the discussion and have prayer for the person in pain. After prayer, group discussion may resume. That's what *Healed and Set Free* is all about: seeking the true Healer when a person is shown the truth or is in pain. AMEN!

Closing Prayer

Take time to pray in thankfulness for God's truth, which allows you to let go, and move beyond the hurt and toward Jesus.

Notes

Two Become One: God's Design for Marriage

Prior to Meeting with Your Group

Complete the assigned chapter in *Healed and Set Free*. Meditate on each passage of scripture or reflection as you formulate your answers. There is never enough time to go over every question, so mark the questions you want the group to answer and discuss in the next meeting.

Pray for the leading of the Holy Spirit to meet the needs of the group and each individual.

Arrange meeting chairs in a circle to give a more intimate setting and allow group members to see one another.

As Group Leader

Always open the discussion with prayer. After prayer, the group leader should respond to the opening question first. This will help members feel more relaxed and at ease when asked to participate.

After the leader has shared, group members will be asked to share (if they are comfortable) one after another. Always remind the group that they are not expected to share if they don't want to. The rule is, everyone works within their comfort level.

Opening Discussion Question for Chapter Eight

If you were called upon to point a hurting person to the true Healer, how can you comfort them with the comfort God has given you through *Healed and Set Free*? Read this week's memory verse: "Therefore a man shall leave his father and mother and be joined to his wife, and they shall become one flesh" (Genesis 2:24).

The opening question is not for detailed conversation. Ask members to keep their comments brief. If a member is in obvious pain at any time during the session, the leader should interrupt the discussion and have prayer for the person in pain. After prayer, group discussion may resume. That's what *Healed and Set Free* is all about: seeking the true Healer when a person is shown the truth or is in pain. AMEN!

Closing Question

What have you learned about God's design for marriage? What changes will you make as a result?

Close in Prayer

End the study with prayer. This can be done by the leader or by a group member.

Notes

Chapter 9

Healed & Set Free

Prior to Meeting with Your Group

Complete the assigned chapter in *Healed and Set Free*. Meditate on each passage of scripture or reflection as you formulate your answers. There is never enough time to go over every question, so mark the questions you want the group to answer and discuss in the next meeting.

Pray for the leading of the Holy Spirit to meet the needs of the group and each individual.

Arrange meeting chairs in a circle to give a more intimate setting and allow group members to see one another.

As Group Leader

Always open the discussion with prayer. After prayer, the group leader should respond to the opening question first. This will help members feel more relaxed and at ease when asked to participate.

After the leader has shared, group members will be asked to share (if they are comfortable) one after another. Always remind the group that they are not expected to share if they don't want to. The rule is, everyone works within their comfort level.

Opening Discussion Question for Chapter Nine

What is one thing you will always remember about this time of healing? Read this week's memory verse: "You shall know the truth and the truth shall make you free" (John 8:32).

The opening question is not for detailed conversation. Ask members to keep their comments brief. If a member is in obvious pain at any time during the session, the leader should interrupt the discussion and have prayer for the person in pain. After prayer, group discussion may resume. That's what *Healed and Set Free* is all about: seeking the true Healer when a person is shown the truth or is in pain. AMEN!

Closing Prayer

Dear Lord,
I love You and I believe in You. Help me to live each day as an open and cleansed vessel. Help me to die to my own desires, thoughts, emotions and will, which are contrary to Yours. I don't want my love to grow cold toward You. I desire more of You in my life and less of me.
In Jesus' name, amen.

Special Meal

When the *Healed and Set Free* Bible study is completed, the group leader is encouraged to organize a special breakfast, lunch or dinner to spend time with the group and celebrate their victory in Christ Jesus.

Notes

**GOD IS A GOD OF TRUTH
AND ONLY THE TRUTH WILL SET YOU FREE!**

Watersprings Church of Idaho Falls
4250 S. 25th E., Idaho Falls, ID 83404
(208) 524-4747

Healed and Set Free International Ministries
www.hsfministries.org

All rights reserved. Reproduction of any part of this publication is prohibited by law without written permission from the author. © 1998, © 2000, © 2012.

Acknowledgements

To My Family:

To my husband, Rick, and to my children, Caleb and Jessica. Rick, I am grateful for your prayers, godly wisdom, patience and encouragement. I couldn't have done this without your support. I love you, sweetness. Caleb and Jessica, the two children who have taken my heart hostage: My love and thanks for all your hugs and smiles of love.

To My Parents:

Ron and Lana Davis: I am so blessed to have your constant source of encouragement and love.

To My Church Family at Watersprings Church:

A pastor's wife couldn't ask for a more supportive and responsive flock of committed believers.

Gordon and Roxanne Boyle: Thank you for your undivided heart toward Christ and your love for our family.

To All:

I would like to express my gratitude to the many people who saw me through this book, particularly Ashley Brown and Christa Landon, and all who provided support, talked things over, read, wrote, offered comments, allowed me to quote their remarks, and assisted in the editing, proofreading and design.

Q & A with Tammy

How did you become a writer?

The Bible says God has chosen "the weak things of the world to put to shame the wise" (1 Corinthians 1:27). He does this so He will get all the glory for the end result. First of all, I am not a writer. Writing was never what I had planned to do with my life. I like to stay in my comfort zone and do things that I know I'm good at, like organizing and decorating. I soon realized God had other plans.

One day while camping at Palisades Reservoir with my family, the Lord put two precious women on my heart. I knew they were hurting, and my heart longed for them to experience the same healing that I had received from God. That beautiful sunny day, as my kids giggled and played in the water, I dug through my bag to find a pen, picked up a yellow notebook, and began to write about how God healed and set me free from all my hurts.

With the help of many friends, *Healed and Set Free* was born and published in 1998. Through the years, I have been blessed to see it used all over the world to help struggling women break free from past hurts that have kept them from living the life God intended them to live.

What would you like people to know about you?

When my daughter turned 18, my entire family went skydiving—something I said I'd never do. I was afraid, but my dear friend Roxanne Boyle said, "When you get ready to jump out of the plane, don't look down. Look up and yell out, 'I praise You, Jesus!'" Needless to say, it was an incredible feeling to move past my fear and trust God as I jumped out of the plane. I am thankful that our family experienced this adventure together.

What's something that people don't know about you?

I was a painfully shy child and teenager, but inch-by-inch God is changing this part of my life. I love to have deep belly laughs with my family and friends. I like to hum the same tune over and over (I have for 20 years). It usually starts when I'm cleaning or working on a project—that's about the time my family loves to start teasing me about my unchanging melody.

I enjoy Sunday afternoon naps with my hubby, bike rides, going on prayer walks, eating a big bowl of kettle-and-butter popcorn with my daughter, Jessica, and having great conversations with my family or friends over a meal.

What's something that people don't know about your family?

Rick and my son, Caleb, are both certified pilots, and I enjoy being Rick's co-pilot. My son became a private pilot at the age of 17 and a commercial pilot at 18. The more I fly with my precious guys, the more I grow interested in having Caleb, who is a flight instructor, give me lessons to become a private pilot. I just have to do it!

What is it like being a pastor's wife?

I love being a pastor's wife! I count it a privilege to support and help my husband, Rick. I love serving Jesus in whatever He has me do! Now that isn't to say that being a pastor's wife is easy! I am often asked how I deal with the huge expectations that come with my position. However, it isn't other people's expectations that keep me up at night; more often than not, it's the expectations I place on myself.

After more than twenty years in ministry, I have learned that the only things of value are the things I allow God to do through me. With this in mind, I am constantly brought to the feet of Jesus, where I ask Him to live, love, move and minister—first in me and then through me.

One of the hardest things to deal with is seeing people walk through difficult and trying times. It is often so overwhelming that all I can do is cry, take them by the hand, and point them to Jesus—the only One who can touch the deepest part of our hearts. But like so many things in life, it is the difficult things that bring the most growth in our lives and keep us looking to Jesus. All in all, it is an incredible thrill and gift to watch people grow in their faith and see the transforming power of God at work in their lives.

What is your life's greatest achievement?

Despite all the struggles I have had, God has used my life in amazing ways to glorify Him. I have traveled all over the world, been involved with television and radio ministries, and authored the *Healed and Set Free Bible Study*. God has used everything in my life to show me His healing power, mercy and love more clearly, and most of all to help others with their own struggles.

But when I think about my life as a whole, the biggest blessing and honor God has given me is to be a wife and mother. My family is my number one priority. I count it a privilege to have married my high school sweetheart, and to be blessed with two of the most beautiful children in the world, Caleb and Jessica. My children are grown up now, and Rick and I can see the fruit of all the labor it took to be parents—the devoted hours of attention, discipline, love and the privilege of sharing God's Word with them. Now they are both married, and we see the blessing passed down to the next generation, which will continue as they raise their own families. It has all been worth it!

> "May the God who gives endurance and encouragement
> give you the same attitude of mind toward each other"
> (Romans 15:5).

About the Author

Rick and Tammy Brown

Tammy is the wife of Rick Brown, senior pastor of Watersprings Church of Idaho Falls. She is the founder of Healed and Set Free International Ministries, a ministry devoted to helping women move from past hurts into new lives of freedom in Christ. She's the author of the *Healed and Set Free Bible Study*, a study born out of her own personal triumph over pain and suffering. She is a homemaker and a conference speaker who has been featured in Calvary Chapel Magazine, and on television and radio ministries. She has been blessed to speak all over the world, and to see the *Healed and Set Free Bible Study* translated into many different languages. Tammy and Rick are blessed with two children, Caleb and Jessica, and their blessings have increased with the addition of their children's spouses, Ashley and Christian.

Tammy's personal testimony of God's healing is told throughout the *Healed and Set Free* study, along with stories from many other women who have experienced restoration from God. Tammy counts it a privilege to serve God and see Him move women from long-standing, paralyzing hurts into freedom.

"But seek first the kingdom of God and His righteousness, and all these things shall be added to you" (Matthew 6:33).

Ordering Information:
Bring *Healed and Set Free* to your church: To order, follow the links at www.hsfministries.org.

Tammy Brown's Speaking Information:
For information on having Tammy as a guest speaker, contact Healed and Set Free International Ministries by email: info@hsfministries.org.

Made in the USA
Las Vegas, NV
10 December 2023

82450760R10195